SHANG YUN-XIANG STYLE XINGYIQUAN

# Shang Yun-Xiang Style
# Xingyiquan

## THE FOUNDATIONS AND SUBTLETIES OF XINGYIQUAN TRAINING

**Li Wen-Bin**

with Shang Zhi-Rong and Li Hong

translated by Lu Mei-Hui

BLUE SNAKE BOOKS
BERKELEY, CALIFORNIA

Published by Blue Snake Books, an imprint of North Atlantic Books
P.O. Box 12327
Berkeley, California 94712

Cover and interior photos courtesy of Li Hong
Cover and book design by Brad Greene
Printed in the United States of America

*Shang Yun-Xiang Style Xingyiquan: The Foundations and Subtleties of Xingyiquan Training* is sponsored and published by the Society for the Study of Native Arts and Sciences (dba North Atlantic Books), an educational nonprofit based in Berkeley, California, that collaborates with partners to develop cross-cultural perspectives, nurture holistic views of art, science, the humanities, and healing, and seed personal and global transformation by publishing work on the relationship of body, spirit, and nature.

North Atlantic Books' publications are available through most bookstores. For further information, call 800–733–3000 or visit our websites at www.northatlanticbooks.com and www.bluesnakebooks.com.

PLEASE NOTE: The creators and publishers of this book disclaim any liabilities for loss in connection with following any of the practices, exercises, and advice contained herein. To reduce the chance of injury or any other harm, the reader should consult a professional before undertaking this or any other martial arts, movement, meditative arts, health, or exercise program. The instructions and advice printed in this book are not in any way intended as a substitute for medical, mental, or emotional counseling with a licensed physician or healthcare provider.

Library of Congress Cataloging-in-Publication Data

Wen-Bin, Li, 1918-
    Shang yun-xiang style xingyiquan: the foundations and subtleties of xingyiquan training / Li Wen-Bin with Shang Zhi-Rong and Li Hong, translated by Lu Mei-Hui.
        pages cm.
    Includes bibliographical references and index.
    ISBN 978–1-58394–759–3 (alk. paper)
    1. Martial arts. I. Title.
    GV1100.W46 2014
    796.8—dc23

                                                                    2013037781

1 2 3 4 5 6 7 8 9   SHERIDAN   19 18 17 16 15 14

Printed on recycled paper

# TABLE OF CONTENTS

It is a great privilege and honor to have been asked by Master Li Hong to be the translator of this highly regarded book, *Shang Yun-Xiang Style Xingyiquan: The Foundations and Subtleties of Xingyiquan Training*. This book is truly a treasure trove of information on Xingyiquan, equally rich and complete in theories, philosophy, practice instructions, and illustrations.

Master Li Wen-Bin was not only a great practitioner of Xingyiquan but also a critical thinker and researcher. His breadth of knowledge and analytical mind allowed him to delve into the history and development of Xingyiquan, solve many mysteries, and bring to light the essence of the art.

To faithfully convey the wealth of information in this book to the English audience, I was required to tap fully into my knowledge of Xingyiquan, the English language, traditional Chinese medicine, and classical Chinese language, literature, and philosophy. It has been a most labor-intensive experience and has been both rewarding and consuming—rewarding because of the precious information I have gained from the book; consuming because of the scope and volume of the content.

It is my hope that English readers will now be able to benefit fully from Master Li Wen-Bin's lifelong learning and understanding of Xingyiquan and be rewarded with the same gratification that I myself experienced while reading this book. I shall feel that I have made a contribution to the world of Xingyiquan and, indeed, Chinese martial arts in general.

Many quotations of common martial arts and Xingyiquan principles and sayings in this book are without the original source. Some are passed down from generation to generation; almost all practitioners of the art know without questioning their origin. This book can serve as a good instructional guide for beginning practitioners and valuable supplementary material for experienced practitioners.

I want to express my greatest gratitude to my dearest friend and wonderful student, Jean Wu, for spending countless sleepless nights in sharing my challenges throughout the entire translation process. Without her help, the completion of this work would not have been possible!

**Lu Mei-hui**
June 2014

Xingyiquan is one of the most famous boxing styles in Chinese martial arts, renowned both for self-defense and health cultivation. Master Shang, the originator of Shang-style Xingyiquan, was well known for his three spectacular techniques: Half-step Smashing Fist, Striking at Dantian, and Big Pole. His closed-door disciple Li Wen-Bin inherited his authentic heritage. Master Li was pronounced one of the top ten martial arts grandmasters in China. He used his unique methods and scientific theories to refine the content of Xingyiquan and developed the Shang style, which has become an important branch of Xingyiquan. Master Li's son, Li Hong, is ranked eighth *duan* and is famous throughout China.

Twenty years ago, Master Li—along with Master Shang's daughter, Shang Zhi-Rong—published the first volume of *Shang Yun-Xiang Style Xingyiquan*. Master Li Hong subsequently published the second and third volumes of the book. These have been very popular and highly praised by martial arts practitioners.

This publication of the English edition of the book is a great event, here in China and overseas. I hereby congratulate the authors on their contribution to and achievements in Chinese martial arts, and I highly recommend this book to martial arts enthusiasts all over the world.

**Cai Long Yun** (蔡龙云)
Vice-chairman of Chinese Wushu Association
Professor at Shanghai Sports Academy

PREFACE

As the name suggests, Shang-style Xingyiquan is the school of Xingyiquan that was passed down by renowned Xingyi master Shang Yun-Xiang. Shang Yun-Xiang had inherited the legacy of Li Cun Yi (known as "Single Broadsword") and Guo Yun Shen (known as "Half-step Beng Fist Conquers the World"). Devoting his entire life to the study of Xingyiquan, Shang Yun-Xiang gained tremendous insight into the art and became a great master of it.

Li Wen-Bin, the last disciple of Shang Yun-Xiang, started his training under Master Shang at age fifteen and mastered his teachings. Li Wen-Bin was known for his uprightness and honorableness. He was brave enough to take on tough challenges, further promoting Shang-style Xingyiquan, and won the good name of "Shang Yun-Xiang Junior" in the Old Beijing martial arts *(wushu)* circle.

Li Hong began training in a variety of wushu styles around the age of four, under the strict guidance of his father, Li Wen-Bin. Li Hong carries forward the essence of Shang-style Xingyiquan with a high level of skill and morality. The two generations of the Li family always held their teacher in high respect and dedicated themselves fully to the promotion of Shang-style Xingyiquan.

*Shang Yun-Xiang Style Xingyiquan* contains the insights gained by the author through decades of hard practice and in-depth research on Xingyiquan. It contains the essence of traditional Chinese martial arts and is a tremendous contribution to the promotion of these arts.

Congratulations to the author, for the contributions he has made to and achievements he has gained through the promotion of Chinese martial arts!

**Shouyu Liang**
Chairman of International Wushu Sanshou Dao Association
Shang-style Xingyiquan Honorary Chairman (Canada)
Former Wushu Chair of Physical Education of University
    of British Columbia

*Counterclockwise from left: Grandmaster Shang Yun-Xiang (1864–1937)*

*Li Wen-Bin and Shang Zhi-Rong*

*Master Li Wen-Bin writing at a desk*

*Shang Zhi-Rong at home*

*Master Li Wen-Bin painting*

*Counterclockwise from left: Master Li Wen-Bin performing Swallow Scraping the Water, initial posture*

*Master Li Wen-Bin performing Blue Dragon Probing with Claws*

*Master Li Wen-Bin performing Golden Chicken Standing on One Leg*

*Master Li Wen-Bin performing Insert a Flower with Cross Legs*

*Conterclockwise from above: Master Li Wen-Bin performing the Coiling Snake form*

*Master Li Wen-Bin performing Blue Dragon Probing with Claws (with Xingyi sword)*

*Master Li Wen-Bin performing Sparrow Hawk Drilling into the Sky*

*Master Li Wen-Bin performing Big Dipper Posture*

*Master Li Wen-Bin performing Embrace the Moon in the Arm*

*Master Li Hong with Master Cai Long-Yun in 1995*

# In Search of the Missing Points in the Origin of Xingyiquan Techniques

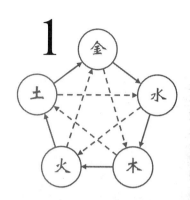

Xingyiquan (形意拳; Shape and Intent Boxing) is one of the most influential boxing styles in Chinese martial arts. Because it has been around for so long, there have been many stages in its evolution and much divergence in its names and techniques and in the theories about Xingyiquan's origin and content in the existing publications on the subject. It is imperative for us to research the process of its evolution, find the differences in the various theories and practices, and discover the essence of each sub-style at every phase; all of these are crucial in the study of Xingyiquan.

Despite some disagreement about the creator of Xingyiquan and its successors in the first few generations, there is now a consensus in the recorded literature and contemporary textual research that Xingyiquan was created by Ji Ji-Ke (姬际可) from Pu Zhou in Shan Xi province during the late Ming or early Qing dynasties. However, the *quan* (拳; fist or boxing style) he created, which is the predecessor of Xingyiquan, is quite different from the Xingyiquan widely practiced today.

Both Xin Yi Ba Shi Er Da Shi (心意把十二大势; Twelve Big Postures in Key Techniques of Mind and Intent Boxing), a form passed down by the Shaolin Temple, and Xin Yi Quan Shi Da Xing (心意拳十大形; Ten Big Animal Forms in Mind and Intent Boxing), a form passed down by Ma Xue-Li (马学礼) in He Nan province, focus on practicing each single technique in order to master fighting skills. They are practical, rather than aesthetically pleasing. They use sideways Bow Stance, which is also used in Xin Yi Liu He Quan (心意六合拳; Mind, Intent and Six Harmonies Boxing), created later by Dai Long-Bang (戴龙邦) in Shan Xi province. However, their focus on movements and techniques draws a clear line between them and the Xingyiquan that we see in later years.

Despite the commonality of using sideways Bow Stance, the Liu He Quan, or Xin Yi Liu He Quan, passed down by Dai Long-Bang has a different focus: the coordination between intent, breathing, internal force, and external movements. In addition, he proposes using *Dantian* (丹田; field of energy/elixir) as foundation, using *yi* (意; intent) to lead *qi* (气; vital energy), coordinating hands with feet, and fusing defense and offense into one. As for the movements, they start natural and relaxed, progressing from slow to fast, aiming to foster strong *nei jing* (内劲; internal force) by fusing internal and external strengths. This nei jing originates from Dantian and circulates throughout the entire body. The ultimate goal of training, according to Dai Long-Bang, is to cultivate an explosive power that can be used effectively in fighting. Dai Long-Bang's great contribution was in shifting the emphasis from movements and techniques to the application of *nei yi* (内意; internal intent), nei jing, *shen* (神; spirit), and qi. Although both Dai Long-Bang and Ma Xue-Li were taught by Cao Ji-Wu, the techniques they passed on were quite different. Dai not only emphasized internal intent, but also added Zhuang Gong (桩功; Post Standing Meditation technique) and Wu Xing Quan (五行拳; Five Element Fist) to the repertoire of movements and forms. In addition, he expanded the Ten Big Forms into Twelve Forms. These changes laid the foundation for the evolution from Xin Yi Quan (心意拳; Mind and Intent Boxing) into Xingyiquan (形意拳; Shape and Intent Boxing).

Li Luo-Neng (李洛能), who trained with Dai Long-Bang, brought Yi Quan (意拳; Mind Boxing) into He Bei province. Yi Quan was later renamed Xingyiquan. Li glorified this newly developed boxing style. He improved Wu Xing Quan by using the shapes of ax, lightning, arrow, cannon, and earth ball to reflect the inner meanings of Chopping Fist, Drilling Fist, Smashing Fist, Cannon Fist, and Crossing Fist;

and he explained the relationships among the five fists. In addition, he changed Ten Big Forms and Seven Small Forms into Twelve Forms, which mimic the shapes and movements of animals. Li also added some forms for solo and dual practice, as well as for weapons. Among his innovations, the most special was a change in footwork: he substituted the sideways Bow Stance for both Huai Chong Bu (槐虫步; Inchworm Stepping), in which the front foot moves forward with the back foot following immediately, and the Ji Tui (鸡腿; Chicken Leg), which requires both legs to be bent and pressed against each other tightly, with 30 percent weight on the front leg and 70 percent on the back leg. As for the body posture, he introduced San Ti Shi (三体式; Three Body Stance)—also called San Cai Shi (三才式; Three Elements Stance) or Ying Zhuo Shi (鹰捉式; Eagle Grasp Stance)—in which the body faces partially forward and partially sideways. Furthermore, Ying Zhuo Shi carries both the physical shape and the character of four animals, referred to as Si Xiang (四象; Four Imitations); they include Ji Tui, Long Shen (龙身; Dragon Body), Xiong Bang (熊膀; Bear Shoulder), and Hu Bao Tou (虎抱头; Tiger Holding Its Head). These broke the norm in Chinese martial arts—which uses Bow Stance, Horse Stance, Crouching Stance, Void Stance, and Resting Stance as the major stances—and established the characteristic of Xingyiquan techniques.

Undoubtedly, this was one of the greatest innovations since the one by Dai Long-Bang. Because he was able to research the subtleties of Xingyiquan and find its essence, Li Luo-Neng reached the highest skill level of this art and could defend himself without having to see or hear the target or plan ahead of time. This level of proficiency has been described as "Punch without being seen where the fists are coming from; attack without having to set up the intent first. All techniques are executed spontaneously. This is the real essence of this art." Due to his high level of skill, Li was nicknamed Shen Quan (神拳; Immortal Fist). In addition to refining the theories and techniques in Xingyiquan, Li also broke the commonly held conservative mindset. He opened his door to students from all over. This is why there have been so many famous successors in his school and the art has been widely spread. His disciples, Song Shi-Rong (宋世荣) and Che Yong-Hong (车永宏), brought the skills that Li learned from Shan Xi back to their place of origination. They have, in turn, had a great many successors, known as the Shan Xi Pai (山西派; Shan Xi sect). At the same time, Guo Yun-Shen (郭云深) and Liu Qi-Lan (刘奇兰) became the head masters of the He Bei branch (河北派). They too passed the art down to many people, among them many talented masters. Although there have only been one hundred and some years of spreading of the art, we already can see the successors of the ninth generation. The whole system is growing stronger and stronger. The Xingyi family has become very prosperous.

Although the Xingyiquan techniques practiced today came from Master Li, the styles and training approaches in the Shan Xi and He Bei branches are quite different. Furthermore, even within the same branch, when it comes to the style—especially the way they make energy hard, soft, long, short, flexible, or solid—different masters teach very differently. Due to these discrepancies, the later generations have developed different levels of understanding about the true ways of doing Xingyiquan and the meaning of classic Xingyiquan. Some of their understanding is deep, but a great many other people have misconceptions. We can see this when reading some publications and watching the movements that some people do. Since we all have passion for Xingyiquan and are willing to research ways to improve its quality, we need to develop a scientific and objective attitude so that we can differentiate the good from the bad. Once the "right ways" are identified, we should follow them, rather than being influenced by the old ideology. Otherwise, we will impede our own progress and mislead future generations. This critical thinking and the courage to choose the right path are things that all contemporary Xingyiquan practitioners should have in common.

When we study the techniques, origin, and development of Xingyiquan, we find answers in the direct teaching of our teachers, the Xingyiquan Classics, and publications by reputable people. Between the late Ming/early Qing dynasties and now, there have been many changes in

Xingyiquan. This has resulted in some difficulties in learning. If we study Xingyiquan without knowing the contents of these changes and just follow the Lao Jing (老经; old classics), Lao Pu (老谱; old names of movements), and publications, we will end up feeling lost. The old literature is precious and beneficial to read. However, these books are not like antiques, which become more valuable as they grow older. For instance, if we follow *Xin Yi Quan Pu* (心意拳谱; *Names of Movements in Mind and Intent Quan*) to study Xingyiquan, we will find a lot of mismatches with what is commonly practiced today. Even more so, if we follow the *Xin Yi Liu He Quan Pu* (心意六合拳谱; *Name of the Movements in Mind, Intent, and Six Harmonies Quan*), which has been revised several times since the year of Yong Zheng in the Qing Dynasty, we will find that many theories in the book are not consistent with the movements and techniques that are currently practiced in Xingyiquan.

An example of this phenomenon is the article *Liu He Shi Da Yao Xu* (六合十大要序; *The Preface of Ten Big Guidelines in Six Harmonies*), from the book *Xin Yi Liu He Quan Pu,* which was changed into *Shi Da Zhai Yao* (十大摘要; *Ten Big Synopses*) by Cao Ji-Wu (see figure 1-1). This article is considered a classic and has had a big influence on many people. However, if we examine its content, we will find that many statements contradict the requirements of Xingyiquan and are confusing and even misleading to practitioners. For example, the article states that "only in our *Liu He Quan,* we practice advancing, defending, and opening techniques as a whole set. That's how our sense organs become very keen and we move very quickly. Even in the dark night, as soon as something comes up, we can sense the energy and respond to it immediately." This last sentence is not convincing, for there is a huge distinction between the ability to "sense the energy and respond to it immediately" and the concepts of training in Xingyiquan. We understand that, before fostering the internal *shen* (神; spirit), *yi* (意; intent), *qi* (气; vital energy), and *nei jing* (内劲; internal force), it is impossible for one to be able to respond to the attacking energy automatically. The Xingyiquan practiced before Dai Long-Bang did not examine this topic. Therefore, if

*Figure 1-1.* Ten Big Synopses *by Cao Ji-Wu*

we learn Xingyiquan today by practicing advancing, defending, and opening techniques, we make the mistake of giving up the root (the crucial part) but searching for the end (the trivial part) of the art.

When discussing the use of San Jie (三节; Three Joints), *Shi Da Zhai Yao* states, "As soon as the end joint moves, the middle joint follows, and the root joint has to chase. The Three Joints echo one another so that there won't be the issues of being too long, too short, too slanted, or too straight; nor will there be worries about the alignment and body posture. Therefore, the use of the Three Joints has to be very precise." The theory of the *qi* (起; starting), *sui* (随; following), and *zhui* (追; chasing) of San Jie is completely different from that in the San Cui Jing (三催 劲; three pushing energies/force) of Xingyiquan. Xingyiquan requires "using the waist to push the shoulder, the shoulder to push the elbow, and the elbow to push the hand." The former theory focuses on the end joint, while the latter focuses on the root joint. This leads to two completely different *jing lu* (劲路; energy paths) and fighting techniques. Xingyiquan requires training the nei jing from Dantian and the power to execute "punching from the Three Joints without the shape being seen." Without San Cui Jing, if we only rely on the method of starting, following, and chasing, it is impossible to obtain this desired effect.

In *Shi Da Zhai Yao,* when they talk about Si Shao (四梢; four ends, or the ends of four limbs), they focus on the external shape of the movement in the technique. Unlike this, Xingyiquan emphasizes Jing Qi Si Shao (惊起四梢; shocking up the four ends), in which the morale would be boosted. It is not difficult to see the difference in the techniques of the two theories.

Although *Shi Da Zhai Yao* talks about the Qi Luo (起落; rising and falling) in hand techniques and footwork, this focus is more on the way and shape of moves. For example, both hands should "come up like lifting a cauldron, fall down like breaking a bottle.... Elbow protects the chest and ribcage area. Hand rises while attacking the genitalia at the same time. When the hands are coming up, it looks like a tiger pouncing at someone. When they fall down, it looks like an eagle grasping its prey." When it comes to footwork, the article explains the way in which the foot comes up while hands are making a drilling movement, and the way the foot looks when it falls down while the palm is turning over: "As soon as the foot rises, the knee comes up and is drawn toward your chest immediately. With your knee up and lower leg raised to strike at the opponent, it forms an upward turn angle and looks like the way you lift your hand upward to attack the opponent's genitalia. As for the falling of the foot, it has the appearance of drilling something with a stone." When discussing the technique of *cai* (踩; stomp, trample), the article states that it "looks like an eagle grasping its prey."

All of the abovementioned concepts have a huge discrepancy from the essence of Xingyiquan. Xingyiquan emphasizes, "When striking with Crossing Fist, the opponent cannot see the trace of crossing. When the fist comes straight downward, you cannot see the path that the fist passes." Within defense, there is offense; within offense, there is defense. It proposes that "the energy expressed when hands are rising up is like the retreating wave; the time when the top of the wave descends is the time that you strike. The energy and power shown are like big moving waves." This is the crucial point in practicing Xingyiquan. Only when you have the key can you have the chance to master the art. This type of *Mo Suo Jing* (摩挲劲; stroking energy/force) is entirely different from that described as "drilling something with a stone" or "eagle grasping its prey."

As for the technique of *cai,* Xingyiquan requires that "when attacking with your leg/foot, you need to have the intent that you are trampling something. The intent is very strong, and it feels like you will never let go of the target." The purpose of executing the technique this way is to develop the skill and power of Juan Di Feng (卷地风; wind whirling over the ground) and Tie Li Fan Di (铁犁翻地; iron plough turning the field). We can see that there is a huge difference in the mental power applied in this type of practicing approach and that in "eagle grasping its prey." They both talk about *qi luo* (起落; rising and falling) and *cai,* yet there are no similarities in the meaning and applications of the techniques between them. *Ten Big Synopses* mentions such terms as "Protecting Technique," "Opening Technique," "Intercepting Technique," and "Chasing Technique." It also mentions terms like "Intercepting Hammer," "Sweeping Hammer," "Soaring Cannon," and "Ground Sweeping Cannon." These terms and names of the movements are not adopted in *Xingyiquan,* nor are the differences in the energy path and the execution of the techniques.

As for nei jing, the article claims that "It actually means *nian jing* (粘劲; sticking energy)." But the so-called nian jing cannot be compared with the forces such as *fan lang* (翻浪; wave turning), *dou sou* (抖擞; shaking), and *zha* (炸; explosive) produced in Xingyiquan. That is why we say that, when trying to learn Xingyiquan, it is inappropriate to refer to the *Ten Summaries in Xin Yi Liu He Quan Pu* or the *Synopses of Ten Methods* by Cao Ji-Wu. During the time when Xin Yi Quan was practiced, the art was considered a rare martial art system and was only passed down to insiders secretly. Although Xingyiquan originated from one person, several different branches and variations of techniques evolved; it would be incorrect to learn Xingyiquan by following the theories and practice formed before this evolution.

One more example is the *Liu He Quan Pu* (六合拳谱; names of the movements in Six Harmonies Quan) passed down from the Dai family in Shan Xi province, which is the blueprint that Li Luo-Neng used to create theories in Xingyiquan. Its content is similar to that in the names of movements passed down from He Bei province, which includes the *Liu He Quan Xu* (六合拳序; the Preface for *Liu He Quan*) written by Dai Long-Bang. However, many stances—such as Cross-Leg Sitting Stance and Character of Human Stance, as well as single-technique training such as Seven Cannons and Seven Shoulders—are no longer adopted in Xingyiquan. Furthermore, the names and substance of many movements and forms have been changed. Some of them are pronounced the same but written differently, and the meanings are completely different. Therefore, if we quote indiscriminately, we create confusion for other people, and the techniques and content may be changed.

The only accurate guidance in Xingyiquan theories is the manuscript of *Liu He Quan Pu* (六合拳谱; Name of Movements in Six Harmonies Boxing), which was passed down from He Bei province and includes the *Liu He Quan Xu* (六合拳序; Preface of Liu He Boxing), written by Dai Long-Bang in the fifteenth year of Qian Long in the Qing Dynasty. Some people call it *Xingyiquan Pu* (形意拳谱; Names of the Movements in Xingyiquan), while others call it *Yue Wu Mu Wang Quan Pu* (岳武穆王拳谱; Names of the Movements in Boxing by King Yue Wu Mu). This manuscript not only keeps the partial content of *Liu He Quan Pu* (see

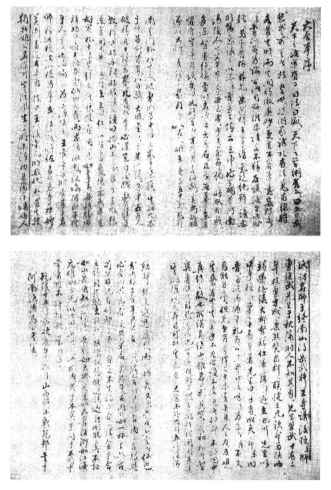

*Figure 1-2. Liu He Quan Pu by Dai Long-Bang*

figure 1-2), but also adds many theories on skills. Although the wording is simple, there is a deeper, more complex meaning. For instance, the term "Qi Luo Zuan Fan" (起落钻翻; rising, falling, drilling, turning) is the same as in other publications, but the meanings of the techniques are quite different. Without guidance from good teachers and experience, it is very difficult to understand the details; it is easy to make mistakes if we interpret the meanings based on our knowledge about other boxing styles, or if we understand the concepts only at a surface level. We must be humble and cautious, lest we impede our own progress and mislead others. Unfortunately, there have been a lot of mistakes in the content introduced by people copying *Liu He Quan Pu.* Some made mistakes or missed some parts of the information because they didn't understand the techniques in the manuscript; others added, cut, or rewrote the content based on their own personal interest.

It is not just the content of this manuscript that has been changed. The preface written by Dai Long-Bang is also different from the original. It's clear that this was done on purpose, not an unintentional mistake made during the copying process. The copy circulating in He Bei—which has been quoted by many famous masters in He Bei branch since Li Luo-Neng, including Matsuda Takatomo from Japan—adapted the preface as follows: "Master Ji, named Ji-Ke, also nicknamed Long-Feng, was born in Pu-Dong Zhu-Feng in the late Ming or early Qing dynasties. One day he visited Zhong-Nan Mountain and obtained *Yue Wu Mu Wang Quan Pu* (岳武穆王拳谱; *Names of the Movements in Boxing Created by King Yue Wu Mu).* At the time, people did not realize how powerful he was . . ."

From this preface, it is clear that the second-generation successor is Huang Ji-Wu. This preface is mostly seen in the old names of the movement copied with brush pens and I have seen many versions of them. However, I read the *Yue Shi Yi Quan Yuan Xu* (岳氏意拳原序; *Original Preface of Yi Quan by Yue*) in *Yue Shi Yi Quan Wu Xing Shi Er Xing Fa Jing Yi* (岳氏意拳五行十二形法精义; *Essential Methods for Five Elements and Twelve Animal Forms in Yue-Family Yi Quan*) by

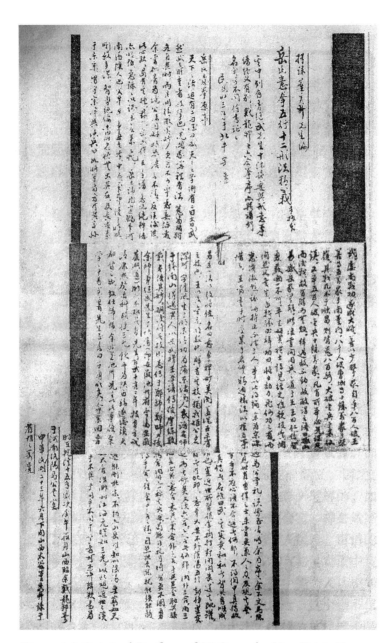

*Figure 1-3.* Original Preface of Yi Quan by Yue Fei *in* Yue Shi Yi *by Dong Xiu-Sheng*

Dong Xiu-Sheng (董秀升) in Taigu, which is actually *Liu He Quan Xu* (figure 1-3). It changed the content into "Master Ji, named Ji-Ke, also nicknamed Long-Feng, was born in Pu-Dong Zhu-Feng in the late Ming or early Qing dynasties. One day he visited Zhong-Nan Mountain and ran into an extraordinary man, who taught him the *Yue Wu Mu Wang Quan Pu* for several years. After learning all the wonderful techniques, he passed them down to Teacher Zheng; Teacher Zheng passed them down to my teacher Cao Ji-Wu in Qiu Pu (Chi Zhou in An Hui province). At that time, people did not realize how powerful it was..." Master Dong not only changed the names of the people but also, at the end of the preface, marked the dates and locations to show when and where the original was written and the copy was made. He did this to take responsibility for his revisions and insights.

Dong Xiu-Sheng's book also included *Cao Ji-Wu Shi Fa Zhai Yao* (曹继武十法摘要; *Cao Ji-Wu Ten Big Synopses for Methods*), which stated that "only Teacher Zheng got the real techniques from Teacher Ji (Ji-Ke)... I am lucky to be a disciple of Teacher Zheng, so I have inherited the real techniques of Teacher Ji..." Dong changed the content in order to put his teacher in a very high position, because he believed that this *Ten Big Synopses for Methods* was written by Cao, and because it was followed by many people and had been copied and spread widely. There is something suspicious about this *Ten Big Synopses for Methods*. We know that it really comes from *Liu He Shi Da Yao Xu* (六合十大要序; *The Preface of Ten Big Guidelines in Six Harmonies*) by Wang Zi-Cheng. Wang's article was written forty years after Cao had won three consecutive national examinations and been appointed the high position of governor; Cao might still have been alive when Wang wrote the article. If the former article was written by Cao, why didn't Wang mention his name, to avoid being accused of plagiarism and earn a good reputation by complimenting Cao's work? In addition, Cao Ji-Wu was known to be respectful of his teachers and the art. In this article, the name and background of his teacher, who had taught him for twelve years, was not mentioned at all. Therefore, it's highly questionable that this article was written by Cao Ji-Wu and that Teacher Zheng was really the successor of this lineage. For now, we can put these issues aside and let the martial arts historians investigate the truth. Still, the confusion created by changing the content of old literature has misled many practitioners. My advice is that we have to choose carefully which texts to follow in learning these techniques.

Some literature is helpful for cultivating health and practicing Gong Fu. However, it can be confusing, to say the least. For example, *Yue Wu Mu Jiu Yao Lun* (岳武穆九要论; *Nine Important Discussions by Yue Wu Mu*) must have been written by someone who practiced Xin Yi Quan, and it was well written, but its true author is unknown. The author claimed he was Yue Fei [also known as Yue Wu Mu] to make the book sound more important. Other literature, such as *Nei Gong Jing, Na Gua Jing, Shen Yun Jing,* and *Di Long Jing,* is helpful in training; in fact, Master Song Shi-Rong loved these books so much that he recommended them to people. However, if we examine their historical background and the content of the techniques, they were written by neither Da Mo nor Yue Fei. Besides, they don't belong to the art of Xingyiquan.

There's no denying that all the literature created by older generations is precious. However, there have been so many differences between publications about Xingyiquan. Some of them exaggerated the power of this boxing art by describing it as having the immortals' magical power, for example. Therefore, we should not be confused by them. We should compare, differentiate, and select those that are reasonable to learn from. If everyone can do this, we can avoid the damage caused by false information and lift our skill level at the same time.

Zhi-Rong and I wrote this book to reveal some secrets and say things that other people are not willing to say. The purpose of this book is to provide something for people to ponder over.

# Features of Shang-Style Xingyiquan

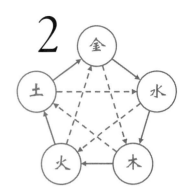

The features we talk about here are unique. However, when it comes to topics such as shape of the movements, energy path, and intent, Shang-style Xingyiquan follows the guidelines stated in the Xingyiquan Classics. Master Shang studied carefully and taught seriously, and that is how the important information has been passed down. It is a pity that many Xingyiquan practitioners do not work hard enough to seek the entire essence. But fortunately, the part we have inherited is enough to guide us to the right path. Instead of criticizing other styles, here we only describe the features of Shang-style Xingyiquan.

The martial arts world values the virtues of respecting its teachers and treasuring the arts we inherit from them. This is the tradition we must keep. However, we need to put aside the ideas that prevent us from becoming better. Concepts such as "whoever comes in first [the first teacher] is the authority" can foster egoism and exclusion. Some people believe that if the teachers are famous, their students must be good. Because of this misconception, they miss the opportunity to learn from people who are better than themselves. If we want to improve our skills, we need to have a scientific mind, select the best concepts to follow, and study carefully to find the essence of the art. Zhi-Rong and I are breaking with tradition by sharing our knowledge with all practitioners, to promote the art passed down by our teacher. I hope all of you can, after reading this book, critique it with an objective attitude, regardless of style and lineage. You can adopt the helpful parts, to enhance your skills or promote the art. If you can do this, I, as the main author of the book, will feel that my mission has been accomplished.

# San Ti Shi Zhuang Gong

*San Ti Shi* (Three Body Stance) extends tendons, expands bones, and has movement within stillness. It is the primary *Zhuang Gong* (桩功; Post Standing Meditation Posture) in Shang-style Xingyiquan. In addition to enhancing the foundation for learning techniques, it includes rich fighting applications. There is a saying in the martial arts world that goes, "If the tendons are long, the force is strong; if the flesh is thick, the body is more solid." Through training, we make joints flexible and stretch muscles, making them expand or contract easily to increase the explosive power. With this power, we can punch hard and fast. Although San Ti Shi Zhuang Gong is done in stillness, it "extends tendons and expands bones" in a subtle way. This contributes to the features of Shang-style Xingyiquan, which include big and flexible movements and the ability to issue fast, hard, solid power.

The Xingyiquan Classics state, "The motion within stillness is the real motion; the stillness within motion is the real stillness." From the perspective of martial skills training, if there is no motion within stillness, what we have is just the empty posture. Zhuang Gong is the foundation for *Gong Fu*. It combines both internal and external aspects, which correspond to substance and applications. The training starts by striving for accuracy in postures and movements, and then proceeds to training the intent. The goal is to seek motion within stillness and initiate intent to move *qi* throughout the body. The highest level of proficiency is the integration of motion and stillness, shape, and spirit, and to be able to "throw punches without setting up the mind to do so. Everything is done so spontaneously, that is the real Gong Fu." Shang-style Xingyiquan focuses on the training of this hidden fighting skill. In fact, the motion we are seeking is the training of intent, and it is also the cultivation of qi, spirit, and internal force. This "motion" is required to regulate the central nervous system so that spirit can be boosted. In addition, the extension and stretching of muscles invigorates blood circulation, nurtures the tissue, and enhances metabolism. Therefore, San Ti Shi is effective for healing and health cultivation. It can improve a person's constitutional quality because it teaches us how to strengthen our body and spirit in a calm and natural way. Use of clumsy, brute force is not allowed.

## EXTENDING THE TENDONS, EXPANDING THE BONES

### Tuck Chin, Lift Head, Sink Qi to Dantian

Tucking in the chin, lifting up the top of the head, and sinking qi down to Dantian are required to stretch the body in upward and downward directions. This allows qi to go up easily through the Three Gates— Jade Pillow Gate, Narrow Vertebrae Gate, Coccyx Gate in the *du* channel of Microcosmic Orbit qi circulation path—and go down to solidify the root of spirits (i.e., Dantian).

In "Dragon Folding the Body" [explained in Chapter 3], our pelvis faces forward and we twist the *yao* to stretch our bodies. This helps Dantian to issue power and send it to the limbs easily.

### Lift Back, Sink Shoulders, Drop Elbows

Lifting up the back, sinking the shoulders, and dropping the elbows are required to stretch the arms. The wrapping inward and dropping downward of the elbows, combined with the palm being concave and facing downward, aim to make the shoulder, elbow, and hand form a straight line and extend completely to produce a twisting and extending force. This alignment increases the holistic power resulting from *San Cui* (三催; Three Pushes). If these movements are integrated with yi, the energy will go to the end joints, creating a tinkling, swollen heat and qi sensation in the hands. You can feel and hear the clicking in the finger joints when you touch them.

When punching in Xingyiquan, we need to follow the principle of "putting the *San Xing* (三星; Three Stars) in the right positions to make your force stronger." When doing *Zuan Quan* (钻拳; Drilling Fist), not only the shoulder pit and the elbow pit need to be formed; the wrist also has to be stretched. When doing San Ti Shi, the front hand reaches out with the palm facing down, but the center of the palm has to be pulled back; the fingers reach forward and *Hukou* (虎口; Tiger Mouth; the curved area between the thumb and the index finger) has to be round to stretch the wrist. If all of these requirements are met, even if we focus on intent instead of force, we still can increase the holistic power and make qi go to the fingers, which lengthens and enhances the force issued.

## Bend Knees, Distribute Weight 30/70

Bending the knees and distributing the weight by 30 percent in the front and 70 percent at the back forms the shape of a pair of scissors and extends the lower limbs. The toes of the front foot point forward, and the front knee has to push forward while the whole leg is squeezed inward. The toes of the back foot swing outward at a 45° angle while the back knee turns inward so that the kneecap is close to the front leg. These movements form a solid and flexible *Jia Jian Jing* (夹剪劲; force of scissors). It has a very good stretching effect on the ankle and knee joints as well as the muscles in the shins and hips. Since the knee joints are more sensitive to energy, we can hear and feel the sound of clicking during San Ti Shi.

Turning the back knee inward, twisting the upper body, and extending the *yao kua* [region between the waist and the groin] increase the drilling force in the upper limbs and the downward- and backward-pressing power in the lower limbs. These postures enhance the power issued from the yao. Although the abovementioned requirements for extension and stretching look ordinary, they bring about the unity of the entire body. This posture makes the power issued from Dantian strike long and far and attack fast, hard, and strong. This is the essence of Shang-style San Ti Shi.

## The Manifestation and Function of "Motion within Stillness"

The Xingyiquan Classics state, "Stillness is the substance and motion is to put it to use"; "The motion within stillness is the real motion, while the stillness within motion is the real stillness." Motion and stillness are closely related; substance and applications actually have the same origin. Standing in San Ti Shi is to integrate substance and application and to seek motion within stillness. Without the real motion, there is no understanding of yi. Without the real stillness, there is no understanding of *xing* (性; nature). Stillness belongs to nature while motion reveals intent. Without being able to stay still, the true intent cannot be triggered. Only when the true intent is triggered can the application of the techniques reach the mastery level. That is why training in Xingyiquan requires the integration of *xing* (形; shape) and *shen* (神; spirit). We are seeking the state when "you reach the ultimate emptiness and stillness, you return to your prenatal nature." And when "you are standing still quietly, the sensation is so keen that you can feel everything. At this point, you can decide when to act and when not to." To reach this goal, we need to learn to use yi to transform shen and qi and put them to use in fighting. San Ti Shi is to build up the foundation for this ability.

If you look inside at the tendons and bones, focus on the end joints of upper limbs, sink the shoulders, and drop the elbows, there will be "movements" in the fingers. There will be tingling, swelling, heat, and the sensation of moving qi. Although we only use *yi,* the power can go through the fingers and qi can flow toward the end joints. If you focus your mind on the lower limbs, with the front knee pushing forward, back knee squeezing inward, and the body twisted, there will be "motion" in the knees. There will be clicking sounds, soreness, ache, heat, and the sensation of flowing qi. The lower part of the body will become very solid, and the back leg will have greater power to press forward. Additionally, since qi can go down to the *Yong Quan* (涌泉; starting point of kidney channel), problems such as arthritis and cold legs will be healed.

When you focus on Dantian, regulate your breathing, and try to bring qi to its root [i.e., Dantian], there will be "motion" in the lower abdomen. You will feel a sensation of heat, which means that Dantian is being filled with Genuine Qi, which strengthens our body, solidifies our root, and increases our ability to generate force. During this process, you will generate a lot of saliva. If you swallow it and use yi to bring it down to Dantian, you will hear the sound of saliva going down and feel a soothing sensation in the lower abdomen. When qi is smooth and the lower abdomen is solid, problems in the internal organs and the abdominal cavity will be corrected. This is what is known as "training qi in Dantian": "If you train your Dantian long enough, you will solidify the root of spirits." It is also described in the phrase, "the Genuine Qi is concealed in a secret place." At the same time, it indicates a state in which the "Primary Spirits and Primary Qi" are integrated. When qi is initiated, internal force is gradually formed and permeates throughout the body. Shang-style San Ti Shi is a vehicle for cultivating motion within stillness, and also for initiating the nurturing process.

After training with movement in forms and reaching the level when "the upper and lower part of the body follow each other; the internal and external aspect are integrated and the qi in the whole body is unified as one," and having developed the technique of issuing hard energy, the understanding of soft energy will follow and the ability to use energies in a flexible way will transpire automatically. Upon reaching this level of proficiency, the practice of San Ti Shi demands even more. It has to "put the realization of spirits and nature as the first priority" and "fuse shen, yi, and qi in Dantian" in order to transport them to all parts of the body. When the situation requires, qi will flow immediately and you will have access to great force. This is the highest level of Shang-style San Ti Shi Zhuang Gong. At this point, we have reached the level referred to in the Classiscs the statement, "It's everywhere; it's always like that; it responds as soon as you touch it; you obtain it without thinking about it." And: "You throw punches without setting up the mind to do so. Everything is done so automatically; that it is the real Gong Fu." These are the guidelines that Master Shang has given us for working toward an advanced level of proficiency.

## Tang Jing and Jiao Da Qi Fen

Another feature of Shang-style Xingyiquan is Tang Jing (趟劲; tang force [this is the energy that comes from pressing the back foot hard against the ground, which creates a forward-springing momentum]) and the special technique of Jiao Da Qi Fen (脚打七分; leg kick 70 percent), meaning that 70 percent of fighting relies on the legs. The Xingyiquan Classics state, "When fighting, your legs have to step firmly as if you are grabbing the ground. The force is initiated by the forward-spring energy from the back foot. You are always ready for a fight, since you have trained this forward-stepping force to the point that it is as powerful and fast as the whirling wind sweeping the leaves off the ground." It continues, "When smashing the punch forward, the power is as crisp and solid as breaking the stem of a bean. When stepping forward, the five toes grab the ground so firmly that the force is as big and solid as that used when turning the ground over with an iron plow." And: "70 percent of fighting relies on the legs and 30 percent on the hands." Because the power generated from stepping forward is greater than that generated by the hands, it makes sense that we put so much focus on footwork. Master Shang was strict about his students developing Tang Jing. Due to his effort, this special feature of Shang-style Xingyiquan has been passed down.

## Offense and Defense Are Integrated, Applied in a Flexible and Smooth Manner

The hand techniques in Shang-style Xingyiquan focus on having "Elbows attached to the ribs, and hands close to the heart." This major defense posture in Xingyiquan can be used as a movement for gathering power. The arm power increases because the body is supporting the arms, and the body power is released through the arms. The power from the *yao* pushes the shoulder, the shoulder pushes the elbow, and the elbow pushes the hand. These "Three Pushing Forces" are formed because of this body posture. The application of "Tiger Holding the Head" is described as follows: "Whether it is entering or exiting from the cave, the hands are always close to the body." With the forearms wrapped inward and held underneath the chin, you are not only protecting the head and the chest, you are also gathering power of "twisting, wrapping, and dropping," and you are ready to attack. This is the manifestation of offense and defense integration.

"When using Crossing Punch to strike, one cannot see the horizontal energy in the punch; when the fist comes downward, one cannot see the straight downward energy." The crossing energy here is for defense. Since it is hidden, it carries the power of offense as well. The dropping energy here is to attack. Although it cannot be seen, there is hidden wrapping energy in it. It can be used to parry the attacking hand from the opponent. Within the "rising and falling" and "crossing and straight" energies, there is a complementary relationship. Following this principle leads to the integration of offense and defense. Shang-style Xingyiquan demands its practitioners to train hard to obtain this technique.

When practicing martial arts, if we can keep the entire body relaxed and natural, without using any clumsy or brute force, the body will be well extended and the movements will become more flexible. Having achieved this, we will be able to find the right way of doing each technique, train internal force, and find the right *jing* (劲; force). If we can apply the foundation of "extending tendons and expanding bones" from Zhuang Gong to the practice of the movements, it will be easy for us to transform soft energy into hard and solid energy, and to extend our limbs farther in fighting. We should follow the principle of "spread out first, tighten later." Shang-style Xingyiquan requires softening the entire body before doing the movements. All the body parts need to be in alignment to create the right jing and yi. Shen and qi are concealed inside Dantian. The movements have to be expansive and flexible, solid and with holistic jing in order to create tremendous, intimidating power over your opponents. If we can do this, the quick [mental] wit and [physical] agility described in the following quotes from the Xingyiquan Classics will be easily obtained: "You are ten meters away from the opponent. You measure the situation, and then move fast toward the opponent. Although you move faster than the opponent by only one inch, you have the upper hand." "I don't hold any fixed posture in fighting. All I do is to evaluate the situation and I will know whether I should use the palm or fist to fight." "When fighting, if you don't know when to advance or retreat, all the Gong Fu you practice is in vain; if you don't know when to raise your fist or punch down, it is of no use even if you are very smart." "You need to be able to advance within one thought. Don't retreat and be defeated because you hesitate." "When encountering multiple opponents, I shake my body three times and move around twice. Then, the job is done."

## Power Issuance Is Fast, Fierce, Hard, and Solid

The most striking feature of Shang-style Xingyiquan is that the movements and power issuance are very fast, fierce, hard, and solid. (This technique is summarized as, "When the trigger is pulled, the object is hit.") Many of my fellow practitioners say that "if you cannot get the explosive jing that is fast, fierce, hard, and solid, you cannot say that you have learned the hard energy." Even in his later years, Master Shang still said, "If I could have thirty more years to live, I would practice thirty more years of hard energy." Not many people understand why he said that. In fact, it reflects the truth that Master Shang discovered from his own experience. Master Shang specialized in Xingyi throughout his life. People know that he was highly respected and famous for the many fights he had been in against bullies. It is rarely known that Master Shang was born with a very small body size and a weak constitution.

When he tried to train with Master Li Cun-Yi, he was rejected, because Li thought that he was not cut out for martial arts. He forced himself to train to obtain that high level of Gong Fu. This is why what he said is so valuable and helpful to our training.

The principle for defeating enemies in Xingyiquan is to "fight hard, advance hard regardless of barrier." Master Shang explained it as follows: "Whether the opponent is moving or still, using hard or soft energy, you always attack. You don't rely on momentum or borrow force from the opponent. Even when he is parrying, as soon as you touch him, you issue explosive power. This is called 'fight hard.'" To own this asset, first you must train to have hard jing. Without using brute and clumsy force, we train to have holistic, harmonious hard jing. After that, we can move forward to train the fast, fierce, hard, and solid explosive jing and reach the level described in the sayings "rising up like the wind, dropping down like an arrow; although the opponent has been beaten, you still don't think that is fast enough" and "rising up like an arrow, dropping down like the wind; chasing the wind and catching up with the moon, there is no letting go." That way, the internal force will be abundant; the strike will be solid, far-reaching, and fast. With all of the power mentioned above, you can then claim to have the real jing in Xingyi and have the Gong Fu of "when the trigger is pulled, the object is hit." Although Master Shang had already reached the level of being able to use soft energy to defeat his opponents, he still worked hard to continue training his hard energy and issuing explosive power. He taught his students to do it in the same way. That is why Shang-style Xingyiquan is able to issue power that is fast, fierce, hard, and solid. Some practitioners have already learned the Fan Lang Jing (翻浪劲; Wave Rolling Energy)—also called Mo Sha Jing (摩挲劲; Rubbing and Rolling Energy) or Hua Jing (划劲; Gliding Energy)—which has the feature of issuing power as soon as it encounters attacking energy. However, such practitioners still practice issuing hard energy. By doing so, the two types of energies can reinforce each other, to enhance Gong Fu. It also feels more fulfilling. In brief: "If you cannot obtain the explosive power that is fast, fierce, hard, and solid, you will not be able to strike at will when your hand touches the opponent." Is this true? Those who are willing to experiment will find the answer to this question.

## Nei Jing (内劲; Internal Force) Allows for "Pushing the Three Joints" and "Shocking the Four Ends"

When it comes to the training of nei jing, there is a theory of "returning to prenatal state." Based on this theory, the movements have to be relaxed, coordinated, and natural. Without using brute force or clumsy energy, we adjust our body posture, get rid of chaotic external energy, and bring wandering shen and qi into Dantian to integrate with the prenatal Genuine Qi. This is a process that can only be mastered by persistent practice. In the end, force will circulate throughout the body in a harmonious way. Eventually, this force becomes a strong nei jing that fuses xing and shen, and hence combines substance and application. In learning Xingyiquan, if the foundation is not good or hard energy is not developed, nei jing cannot be fostered. When nei jing is applied to movement, we need to use yao as the core, to transport the nei jing to all parts of the body. Once nei jing is abundant, applying Xingyi techniques will become very efficient. When teaching Xingyiquan, instead of emphasizing forms and strategies, Master Shang focused on practicing internal work and searching for jing. The purpose is to integrate the internal and external aspects and to look for the true jing. That is why he could achieve such a high level of proficiency.

The integration of xing and shen, as well as the abundant nei jing expressed in Shang-style Xingyiquan, results from following strictly the concepts of "pushing the Three Joints" and "shocking the Four Ends." The Xingyiquan Classics state, "When you punch with the Three Joints, people cannot see the attack in action. If it can be noticed, then your technique is not good enough." We all know that in our torso, arms, and legs there are three joints: the root, middle, and end joints.

In our arms, they refer to shoulder, elbow, and hand. In the legs, they refer to groin, knee, and foot. If all the three joints are integrated and use *yao* to move, the whole body will be filled with holistic energy. Independently, each joint has its own function. "When you punch with the three joints, people cannot see the attack in action" does not mean that, when you are punching with your fist and are intercepted, you shift into using your elbow to strike. Or that when you are using the elbow to strike and are intercepted, you use your shoulder to fight. These are techniques that use visible energy. Instead, it means that you use the Three Pushing Forces to have the yao push the shoulder, the shoulder push the elbow, and the elbow push the hand. When the attacking hand is intercepted, you still push with your shoulder and elbow. You issue power at the point where it is intercepted. We change the the source of power instead of changing the hand technique. This way the opponent cannot see the type of technique you are using and will remain unaware when he is attacked. This is the wonderful effect of this concept. Yi, qi, and li (力; force) are fused in Dantian. The power is also issued from Dantian and transported to the Three Joints. Under the guidance of this rule, all the three joints will form free passages for nei jing and the body shape will be integrated with the energy path. This way nei jing will become abundant.

As for the Four Ends, they refer to the following: 1) the hair is the end of the blood; 2) the finger- and toenails are the end of the tendons; 3) the teeth are the end of the bones; 4) the tongue is the end of the flesh. We use the term "shock" to describe the initiation of the Four Ends, implying that stimulating spirit is required to make them work. The following statements from the Xingyiquan Classics indicate how they function: 1) Whenever your mind senses something, your spirit reacts to it; 2) When one is filled with anger, his or her hair will stand up so high that the hat will be pushed off. The blood will circulate a lot faster; 3) When the tongue is curled, qi will sink down. The flesh will become so tough that even the mountain is impressed; 4) Tigers are powerful and eagles are vicious. They fight by using the claws as their main weapon; 5) Courage lies in the bones. As soon as you clench the teeth, it is released. All of these statements explain the spiritual power of the Four Ends. If we can apply these concepts to our daily practice, our shen will become very strong. In fighting situations, lifting up the head, pushing the tongue against the upper palate, keeping the jaw tight, and hooking the fingers will boost our courage and intimidate our enemies. Because of this, Master Shang emphasized the application of shen to "shock up" the Four Ends and the five internal organs. When combined with body movements and *jing lu* (劲路; energy path), xing and shen will be integrated and nei jing will become abundant. If you practice consistently, you will feel energized as soon as you start practicing, even when you are very tired. These techniques are valuable for both self-defense and health cultivation.

## *Ying Zhuo* (鷹捉; Eagle Grasp) Expresses the Special Function of Pi Quan

In the first hand form of Xingyiquan, you drill up with a fist and press downward with a palm to form San Ti Shi. Many people call this "Pi Quan," but Master Shang called it "Ying Zhuo." He had a point. First, since it is a palm instead of a fist, it should not be called "quan." Second, the definition in the Xingyiquan Classics says, "The shape of Pi Quan is like an ax. It has the property of metal." Pi Quan is a downward-facing palm. It does not have the shape of an ax, nor is it possible to train the power of an ax by holding this hand posture. This does not match what is described in the Xingyiquan Classics, and that is why it is not Pi Quan. Third, the Xingyiquan Classics state, "When encountering an enemy, the first technique you use is Tiger Pouncing; when starting a form, the first hand technique you use is Ying Zhuo." Since Ying Zhuo is the initial movement of *Wu Xing* (五行; Five Element) and *Shi Er Xing* (十二形; Twelve Animals) *Quan,* we should call it *Ying Zhuo* instead of *Pi Quan.* Ying Zhuo looks ordinary, and many Xingyiquan practitioners practice it. However, it is not easy to master. Why is this the case? We need to look at it from the perspective of jing in Xing-yiquan. Each technique of Wu Xing and Shi Er Xing has its own jing. Sometimes there are several *jing* within one form. The most common jing in Xingyiquan are *qi* (起; rise up), *luo* (落; falling down), *zuan* (钻; drilling up), and *fan* (翻; turn over). In the Xingyiquan Classics, there is a warning about the importance of *qi luo* (起落; rising and fall-ing), which says, "If you don't know the energies of rising and falling, no matter how smart you are, your training in Xingyi Gong Fu is in vain." If we interpret *qi luo* as simply an up-and-down movement, we are missing a lot. The essence of qi luo is manifested in "Mo Sha Jing," which is the rarely known "Fan Lang Jing." Ying Zhuo is the form that trains this energy. That is why it is called the Mother Fist of Xingyiquan. The Xingyiquan Classics state, "When the fist goes upward, it is a drilling punch; when it goes downward, the palm needs to turn over," and, "Qi is the issuance of the energy, while luo is time to strike. Using the energies of rising and falling to fight is just like the way ocean waves roll." If we do not understand the energies of qi, luo, zuan, and fan in Ying Zhuo, we will not be able to get the essence of Xingyiquan. Master *Shang* always said that without understanding qi luo, you are practicing blindly. At most, you just get a strong body. Shang-style practitioners look at Ying Zhuo as the key to the mystery of Xingyiquan, the transition from hard energy to soft and the ability to issue power at will. Therefore, they practice it very hard. Because the technique of Ying Zhuo is not included in Wu Xing Quan, it thus becomes a noteworthy feature of Shang-style Xingyiquan.

The Xingyiquan Classics state, "The shape of Pi Quan is like an ax. It belongs to metal, connects with the lungs, and its energy goes out through the nose." The movements of Pi Quan that Master Shang taught are similar to those in Ying Zhuo, except that he changed the downward-facing palm into a standing fist (Hukou is facing upward). This is an important difference, because when you combine it with the use of yi and li, they become two completely different techniques. The palm in Ying Zhuo goes through drilling up and turning over movements to create "Mo Sha Jing." Pi Quan uses the forearm like the blade of an ax. It drills upward and then chops downward to issue a power similar to that created by an ax. They are obviously two different techniques. Most notably, the focus of Pi Quan's power is not on the fist and elbow joint. Instead, it is on the forearm. This forms an additional striking tool besides the head, shoulder, elbow, hand, groin, knee, and foot. In addition, it goes beyond using the joints to strike.

## Other Unique Concepts and Practice Methods

In addition to Ying Zhuo and Pi Quan, mentioned above, there are more movements and theories that are different from other styles. If you cross-check with the Xingyiquan Classics, you will find the consistency between them. The different points are listed below for your reference and research.

### THE ORDER OF WU XING QUAN

Most people practice Wu Xing Quan in the order of metal, wood, water, fire, and earth; the characteristics of these elements are reflected in the boxing technques of Pi, Beng, Zuan, Pao, and Heng Quan. Master Shang was different. He said, "When we talk about Wu Xing, we need to focus on the principles of generating, controlling, restricting, and transforming." The purposes of practicing Wu Xing Quan are to treat disease, enhance health, transform constitution, and increase skill level. Therefore, we must follow the principle of generating—metal generates water; water generates wood; wood generates fire; fire generates earth—to form the order of Pi, Zuan, Beng, Pao, and Heng Quan. From the Chinese medical perspective, it is beneficial to health if we follow this order. From the perspective of training internal force, it is more efficient if we can cultivate both internal and external aspects. If we reverse the order of Zuan and Beng, there will be problems, because Pi Quan belongs to metal and Beng Quan belongs to wood. If we practice Beng Quan after

Pi Quan, it becomes metal controlling wood. Zuan belongs to water, while Pao belongs to fire. If we practice Zuan Quan before Pao Quan, it becomes water controlling fire. If we violate the principle of generating when practicing quan, it will not be an effective training scheme.

Zuan Quan is one of the Wu Xing Quan. Generally, there are two ways of practicing Wu Xing Quan; the major difference is in the hands. In the first method, the front fist turns inward (with the wrist turning inward and pressing downward) and pulls back to the front of abdomen (palm facing downward). Meanwhile, the back fist comes up over the chest to drill out from the mouth. The two fists alternate in their movements. In the second method, the front fist changes into a palm before folding into a fist and turning inward (with wrist turning inward and pressing downward), pulling back to the abdomen (palm facing down). Meanwhile, the back fist drills upward above the front fist. Both ways are different from what Master Shang taught.

The Xingyiquan Classics state, "The shape of Zuan Quan is like electricity or lightning, and it has the property of water. Its energy is connected with the kidneys. Its manifestation is through the ears." There is no doubt that we mimic the shape and then come up with the meaning. "Zuan Quan is like electricity" does not refer to the speed of electricity but to its shape. In ancient times, people used the word "electricity" to refer to the lightning in a thunderstorm. Based on this, we know that Zuan Quan copies the shape of lightning. The saying "Its energy is connected with kidneys" means that the movements of Zuan Quan help the functioning of the kidneys. In the Zuan Quan that Master Shang taught, before the front foot takes half a step forward it retreats half a step. At the same time, the front fist changes into a palm and hooks in toward the front of the chest. When the front foot takes half a step forward, the palm hooked in continues to swing to the side of the body, then forward and upward to become a standing palm (with the Hukou open and the palm facing forward). When the back fist follows the front palm to drill upward, the front palm changes into a fist and turns inward with a twisting energy, pulling backward to the side of the navel. The fist is facing upward. This series of movements derives energy from swinging the arms and shaking the waist. Zuan Quan relaxes the waist region to enhance kidney function. In addition, it includes the unique wrapping energy that is required in the Xingyiquan Classics (see photos of Zuan Quan in Chapter 4 for details).

## TUO XING QUAN

*Tuo Xing Quan* (鮀形拳; boxing that mimics the movement of *tuo* [鮀]) is one of the Twelve Animal Forms. Most people say that we are copying the movements of *tuo* (鼉), also named *tuo long* (鼉龙; tuo dragon) and *yang zi e* (扬子鳄; yang zi crocodile) or *zhu po long* (猪婆龙; zhu po dragon). However, we know that Ma Xue-Li and Dai Long-Bang passed down *Shi Da Xing* (十大形; Animal Forms), which already included *Long Xing* (龙形; dragon form)." There is no need for us to learn any other "dragon" animal form. Later on, Li Luo-Neng added two more animals to make the form include twelve animals, which became widely practiced in He Bei. 鮀 is one of them. The old manuscript passed down from He Bei with the *Liu He Quan Xu* by Dai Long-Bang did not record the word 鼉; instead, it used 鮀. It stated that this animal has "the mastery of floating on the water." This discovery draws a big distinction between 鮀 and 鼉. Master Shang said,

> When they are learning 鮀形, many people don't know what animal 鼉 is. They think that it is the 鼉 in 鼉龙, a very fierce animal that is the most agile among the animals in the water. So, they believe that we are learning the movements of this animal. In fact, 鼉 is a crocodile. Its body is *not* the most agile in the water. In fact, it is very clumsy. In addition, instead of floating on the water, it swims with its body under the surface of the water; only its head and the upper back are exposed above the water. Moreover, it swims in a straight line. Its claws are wide and big. They are not light and agile at all. 鮀 is transcribed as "Scissors' Leg" in the old manuscript. It is also called "Fragrant Oil" or "Oil Salesman." In *Animals' World,* it is called "Traveler on the Water." People transcribed the pronunciation of its name as *"yin*

*lu.*" Since its nickname is "Traveler on the Water," we can infer that it is the one that has the mastery of floating on the water. This is the animal we should be trying to learn from instead of the fierce 鼍.

Master Shang also said,

The color of 鮀 is gray. Its body length is shorter than one inch. It has six long and thin legs. People can often see it on the surface of static water after rain. It floats on the water and moves forward very fast, in a curving pattern that goes left and right. 鮀 and 鼍 are definitely not the same. According to the Xingyiquan Classics, we are trying to learn "the mastery of floating on the water," not the fierce force [of the crocodile]. When we practice Tuo Xing Quan, we move in a zigzag instead of straight forward. The thumb and the index finger are separated and the other three fingers are curved, which shows that obviously we are copying a claw instead of the big, wide paw of a crocodile.

Based on this description, we know that what Master Shang said and taught was right. Since 鼍 has the same pronunciation as 鮀, swims in the water, and is very fierce, people mistake it for the animal they should learn from. If we really follow the shape of 鼍 and copy the way it moves, the movements and meaning of the technique will be completely different from what the Xingyiquan Classics described. It is fortunate that Master Shang was able to differentiate the two and clarify this for Xingyiquan practitioners!

*Tai Xing Quan* ([鸟台]形拳; boxing that mimics the movement of [鸟台]) is one of the twelve animals in the form. It is one of the two animals that Master Li Luo-Neng added to the original Shi Da Xing. The majority of Xingyiquan practitioners recognize that we are copying the movement of a bird instead of an animal with four legs. However, there is no such character in modern dictionaries. Master Shang said, "*'Tai'* is also named *'tu hu'* (兔鹘). In many copies of *Quan Jing* (拳经; *Classic of Quan*), it is mistakenly written as *'tu hu'* (兔虎). Tu hu is a small eagle, also named *'tu wei ba ying'* (禿尾巴鷹). It has a very short tail. Hunters feed it with live poultry to improve the agility of its claws, and they use it to catch wild rabbits." The Classics stated that a *tai* has the ability to stand its tail up. People do not know what this animal is, or why it can stand its tail up. They either make a wild guess or deny that it has this ability. Master Shang has made this very clear. He explained, "The wild tai often hang upside down from a branch watching the moves of rabbits and birds in order to catch them at the right moment. This is the feature that other animals do not have. It is why we are learning from it."

Some published articles mistakenly used the character of "駘" for "[鳥台]", which is a very big mistake. 駘 is a bad horse. In the Twelve Animal Form, there is already a horse routine. Since we are learning the power of a "good horse," there is no reason for us to mimic the movements from 駘. Other articles or oral traditions considered tai as *ge* (鴿; pigeon), which is definitely a mistake. Some people describe tai as "a legendary animal that looks like an ostrich." But if it were really like an ostrich, it would be good at walking but would not have the ability to stand up its tail or land to grab prey. Still other people mistakenly used the word *hu* (鶻) for [鳥台] in the books they wrote. Although it is true that there is no character for tai in modern dictionaries and tai is also named *tu hu* (兔鶻), we shouldn't mix them up, because the name *hu* is not consistent with the name tai in the Xingyiquan Classics. The mistakes mentioned above are important and should be clarified.

As for the technique and power issuance of Tai Xing, there has been even more guessing and distortion. Some people say that "the end of its tail is considered a punching tool" and "strike with kua" are at the core of this technique; even more people say that "it has the power of landing down to destroy the target" is the core. They are all wrong. Master Shang said, "Tai Xing uses neither the tail nor kua to strike. Instead, it uses Dantian energy and the power from the ribs and abdomen to strike. You drop both arms and wrap inward to attach to the ribs and create a combined force pushing forward and upward to issue power. This is to mimic the tai's ability to stand its tail up. If this is the technique we are trying to learn, then the power of landing down to destroy the target should not be our focus, because it was not stated in the Classics and is not the feature of Tai Xing." This Lei Fu Da (肋腹打; strike with ribs and Dantian) technique is the root of power issuance in Tai Xing.

## QI QUAN / QI XING / QI YAO

On striking methods, the Xingyiquan Classics state, "the head, shoulders, elbows, hands, groin, knees, and feet are the *Qi Quan* (七拳; Seven Fists), also called the *Qi Xing* (七星; Seven Stars), or the *Qi Yao* (七曜; Seven Suns)." However, some books count the head twice, plus both sides of the rest of Qi Quan, to make it fourteen places as the main tools to attack with. This is a mistake. In the Xingyiquan Classics, the "Fourteen Places to Strike With" refer to all the Qi Xing plus the hip and tail strike. The issuance of power in all fourteen places comes from Dantian qi. As a matter of fact, it still misses Lei Fu Da, which is what made Guo Yun-Shen and Shang Yun-Xiang famous in the martial arts world. If we add it, there should be "Fifteen Places to Strike With." Because people know very little about Lei Fu Da, the misunderstanding about "standing the tail up" thus arose. In the movements, we use the two arms in place of the tail, by wrapping them inward against the ribs to form the shape of a tail. In addition, this combined force of arms and body pushes forward and upward. This is to imitate its power to stand up its tail. (In the rest of the twelve animals, you cannot find this way to issue power. This is its special feature.) The tai has a very short tail, so the punch with the arms in Tai Xing is also short. However, because it issues power directly from Dantian and involves the ribs and abdomen to strike, its attacking power is tremendous. Using both fists to attack the opponent's abdomen is very effective in intercepting the opponent's qi but also in hurting the person. In general, older masters used palms (instead of fists), called *Yan Shou* (掩手; Covering Hand). There is defense within offense. It is easy to control the opponent but does not hurt people so easily. You issue power to off-balance the opponent as soon as you touch his abdomen. The level of damage it may create depends on the part of the body and the method of issuing power. This is what Master Shang taught in Tai Xing.

## Quan and Weapon Are Integrated; They Reinforce Each Other

There is a motto that goes, "If you can train your Gong Fu to reach the point of having internal and external aspects integrated and using hands and weapons at the same level of proficiency, then whatever techniques you use for fightingwill be just right for the situation." The use of jing is the most crucial when training in Xingyiquan and weapons. Weapons are the extensions of the arms and legs. If you learn quan well, it will be very efficient when learning to use weapons. They will supplement and reinforce each other. After practicing for some time, you will be able to apply what you learn from quan about the use of shen and yi to the use of weapons, whether it is a long or short weapon. Each weapon has its own nature. As long as we understand them and combine them with the shen, yi, and Gong Fu in quan, they will reinforce each other and function very well in fighting. Master Shang devoted his entire life to studying Xingyi, so he inherited and passed down a lot of weapon techniques. His followers have experienced the merits of both his quan and his weapon skills.

Each technique in Wu Xing Quan has its own unique jing and movement. Practicing them repetitively is necessary to lay a solid foundation of basic Xingyiquan techniques. There are also pi, zuan, beng, pao, and heng techniques in traditional weapons like dao (broadsword), jian (sword), gun (staff), and qiang (spear). We must practice the weapon forms with the same approach. In addition, there is a series of forms of Wu Xing, Lian Huan, and Liu He that use the same weapons. Some special traditional weapons such as Unicorn Horn Dao and Phoenix Wing Tang have rarely seen features. All of the abovementioned weapons have the same jing as the corresponding quan. They reinforce one another.

Since there are not many people who know about the traditional Xingyi weapons, I am planning to promote them through future publications. Due to the limited space of this book, only the forms that are better known to people—such as Lian Huan Dao, jian, gun, and qiang—are introduced. To benefit more practitioners, other materials will be published in the near future.

# The Foundation for Xingyi Gong Fu

*SAN TI SHI ZHUANG GONG AND YING ZHUO*

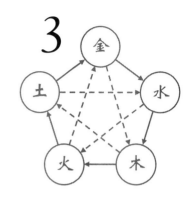

There is a famous saying in Xingyiquan that says, "There are tens of thousands of methods, all of which originate from *San Ti Shi* (三体式; Three Body Stance)." This statement points out that San Ti Shi is a main gate to Xingyiquan. It is thus called *"Xingyi Mu Shi"* (形意母式; Xingyi Mother Form). But both the movements and the internal substance of San Ti Shi have become very different from school to school; we must examine them in order to make comparisons and choices. For example, when it comes to *Zhuang Gong* (桩功; post standing meditation technique), which looks simple and boring, our ancestors insisted that, "Zhuang Gong is a treasure. Only when you have mastered it can you become good." They emphasize that we should learn it, practice it consistently, and most important, become very good at it. Why is San Ti Shi Zhuang Gong so important? In Shang-style Xingyiquan, San Ti Shi is considered to be the Mother Form while *Ying Zhuo* (鹰捉; Eagle Grasp) is considered to be *Mu Quan* (母拳; Mother Fist). Together, they form a key to the mystery of Xingyiquan. That is why it is imperative for us to learn these techniques. Master Shang has analyzed them in great detail. The following sections are a synopsis of his inspirational study.

# San Ti Shi (Three Body Stance)

## THE MEANING AND FUNCTIONS OF SAN TI SHI

"*Dao* (道; the way) originates from nothing but it generates *Yi Qi* (一气; One Unified Energy). From Yi Qi, Yin (阴) and Yang (阳) energies arise. Yin combines with Yang, and then *San Ti* (三体; Three Bodies) are formed. The Three Bodies interact with one another, and thus all things in the universe start to grow and become prosperous." Xingyiquan uses the Yin Yang and Five Element theories as a basis, Nei Jing (内经; Internal Classics) as a guideline, and concepts of generating—such as *Yi Qi, Liang Yi* (两仪; Two Polarities), *Yin Yang* (阴阳), *San Cai* (三才; Three Elements) or *San Ti, Si Xiang* (四象; Four Phenomena), *Wu Xing* (五行; Five Elements), and *Liu He* (六合; Six Harmonies)—as a means of regulating fighting-technique training as well as to achieve mastery in this art. The so-called *Yi Qi* refers to the fused energy that is the combination of prenatal Genuine Qi within the human body and the postnatal qi coming from the breathing activities. When we apply the concept of Yin Yang in martial arts, it refers to the opposite position of body parts and the changing of movements. Any contrasting concepts—such as up vs. down, forward vs. backward, left vs. right, inside vs. outside, advancing vs. retreating, facing vs. turning away, leaning forward vs. bending backward, pulling back vs. letting go, rising vs. falling, entering vs. exiting, extending vs. contracting, moving vs. stillness, hard vs. soft—are energies following the Yin Yang theory. In the application of techniques, the two components are opposite but complementary. They are antagonistic toward each other and yet they support each other. The so-called San Ti, also named San Cai, refers to heaven, earth, and human. We consider the human body as a small universe. Thus, in our body we have three elements. In Xingyiquan, *San Ti* refers to three sections of the body: the upper, middle, and lower sections. In other words, it refers to our head, upper limbs, and lower limbs. In fact, it also includes the upper, lower, inside, and outside of human bodies. Through training, if we can harmonize Yin and Yang energies, coordinate the qi from inside and outside, and integrate the three parts of our body, then positive outcomes will follow. That is why we say that if the Three Bodies are successfully integrated, myriad things will grow and become prosperous.

Chinese medicine uses Yin Yang and Five Element theories to explain the functioning of many [body] mechanisms, differentiate between syndromes, and come up with treatment approaches. Xingyiquan uses the same theoretical framework to practice techniques for healing and enhancing health. We can say this because we can find interpretations from Nei Jing (内经; Internal Classics). For instance, *Su Wen: Yin Yang Ying Xiang Da Lun* (素问:阴阳应象大论; *Plain Inquiry: A Big Discussion on the Changing of Yin and Yang;* the first part of the Internal Classics) mentions that "Yin and Yang are the way in which heaven and earth operate. It is the rule that governs everything, the parents of change, the causes for things' growth and destruction, and the key to reveal the mystery of all living things. When treating diseases, we need to seek the root." The meaning of change that Su Wen talks about is twofold. The natural growing process of everything is called *hua* (化; transformation). When something reaches an extreme state, it will bounce back and turn into its opposite state. This is called *bian* (变; change). We call Yin Yang "the parents of change" because they are the origin of bian and hua. *"Sheng Sha"* (生杀; growth/birth and damage/death) refers to two things: the natural growth of things is called *sheng* while the damage or destruction of something is called *sha*. "Sheng sha zhi ben shi" ( 生杀之本始) indicates that Yin and Yang are at the root of the birth or death of everything. In the phrase "Shen Ming" (神明), *shen* refers to the unpredictability of changes while *ming* refers to the obviousness of this. The phrase "Shen ming zhi fu ye" (神明之府也) expresses the phenomenon that all living things grow without our seeing how they are nourished, and that they die without our seeing them having been damaged by anything. Yin and Yang are the keys to reveal the mystery of this obvious but unpredictable phenomenon.

When we treat diseases, we need to differentiate Yin from Yang so that we can determine the root of the problem. By the same token, when practicing Xingyiquan we need to master both substance (Yin) and application (Yang). The integration of Yin and Yang and the unity of San Ti govern principles such as the upper part and the lower part following each other, the integration of the internal and external aspects, filling the body with holistic energy, and even the ability to control changes and to decide when to spare or kill. There is one more statement in Su Wen, which says: "Yin is inside and it provides Yang with substance. Yang stays outside and acts for Yin." What it means is that Yin needs protection from Yang and Yang needs support from Yin. Yin and Yang are opposite but also the root of each other. San Ti Shi uses the theory of "One Unified Energy produces Yin and Yang; Yin and Yang generate the Three Bodies" to start the training. Since San Ti Shi is the Mother Form of Xingyiquan and the gate to the art, we need to be good at it to build a good foundation of Yin Yang, San Ti, and Wu Xing. That way we will be able to control Bian Hua, judge the time for Sheng Sha, and master Shen Ming for treating diseases, all of which are foundations for defeating the enemy.

"Zhuang Gong is a treasure." It is no wonder that the ancestors in Xingyiquan repeatedly said this. Without even mentioning how it can help us learn Xingyiquan well, it is enough just to think about the functions it has in fighting and healing. As soon as we start training in Zhuang Gong, we hear stories about the Zhuang Gong of San Ti Shi. For example, it is said of a master who does San Ti Shi: People try to push him, pull him, hold him up, or take him down. None could do it. He is like a tree rooted in the ground. Where does this power come from? According to this master, "This is nothing special, it is the result of doing Zhuang Gong." Guo Yun-Shen (郭云深) once had people test his skill by standing in San Ti Shi and making five big strong men push against his abdomen with white wax wooden staffs; they could not move him at all. But when Guo used a little force, he threw all of them ten meters away. There was also a person who worked in the Beijing Martial Arts Academy whose feet were so powerful that he could kick a wall to rubble. Once he challenged Master Shang. Master Shang stood in San Ti Shi, to be kicked by this challenger. Nothing happened the first time. When the challenger dashed forward to kick the second time, the only thing Master Shang did was to issue a little bit of force; the challenger was thrown far away and could not get up on his own. These are examples of the power from Zhuang Gong that our ancestors applied in self-defense. When it comes to issuing power to defeat the enemy, the role of Zhuang Gong is even more crucial—and there are numerous stories about this as well. We all know that if our Zhuang Gong is not solid enough, we cannot issue power. The reason those Xingyiquan masters have such great power is that there are deep roots in their feet. It is issued upward through the legs and manipulated in yao. Zhuang Gong is the foundation of this power. There are many more stories and legends about this, all of which exist to encourage people to strengthen their belief and practice hard. However, those results did not come from practicing blindly. Instead, it is the crystal formed from the combination of skills, dedication, and wisdom. It is obtained by following the requirements of the techniques and grasping the subtleties in their essence. Therefore, when we are practicing it, not only do we have to work hard, but we also need to delve into the deeper, finer part of it, in order to achieve Gong Fu.

The effect of San Ti Shi Zhuang Gong is not just apparent in fighting situations. Its functions of treating diseases and enhancing health are also well known. Many research findings have indicated that Zhuang Gong is very effective in treating chronic diseases, senility, and diseases of the female reproductive system. In many cases, it seems to work even better than practicing hand forms. Although it is a static body posture, there is motion within stillness. In addition, the techniques require that tendons be extended and bones be expanded, which trains our body to resist pressure very well. There was an ex-captain of the National Hockey Team who could lift heavy weights easily for hundreds of rounds. However, when he tried to do San Ti Shi, before he could get to the right posture, he collapsed and kept saying, "Incredible! Incredible!" The level of difficulty and intensity in San Ti Shi are very high. The strengthening of tendon, bone, and muscle, and bringing qi to Dantian can promote blood circulation, enhance metabolism, and massage internal organs. The techniques, particularly "shocking the four ends of limbs" and "initiating the function of five internal organs," boost the spirits. It stimulates the mind to move qi around the body. This regulates the central nervous system, which enhances breathing, heart function, and the digestive system. Due to all these benefits, Zhuang Gong is useful for healing.

## The Techniques and Applications of San Ti Shi

The *Ba Zi Jue* (八字诀; Eight Character Formula) and *San Cai Jiu Shi Ge* (三才九式歌; Three Elements Nine Postures Song), which describe San Ti Shi technique requirements, were widely spread. However, the techniques described in those books are not the same as those they are not recorded in the Classics. In addition, they are too voluminous and too full of repetition and redundancy to memorize and apply. In his teachings, Master Shang never quoted anything from them except for the principles of straightening the back, sinking the shoulders, dropping the elbows, keeping the knees together, lifting the rectum, keeping the pelvis area concave, *San Yuan* (三园; Three Rounds), *San Ding* (三顶; Three Pushing Against), and *San Kou* (三扣; Three Hooks). And the techniques of San Yuan and San Kou taught by Master Shang are different from what is said in those songs.

San Yuan is the required palm shape in Xingyiquan, primarily when doing San Ti Shi and Ying Zhuo. First, the center of the palm needs to be concave, as if to bring the center of the palm inward. This will increase horizontal power and make it easier to change hand techniques when encountering the opponent's palm. Second, the back of the hand needs to be round so that power can permeate to the fingers, the "Three Joints" will have more holistic power, and the process of San Cui is more easily achieved. The palm and the back of the hand have the relationship of interior and exterior. However, their jing and application can be different for different applications. Third, the Hukou needs to be round. This will enhance the palm power when turning outward and inward. Furthermore, the area that the palm can control increases because of this palm shape. Since we have mentioned that the back has to be straightened and the shoulders need to be dropped, the chest and the back will thus be round automatically.

As for *San Kou* (三扣; Three Hooks), three parts of the body are involved. First, we need to keep the teeth clenched. This is to issue power at the end of the bone [see Chapter 2]. Clenching the teeth can tighten the tendons and bones and create more force. This is what is meant in the saying, "Courage lies in the bones. As soon as you clench the teeth, it is released." Second, the hand has to be hooked. The purpose is to initiate power at the tendon end of the upper limb [see Chapter 2]. By doing this, force can reach the fingers and qi will be able to get to the end of the joint, which will increase the power issuance when turning the palm and dropping it downward. Third, the feet need to be hooked and the toes need to grab the ground. This is to issue power at the tendon end of the lower limb. When the force reaches the lower limbs, qi will penetrate through the toes to strengthen the foundation of the posture.

As for *San Ding* (三顶; Three Pushing Against), the way that it is generally discussed and practiced is correct... First, the head has to pull upward. This allows the energy to soar upward. It initiates power at the end of the blood [i.e., the hair; see Chapter 2] and boosts essence and spirits. Because the head pulls upward, the neck is erect, qi sinks to Dantian, and the trunk is extended, it is then easy for the *San Guan* (三关; Three Gates) to open, and for kidney qi to go up to *Ni Wan* (泥丸; an acupuncture point) to nurture qi and shen. Second, the tip of the tongue has to touch against the upper palate. This will make you look like a roaring lion getting ready to swallow an elephant. It produces power issued from the end of the flesh [i.e., the tongue; see Chapter 2]. Since the tongue is curled and qi is sunken, breathing becomes even and qi goes down to Dantian, which brings kidney qi back to its root to nourish the whole body. Furthermore, due to the increase of saliva, the throat is moistened, and when using intent to lead saliva downward to Dantian, the qi flow becomes smooth and the digestion system functions better. Third, the hand has to push forward, as if pushing against a mountain. This will help to produce power at the end of the tendon [i.e., the fingernails and toenails; see Chapter 2] and the waist strength can be released. The San Cui force becomes holistic, and qi can go to the fingers. As a result, the palm power in a drilling punch increases.

When Master Shang's students were first learning to do Zhuang Gong, he only mentioned these guidelines to help them memorize and internalize them. Later, when they became better, he would guide them with the theories in the Xingyiquan Classics. This combination helps them to grasp the essence of San Ti Shi. The purpose is to combine Zhuang Gong with boxing techniques, theories, and practice so that training can become more effective.

**Theories of San Ti Shi**

"San Ti Shi" is also called San Cai Shi or Ying Zhuo Shi. Since the beginning movement of both Wu Xing Quan and Shi Er Xing Quan is Ying Zhuo, the Xingyiquan Classics point out, "As soon as you start to attack, you use Tiger Pouncing. As soon as you use hand techniques, you use Eagle Grasp." The final posture for Ying Zhuo is San Ti Shi. That is why it is called "Ying Zhuo Shi" (鷹捉式; Eagle Grasp Stance).

The Xingyiquan Classics state: "In Yin Zhuo, four things must be even." This means that when doing San Ti Shi, four parts of our body need to be kept even. The upper part of the body cannot lean forward or bend backward; neither can it be slanted to the side. It must be centered, upright, and well balanced. Specifically, the four evennesses include the following characteristics:

1) The top of the head has to be even, while the chin has to tuck back. This forms an uprising energy on the top of the head, which can stimulate the end of the blood [hair] to boost energy.

2) Both shoulders have to be even, symmetrical, and support each other. This helps to release power from the yao.

3) The forearm has to be even; in particular, the elbow has to be wrapped inward so that the ulnar side of the elbow joint faces upward. This way the shoulder, elbow, and hand will form a

straight line, which can extend very long. The purpose is to make the San Cui energy smooth and qi flow to the hand. This can increase the power of the upward drilling punch and the forward pushing force when the palm drops down.

4) Both feet need to grab the ground evenly. This will initiate power from the end of the tendon [fingernails/toenails] at the lower limb, and will solidify the stance to prevent the back foot from shaking, which results when the back knee comes in and the groin area is sunken and wrapped inward.

The character *Xia* (下; underneath, below) in *Zu xia cun shen* (足下 存身; put the body underneath the foot) means "Fang Ren (放人; to put down a person)." Although San Ti Shi is single-weighted, with 30 percent of body weight in the front and 70 percent at the back, it is required that we put the center of the upper body inside the heel of the back foot. That way the whole body is balanced, even though the upper body weight is shifted more toward the back. With this, the front leg becomes more flexible and easy to change stance. There is substance within the void, and the back leg has strong support to preserve energy for use.

The following three requirements for San Ti Shi—Si Xiang, Wu Jia, and Liu He—come from the *Quan Jing* (拳经; a Classic in Xingyiquan).

## Si Xiang (四象; Four Mimics)

"Si Xiang" refers to Ji Tui (鸡腿; Chicken Leg), *Long Shen* (龙身; Dragon Body), *Xiong Bang* (熊膀; Bear Shoulders), and *Hu Bao Tou* (虎抱头; Tiger Holding Its Head). Si Xiang requires that we internalize and incorporate the unique strength of each animal into the technique, making those traits part of our martial skills to be applied in combat. Although San Ti Shi is a still-standing posture, there are actually movements hidden within stillness. This is to lay the foundation for building up those special skills.

"Ji Tui" means that we are imitating the shape of a chicken standing on one leg. Despite being on one leg, it is as stable as if it were standing on both legs. It also means that we are imitating the way a chicken walks: "Two legs press against each other, walking with the inside of the legs rubbing against each other." Because the legs are close to each other, the legs are streamlined, which increases the speed of moving forward. Besides, since they are close to each other, the path is linear and direct. The support they get from each other increases the momentum for moving forward. When used for fighting, this feature complements very well with the unique trait of Tang Jing in Xingyiquan. In practicing San Ti Shi, we are training in the single-leg stance with the legs rubbing against each other, to develop the ability to move with the inside of the legs touching each other tightly.

"Long Shen" means to learn from the dragon, which has "the power of folding its body into three sections." During fighting, most animals would get injured and lose power if their bodies were pressed, bent, or partially cut off. Dragons are different; bending enhances the release of the strength from their bodies, which makes them even more powerful. This is what we want to learn from this animal. When standing in San Ti Shi, the front knee is required to push forward and the back knee has to come inward. However, due to the inward position of the back knee, oftentimes the upper body will lean forward. The force coming from wrapping the kua area inward will thus be missing, which prevents the yao from issuing power and the upper and lower limbs' San Cui Jing from happening. That is why it is crucial to learn *Long Zhe Shen* (龙折身; Dragon Folds the Body). "Long Zhe Shen" means that when the back knee comes inward, the upper body is able to turn in the opposite direction to stretch the yao and the legs. This makes the top part of the body partially facing forward and partially turning sideways, which helps the yao issue power more easily. The force coming from the yao pushes downward to the groin area, so the San Cui force for the lower limbs can be obtained. In addition, the force from the yao pushes upward to the shoulders, which enhances the San Cui force for the upper limbs and makes it a lot easier for Dantian to issue power.

"Xiong Bang" means that we are trying to develop the two strengths that bears have, which are to derive power by erecting the neck and by drooping arms. Bears' shoulders droop down as if to embrace something. In San Ti Shi, we imitate this by lifting up the spine and dropping the arms. Because the neck is erect, the head is pulled upward, which boosts energy and enables power from the hair to be released. At the same time, since the arms are well extended and dropped, energy can go down to the elbows and hands, which makes the San Cui force holistic and immense.

"Hu Bao Tou" means that before tigers pounce at their prey, they hold their head and gather energy, waiting for the moment to attack. The tiger's confidence in catching its prey comes from holding its paws underneath its chin, appearing to hold its head, to gather energy, waiting to explode. Since its attacking movement is fast and powerful, and the paws and mouth arrive simultaneously, it is very hard for the prey to escape. Xingyiquan incorporates this technique by emphasizing that "the elbow does not part from the ribs; the hand does not part from the heart. They follow the body tightly when exiting or entering the cave." This is both an offensive and defensive technique. Although we cannot see this in the final posture of San Ti Shi, we do use Hu Bao Tou as soon as we extend our hands to do the stance.

## Wu Jia (五夹; Five Press from Both Sides)

Wu Jia is the fifth method among "The Training Methods for Sixteen Areas" in the Xingyiquan Classics. *Jia* means clip. It's a short form for "Jia Jian" (夹剪), which refers to the scissors people used to cut silver in ancient times, when silver was used as currency. Traditionally, the major stances in martial arts include Bow, Horse-Riding, Crouching, Void, and Resting stances. Xingyiquan breaks this convention and creates a stance that has Jia Jian energy. In Jia Jian Stance, 30 percent of body weight is on the front foot, while 70 percent is on the back foot. This is also the stance used in San Ti Shi.

In San Ti Shi, the front leg is like the front, upper blade of the scissors. So the knee faces forward and the front foot is light. The back knee comes inward and the tip of the knee points forward. It is like the lower, back blade of the scissors. That is why the back foot carries more weight. Both legs are stretched to the utmost and have a force pressing from both sides. Despite the immense power it has, it is not easy to achieve. You must twist the waist to make the kua form a straight line so that Jia Jian energy can be obtained. This energy is crucial to Xingyiquan Zhuang Gong and the training of lower-limb techniques. Because the stance is small and single-weighted, it is more flexible and faster than the traditional Bow Stance and Horse-Riding Stance. However, it is much harder to do this stance than it is to do the other two stances. We have to cultivate the real Jia Jian energy so that the foundation of Zhuang Gong will be solid, the yao power will be released, and the San Cui force will be holistic, thereby facilitating Tang Jing.

## Liu He (六合; Six Harmonies)

Although Xingyiquan originates from Yin Yang and Five Element theories, we need to pursue Liu He if we want to get its essence. Liu He includes *Nei San He* (内三合; Three Internal Harmonies) and *Wai San He* (外三合; Three External Harmonies). "Nei San He" refers to the harmonies between mind and intent, intent and qi, and qi and force. "Wai San He" refers to the harmonies between hand and foot, elbow and knee, and shoulder and kua. Wai San He shows the visible coordination of body parts. The body part pairs are not opposed to each other; rather, they are unified. When it comes to the *San Jie* (Three Joints), in the upper and lower limbs, both hand and foot are end joints; elbow and knee are middle joints; and shoulder and kua are root joints. Yao dominates the entire body. As soon as we start moving, the body is the part that moves first. Then, it will initiate the movements in the limbs. In the upper limbs, the power in the yao pushes through to the shoulder, the shoulder pushes to the elbow, and the elbow pushes to the hand. In the lower limbs, the power from the yao pushes through to the kua, which pushes to the knee; power in the knee pushes to the foot. Upper and lower limbs aim at the same target. Power is initiated by the yao, the root joint pushes the middle joint, and the middle joint pushes the end joint. Due to this trait, the root, middle, and end joints of the upper limbs have to be coordinated with those in the lower limbs so that the power they send out can be holistic. Since "stillness is the substance and motion is its application," we need to understand the importance of Wai San He in its still state, particularly when standing in San Ti Shi. After accomplishing Wai San He, the upper and lower part of our body will be able to follow each other, qi will flow throughout the entire body, and the power we send out will be holistic. With this strength, yi and qi will return to Dantian, and nei jing will thus arise.

"Nei San He" refers to the harmonies between mind and intent, intent and qi, and qi and force. This is the invisible part of "motion hidden within stillness." It is intent that initiates the function. However, the whole process can only happen when the Wai San He is appropriately executed. When the internal and external aspects are integrated, qi will flow actively throughout the entire body; the highest level of Xingyiquan skills come from this integration. That is why in San Ti Shi, we search for motion within a static standing posture.

The Xingyiquan Classics state, "Ming le si shao duo yi jing (明了四梢 多一精; making the four ends clear adds another mastery in the skills)." The end points of our blood, flesh, tendon, and bone are called shao (梢; end point) Hair is the shao of blood; tongue is the shao of flesh; fingernails/toenails are the shao of tendons; teeth are the shao of bone. When the four shao are stimulated, a person's qi level and appearance will be suddenly changed. You will feel your spirit uplifted, confident, and abundant with qi; this can intimidate your enemies. The Xingyiquan Classics mention the term "Shocking the Four Ends," which means that "whenever intent arises, spirit will react to it." This is the function of internal spirit. The Xingyiquan Classics state,

> The end of blood: When one's heart is filled with anger, the hair will stand up so high that the hat will be pushed off the head, and the blood will circulate much faster. This will intimidate the enemies. Hair is just a small part of the body. Yet it can destroy the enemies. The end of flesh: When the tongue is curled, qi will

sink down. The flesh becomes so tough that even the mountain is overwhelmed. One becomes very brave. The power of a small tongue can be so big that enemies lose their nerve to fight. The end of tendon: Tigers are powerful and eagles are vicious. The way they fight is to use extremities as the main weapon. They use the paws/claws to grasp and feet to stomp on the prey. The energy and power are both strong. Wherever the paws/claws reach, they always succeed. The end of bone: Courage lies in the bones. When the teeth are clenched, power is released; they are so strong that you can eat the enemies' flesh. When you do this, you feel as if you are cutting something down with teeth, and your eyeballs are bulging. All of these amazing effects are from the functioning of the teeth.

There are other descriptions of the power of Four Ends, such as "Tongue can break teeth; teeth can break tendons; nails can penetrate through bones; hair can push a hat away." When the mind is ready to fight, all the internal aspects will be initiated automatically, and qi will come out from Dantian. As soon as the Four Ends are in place, the internal force will be released. There is a saying that goes, "As long as the Four Ends are initiated, the internal force will arise." This explains how much impact the Four Ends have on one's spirits. If we use it in fighting, it will boost our courage and intimidate our enemies. That is why the Xingyiquan Classics state, "Once the Four Ends are made clear, you will never be afraid." This type of power needs to be developed and applied as soon as you start practicing Zhuang Gong. In Shang-style Xingyiquan, when practicing San Ti Shi, we are pursuing the goal of "moving in a motionless state." When doing Zhuang Gong, it is easy for some people to be distracted and feel uneasy, and they thus cannot hold it too long. This is because they don't have intent; therefore there is no motion within the static posture. If you practice without intent, even if you do it for a long time, there will be no result. If we can understand the function of Four Ends and master them, we will be able to concentrate and avoid having qi rise. To issue power from the end of blood, you need to lift your head and hold your neck erect; your hair stands up like it is going to push a hat away. To issue power from the end of flesh, the tip of your tongue needs to touch the upper palate, so that qi will sink down. Furthermore, your tongue must push hard against the teeth, as if you are going to smash them. To issue power from the end of tendon, your hands push forward and the toes grab the ground tightly. To issue power from the end of bone, your teeth are tightened like you are going to break the tendons and your bones are contracted. We use yi and shen to shock up the Four Ends, which can then integrate with movement, postures, and force. Whether you put this mindset into Zhuang Gong or movement, you will feel power and spirit. When used in fighting, it will give you the upper hand.

## Motion within Stillness Is the Real Motion

The Xingyiquan Classics say, "Stillness is in the nature while motion is the manifestation of yi. Stillness is the substance while motion is the functioning of the essence. Motion within stillness is the real motion; stillness within motion is the real stillness." From these interpretations of the Xingyiquan Classics, we know that, besides learning how to move, we need to pursue the "motion within stillness," for this is the "real motion." If we don't know the "real motion," we cannot understand the use of yi. Furthermore, if we don't pursue the "real stillness" through motion, we will not understand the nature of the art. Yi and *xing* (性; nature) are two important components in practicing Xingyiquan. Only when we understand the function of yi can we "keep ourselves still and yet issue explosive power upon being attacked." Through this, we can achieve a very high level of proficiency in applying the techniques. Only when we understand xing can we "find the supreme tranquility and easiness in our minds and regain the prenatal nature." Equipped with this, we can return to the prenatal state of mind and respond to incoming energy spontaneously.

In practicing San Ti Shi, we start with the substance (i.e., stillness), and then pursue its function (i.e., motion). We follow the requirements of having right postures and movements, to lay a good foundation for learning Xingyiquan and weapons. This is just the beginning. We need to take a further step by pursuing motion within stillness, which means to move with yi. Then, we continue with fostering shen and qi and the cultivation of nei jing. We need to shift focus from body shape and energy path to utilizing yi to pursue motion within stillness. The precondition for achieving this is to be able to "keep the essence and spirit inside" by using yi to form inner vision, to look at *cou li* (腠理; the area between the skin and flesh). In the Internal Classics there are statements such as "yang transforms into vital energy," "the clean yang energy is issued from cou li," and "the clean yang energy can strengthen the four limbs." That is why our ancestors taught us to look at cou li, so that we can have our qi permeate the limbs. After that, we focus on Dantian in order to solidify our root of spirit. All of these have to be done in a completely relaxed manner, by directing qi to all parts of our bodies. The specific ways of doing that are as follows.

## 1. Focus your mind on the end joint of the upper limb—the hand.

With the back erect, shoulders and elbows dropped, use intent to search for the sense of motion in the palm, fingers, and *Lao Gong* (劳宫; an acupuncture point located near the center of the palm). There is a tingling, a swollen and hot sensation. Very often, a clicking sound can be heard in the finger joints. Since everyone has a different constitution, there are differences in the location, volume, and length of the clicking sound in the joints. Not only can you feel the movements with your fingers, but the sound can also be heard by just getting your ear close to the joints. Although we only use yi instead of force in this type of training, power can penetrate through the palm and fingers. This lays a solid foundation for cultivating power in the "drilling up" and "turning to chop down" palm techniques.

## 2. Focus your mind on the lower limbs.

When the front knee is pressing forward, the back knee is squeezed inward, and the body folds in three sections, you will find motion in the knee joint. There is a full, tingling heat and qi sensation. It is so strong that the clicking sound can be heard in the knee joints and the legs are filled with qi. The feeling can go down to the Yong Quan point. After practicing this way for some time, the legs will become well rooted. Although the front leg is void, it is still very solid. The back leg comes in to get close to back of the front knee and form the shape of a pair of scissors; the forward springing power is thus increased. This is also a good way to treat arthritis, cold legs, and sciatica pain.

### 3. Regulate your qi and focus on Dantian.

Regulate your qi, bring it back to its root (i.e., Dantian), and focus your mind on Dantian. There will be motion in the lower abdomen, accompanied by heat and a qi sensation. When saliva increases, swallow it and use your yi to direct it to Dantian, creating sound in the process. This will make your qi smooth and the lower abdomen relaxed and solid. This process will fill Dantian with abundant Genuine Qi, which makes our body strong and the root solid. The internal force is thus generated. We can then "solidify the root of spirit" and allow "Genuine Qi to retreat and hide inside." This is how Shang-style Xingyi Zhuang Gong helps us train in the techniques and nurture ourselves.

Through the training of the forms, "Upper body and lower body follow each other and internal and external aspects are integrated; qi of the entire body will be united," and clear, hard energy will be fostered. This is the right time for us to move to the next level. After obtaining the ultimate hard power, we need to pursue "Rou Ji Zi Hua" (柔极自化; When the ultimate soft energy is fostered, the ability to transform will transpire). At this stage, we demand even more in doing San Ti Shi. We need to put spirit and nature as the top priority; fuse shen, yi, and qi in Dantian; and direct it throughout the body. "Motion and stillness integrated; intent and nature fused as one" is now achieved. This is the highest level of Shang-style San Ti Shi Zhuang Gong practice. We have moved from "motion within stillness" to "stillness within motion" and finally to "realizing the spiritual property of genuine stillness, finding emptiness within substance and existence of substance within nothing." Having reached this level, we will be able to apply the techniques anywhere, anytime, in a spontaneous manner. This level of proficiency can be described as, "Realizing the free nature of a baby, the applications of all the techniques reflect the way of a baby who reacts to everything in a true, natural, and spontaneous manner" and, "When a punch is thrown, it is not observed as a punch. It feels like there is no punch and no intent involved, because every technique is executed in a fast and spontaneous manner. This is the true manifestation of yi." This is the tool that Master Shang gave us to cultivate power, which focuses on both substance and applications in Xingyiquan.

## THE SPECIFIC WAYS OF TRAINING IN SAN TI SHI

Before performing the movements of San Ti Shi, we must completely understand the meaning and functions of San Ti Shi described above so that we will be more motivated and determined to learn Xingyiquan. To grasp these details and improve training, we need to explore the techniques and applications of San Ti Shi in more depth. We need to be able to fulfill its requirements regarding the positioning of the head, arms, hands, legs, and upper body. In addition, we need to apply those principles in the movements of San Ti Shi and combine them with such guidelines as *Si Ping* (四平; four flat), *Si Shao* (四梢; four ends), *Si Xiang* (四象; four mimics), *Wu Jia* (五夹; five clips), *Liu He* (六合; six harmonies), *Dong Jing* (动静; motion and stillness), *Yi Xing* (意性; intent and nature), and *Qi Shen* (气神; vital energy and spirit). If we can find the subtleties in these principles and practice consistently, we definitely will succeed.

The result of experimentation has proved that it helps to increase the effect of Zhan Zhuang if we do some preparation activities to warm up the waist, lower back, legs, and joints. After that, the heel of the front foot must be aligned with the ankle of the back foot. This is crucial, because if the front foot turns too far inward, we will feel off balance. If it turns too far outward, the energy will not be focused. Either one will affect the stability of the stance. Traditionally, the right side governs qi and the left side governs blood. Therefore, both the beginning and closing of San Ti Shi are done with the left foot in the front and right foot at the back, so that qi will move blood.

The specific ways of practicing San Ti Shi are as follows.

## Step 1

Relax the entire body. Stance is erect. Arms are naturally dropped down. Chin is tucked back. Head is straight. Eyes look straight forward. Jaw is closed but relaxed; tip of the tongue touches the upper palate. The front foot points forward; its heel touches the inside ankle bone of the back foot; the back foot points slightly outward. The two feet thus form a 45° angle (picture 3.1).

3.1

PRINCIPLES

   i. The Xingyiquan Classics state: "Harness the monkey mind and the horse intent, focus on establishing the sea-depth foundation." This is to say that to master Gong Fu, one must block out all thoughts, concentrate, and follow training techniques faithfully.

  ii. The stance must be stable and erect. The head must be straight, and the breathing natural. The entire body must be relaxed.

## Step 2

Raise both forearms naturally to the chest with palms facing downward (picture 3.2).

PRINCIPLES

   i. Forearms must remain in contact with the body while they are being raised; the outside of the thumbs must remain in contact with the center of the chest. This is to follow the principles of "have elbows attached to the rib, palms attached to the heart" and "massage the channels and the five internal organs."

  ii. Do not raise the shoulders or stick out the elbows.

 iii. Do not raise qi with exaggerated force.

3.2

3.3

## Step 3

With forearms and thumbs remaining in contact with the body, press palms downward to Dantian level while exhaling naturally. Knees are together and bent down at the same time (picture 3.3).

PRINCIPLES

   i. While pressing downward, upper body must remain straight. Head must also remain erect. Shoulders are relaxed. Elbows are tucked in.

   ii. Follow the breathing. Forearms and thumbs must remain in contact with the body. Lao Gong point presses the root of the palm to keep all fingers level. Qi must sink down and be gathered into Dantian. Elbows hug the ribs; thumbs are level and rest by Dantian. While kneeling downward, knees are bent, ankles are pressed; the front knee points forward while the back knee presses tightly against the inside of the front knee, thus forming a semi-squat posture.

   iii. Hips must not protrude; naturally lift the rectum instead. The waist region should be collapsed. The upper body must remain at a right angle to the ground.

## Step 4

Both palms change into fists and simultaneously turn outward, fists and forearms remaining in contact with the body, ending with the fists facing upward (picture 3.4).

PRINCIPLES

   i. Fists are formed by folding the fingers in order, starting with the small finger, resulting in solid fists (the small finger and ring finger must hold tight), while remaining natural, without exaggerated force.

   ii. While turning outward, there should be a slight twist and pull intent; the fists stay by the navel (picture 3.5). Forearms remain in firm contact with the ribs.

3.4

3.5

## Step 5

Left fist and left forearm drill upward, while remaining in close contact with the body, moving above the chest center and under the chin (picture 3.6).

PRINCIPLE

When drilling upward, shoulders must be sunk and elbows must be tucked in. Furthermore, "elbow does not detach from the rib, palm does not detach from the chest"—this is referred to in the *Quan Jing* (拳经; *Quan* Classic) as the Hu Bao Tou (虎抱头; Tiger Holding Its Head), or the "defense first, offense after" principle; it is also known as the "to defend and attack, gather energy and wait to issue" principle.

## Step 6

Do not pause from the preceding step. Left fist and left forearm continue to drill upward from under the chin, then outward, ending with the fist facing upward, not exceeding eyebrow height. Simultaneously, the left foot steps forward to form the Scissor Stance, with 30 percent of body weight on the front leg and 70 percent on the back leg (pictures 3.7 and 3.8). This is the *Zhuang Bu*.

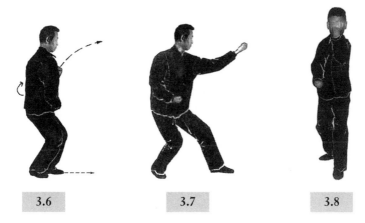

| 3.6 | 3.7 | 3.8 |

PRINCIPLES

i. The left fist, while remaining in contact with the body, drills from under the chin, then out from the mouth—this is the application of *Hu Bau Tou,* also described as "exit and enter the cave by remaining attached to the body" in *Quan Jing.* "Cave" refers to the mouth.

ii. In drilling the fist outward, the fist must twist outward. The power is horizontal, yet not observed as horizontal. Eyes follow the curvature of the small finger.

iii. When issuing the punch, the waist region should be forward-facing; the back must be erect. The power of the punch originates from the shoulder, which in turn pushes the elbow, which in turn pushes the hand.

iv. The upper body is both forward-facing and side-facing.

v. In stepping, it is the waist region that pushes the kua, which in turn pushes the knee, which in turn pushes the foot. The foot and the fist must arrive simultaneously.

vi. The distance between the heel of the front foot and the heel bone of the back foot should be greater than the combined length of both feet. Both feet must grab the ground and be firmly rooted.

vii. The front knee presses slightly forward while the back knee points inward. The waist region is twisted while the two kua are forward-facing. Body weight is on the back leg.

## Step 7

Once the preceding stance is stabilized, change fists to upward-facing open palms (picture 3.9).

3.9

## Step 8: *San Ti Zuo Shi* (三体左式; **Three Body Left Stance**)

Do not pause from the preceding movement. With eyes fixed on the curvature of the front elbow, which remains fixed, turn and twist the front forearm and palm inward and downward, ending with the palm facing downward at the heart level. Simultaneously, the right forearm and right palm also turn inward, ending with the palm facing downward; the root of the palm touches the navel, the outside of the thumb touches the abdomen. This is the fixed posture of San Ti Shi, also called San Cai Shi, also called the Ying Zhuo Shi. This is the Mother Pose of Xingyi (pictures 3.10 and 3.11).

3.10    3.11

PRINCIPLES

i. When turning the palm, shoulders must be sunk; elbows must be dropped. Twist and sink at the same time while reaching forward. Upper body must not lean forward. Arms must not be stretched.

ii. The left shoulder, left elbow, and left palm must form one forward-facing straight line.

iii. The tip of the nose, the tip of the palm, and the front of the foot must all point in the same direction. This is referred to as the *San Jian Dui* (三尖对; Three Point Alignment) in Xingyiquan.

iv. The back arm must remain in firm contact with the side of the ribs. When turning the palm, it must twist and hook in at the same time, but without exaggerated force.

v. Fingers in both palms should part naturally. The shape of the palms is round, with the back of the palms and the Hukou being round as well (pictures 3.12 and 3.13).

3.12

3.13

vi. Fingers of the front hand point upward at about a 45° angle. There is a pushing forward and hooking energy.

vii. Fingers of the back hand point slightly upward so that the side of the thumb touches the navel with the palm pressing downward. In addition to the arms and the palms, the rest of the body must also follow the general principles.

viii. Head must be straight. Chin is tucked in. Neck is naturally stretched. Eyes look forward through the index finger. Jaws are closed but relaxed. Tip of the tongue touches the upper palate.

ix. Mind must be focused. Breathing is natural, while chest is relaxed and abdomen is solid. Qi is sunk to Dantian, but do not consciously hold the breath.

x. Upper body must be aligned with the kua (two kuas are now forward-facing), the waist region is twisted (in opposite direction of the knee formation, this is the so-called Dragon Folds the Body). The resulting pose is both forward-facing and side-facing; upper body is perpendicular to the ground, shoulders are dropped, chest is concave, back is erect. Do not lean forward or backward or sideways; rectum is naturally lifted; arms must be tucked in.

xi. The body weight distribution is 30 percent on the front leg, 70 percent on the back leg. Front knee pushes slightly forward; back knee turns inward as much as possible. Front-foot toes point forward; back-foot toes point outward, forming a 45° angle with the front foot. The front heel is in line with the inside ankle bone of the back foot. While body weight rests more on the back leg, the upper body and the hip must not protrude beyond the heel. Both feet must grab the ground and be firmly rooted.

xii. These principles must be followed faithfully. While training in the basic techniques, "The Meaning and Functions of San Ti Shi" (page 38) must be reviewed frequently, to enhance your understanding and to appropriately apply the techniques as you progress.

## Step 9

When the back foot is tired from the preceding movement, change the pose. Both palms change to fists at the same time. Left fist twists and pulls inward and downward, ending with the fist resting close to the left side of the navel. Simultaneously, the right fist turns and twists, resting at the right side of the navel. Both fists are now facing upward. Simultaneously, the left foot pivots on the heel toward the inside, facing the right foot. Weight distribution remains the same. Eyes look toward the left (picture 3.14).

**3.14**

PRINCIPLES

i. It is the left elbow that pulls the left fist; with the elbow maintaining contact with the body, it pulls and turns outward at the same time. Only when the fist reaches the navel does it turn completely upward. The right fist turns simultaneously outward until it reaches the navel.

ii. The pivoting of the left foot and the pulling back of the left fist must be synchronized, such that the hand and foot and the elbow and knee are in line with each other. Upper body must not lean; elbows must not protrude.

## Step 10

No pause from the preceding step. Shift body weight to the left leg, and the upper body turns around to the right. The right foot steps back so the right heel touches left foot's inside ankle bone. Left knee pushes slightly forward to press on the inside of right knee (picture 3.15).

PRINCIPLE

When shifting body weight to the left leg, the hip should not protrude. Also, the body should not rise—maintain the original height.

**3.15**

## Step 11

Right fist and right forearm drill upward to the center of the chest, while maintaining close contact with the body throughout (picture 3.16).

PRINCIPLE

Shoulders and elbows must drop. Fist and forearm maintain contact with the body while drilling upward. This is the same as Step 5, substituting "right" for "left."

## Step 12

Do not pause from the preceding movement. Right fist and right forearm continue to drill upward from under the chin, then outward from the mouth, ending with fist facing upward, not exceeding eyebrow height. Simultaneously, right foot steps forward to form a Scissor Stance, with 30 percent of the body weight on the front leg and 70 percent on the back leg (picture 3.17).

PRINCIPLE

This is the same as Step 6, substituting "right" for "left."

## Step 13

When the preceding movement is stabilized, change both fists to upward-facing open palms (picture 3.18).

3.16                    3.17                    3.18

## Step 14: *San Ti You Shi*
## (三体右式; **Three Body Right Stance**)

Do not pause from the preceding step. Fix eyes on the curvature of the front elbow, which should remain stable. Turn and twist the front forearm and palm inward and downward, ending with the palm facing down at heart level. Simultaneously, the left forearm and left palm also turn inward, ending with the palm facing downward; the root of the palm touches the navel, and the outside of the thumb touches the abdomen (picture 3.19).

3.19

PRINCIPLE

This is the same as Step 8, substituting "right" for "left."

## Step 15

To change from Three Body Right Stance to Left Stance, the turn/twist principles are the same as for those described in Steps 9, 10, 11, 12, 13, and 14, but reversing "right" and "left." Refer to figures 3.20 through 3.23; the left and right turns and twists follow the same principles.

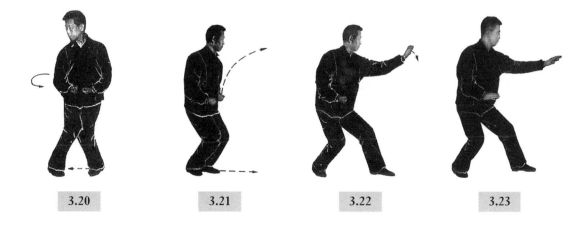

3.20          3.21          3.22          3.23

## Step 16: Closing Stance

1) Both palms change to fists (picture 3.24).

PRINCIPLE

Xingyiquan's opening movement must have the left foot and left hand in the front. It is the same for the closing movement.

2) Front fist rotates outward as it lifts up to the height of the brows; fist is facing upward. Simultaneously, the back fist, using the elbow as the axis, rotates downward, then outward, then upward, also up to the height of the brows; fist is still facing upward. Two arms now form a symmetrical curve (picture 3.25).

PRINCIPLE

When turning the arms, shoulders must sink, elbows must drop, be relaxed and natural.

3) Both fists hug inward so that the knuckles are locked against each other, resting at the center chest (picture 3.26). When the preceding step is complete, while exhaling, both fists and elbows continue to press downward, ending with the fists resting at Dantian (picture 3.27).

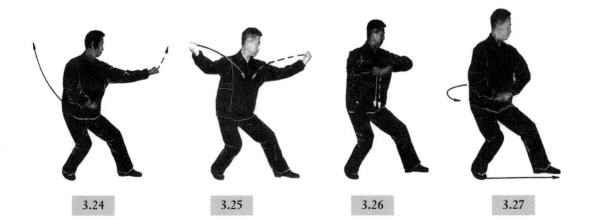

3.24            3.25            3.26            3.27

PRINCIPLE

When hugging the fists inward, body sinks slightly. Fists must be in contact with the body while resting at the chest. Press the fists downward only when exhaling; qi must sink to Dantian. The movement must be relaxed and natural.

4) Upper body turns slightly to the left, body now faces directly forward; back foot steps forward to be in line with the front foot (picture 3.28).

5) Simultaneously: fists open naturally into palms; knees straighten naturally; elbows drop down. Stand Up with Feet Together pose is formed (picture 3.29).

3.28 3.29

# The Mother Fist—Ying Zhuo
# (鷹捉; Eagle Grasp)

## THE MEANING AND FUNCTIONS OF YING ZHUO

Zhuang Gong San Ti Shi is considered to be the fixed posture of Xing-yiquan, which is the static type of fundamental Gong Fu. In contrast, Ying Zhuo put many techniques in San Ti Shi, which is the fundamental moving Gong Fu. It covers important guidelines for execution of the techniques. That is why it is a crucial training in this art. The Xingyiquan Classics state, "Whenever you use a hand technique, you always start with Ying Zhuo." People always say that "San Ti Shi is the Mother Form," while "Ying Zhuo is the Mother Fist." Both are keys to master Xingyiquan.

All the important requirements in San Ti Shi, such as moving qi as one unit, changing Yin and Yang energies, coordination of the three parts of our bodies [i.e., head, hands, and feet], Four Imitations, Five Elements, and Six Harmonies have to be met by moving the three sections of our body (i.e., the upper, middle, and lower level at which we hold our stance, or the head, upper limbs, and lower limbs). We use Ying Zhuo, the moving form of San Ti Shi, to implement the ideas of technique execution. This has been proved as the shortcut, the most efficient approach. In the previous section, we mentioned that San Ti Shi is the essence of Xingyiquan. However, you must rely on the training of Ying Zhuo to make all the techniques applicable. Its importance is described in the saying, "All hand techniques cannot be done without Ying Zhuo; all footwork involves Chicken Leg."

## THE SPECIAL TECHNIQUES AND APPLICATIONS OF YING ZHUO

People might question if there are still other techniques in Ying Zhuo besides expressing the ideas required in San Ti Shi. The answer is yes. Since Ying Zhuo is the Mother Fist, it definitely includes the core of the art. The core of Xingyiquan techniques is Qi, Luo, Zuan, Fan Jing (起

落、钻翻劲; the uprising, falling and drilling up, turning over/downward energies). We work very hard practicing Ying Zhuo to obtain these energies. Although Five Elements Fist and Twelve Animal Form are very unique and dynamic in movements, Ying Zhuo is still the form that best expresses the energies of Qi, Luo, Zuan, and Fan. In other words, without practicing Ying Zhuo, we will never be able to find the essence of Xingyiquan. Many people in the field worship and pursue the Fan Lang Jing (翻浪劲; wave rolling energy). [People had no idea about what it is. They just call it "Mo Sha Jing" (摩挲劲; rubbing and rolling energy) or "Hua Jing" (划劲; gliding energy) based on the way the movements look.] By either name, this is actually the representative of the Zuan Fan Jing that we just discussed.

When we learn Ying Zhuo, we need to cultivate the holistic power of having "The upper part and lower part of the body follow each other; the internal and external aspects are integrated" through a natural and harmonious practice. After that, we can foster the fast and solid explosive power by extending our body in a relaxed manner. That way, the internal power will be developed gradually and eventually become very strong. The Xingyiquan Classics state, "When being quiet, you are like a virgin lady; as soon as you move, you are swift as an escaping rabbit" and "When you are not issuing power, the energy you have is as light as a breeze; when doing it, the force is as strong as a roaring thunder." This is the rhythm and power that we are learning to cultivate! Only when we reach this level can we realize the skills and energy paths in Xingyiquan. "Once you learn the ultimate hard energy, the soft energy will arise. The ability to use the ultimate soft energy will enable you to apply hard and soft energies at will." Since now we know how to issue the fast, strong, hard power, if we observe more carefully and practice hard, the soft (hidden) power will eventually come out. In Xingyiquan, there is a middle-level Gong Fu called *Zhan Shen Zong Li* (沾身纵力; You issue power spontaneously upon attack). Practicing Ying Zhuo, you will have this Gong Fu. Although people have heard of the term, they don't know that this Zhan Shen Zong Li is the application of Qi, Luo,

Zuan, Fan. To obtain this Gong Fu, you need to have guidance from good teachers. Afterward, you will be able to transfer the skill to other forms. That is why Ying Zhuo is the Mother Fist of Xingyiquan. In my opinion, it definitely deserves the name.

Many people mistake Ying Zhuo for *Pi Quan* (劈拳; chopping fist) and practice it as Pi Quan. In Ying Zhuo, there is no movement of holding the fist and the technique is executed with the palm facing down. This does not form the shape of an ax, as the Xingyiquan Classics say that Pi Quan should have. In addition, since there is no "blade of the ax," how can it create the power coming from something like an ax? All the boxing forms in Xingyiquan use Ying Zhuo to start with. The concept of "Qi Shou Ying Zhuo" has been well established. It is thus a serious mistake to mix Ying Zhuo with Pi Quan. More important, because of this mistake, we lose the invaluable essence of Pi Quan, which focuses on striking without using the joints. This is really a pity.

## THE SPECIFIC WAYS OF TRAINING IN YING ZHUO

### 1: *Yu Bei Shi* (預备势; **Preparation Stance**), or *Yuan Di Zuo Ying Zhuo* (原地左鹰捉; **On-Spot Left Eagle Grasp**)

1) Stand up straight with heels together. All principles are the same as in Step 1 of San Ti Shi (三体式) (page 55) (picture 3.30).

2) Same as Step 2 of San Ti Shi (picture 3.31).

3) Same as Step 3 of San Ti Shi (picture 3.32).

4) Same as Step 4 of San Ti Shi (picture 3.33).

5) Right fist and right forearm, while maintaining contact with the body, drill upward along chest center line up to under the chin (picture 3.34). Without pausing, right fist and right forearm continue to twist and drill upward then forward from under the chin, ending with the fist not exceeding brow height (picture 3.35).

PRINCIPLES

i. As in figure 3.34, this is the "gather energy and wait to issue" pose of Hu Bau Tou.

ii. When the right fist is drilling outward from under the chin, it must maintain contact with the body, then drill outward from the mouth; this is the "exit and enter the cave by maintaining contact with the body" technique requirement, and is also the correct application of Hu Bau Tou. Whether it is single-arm or with both arms, the same meaning applies.

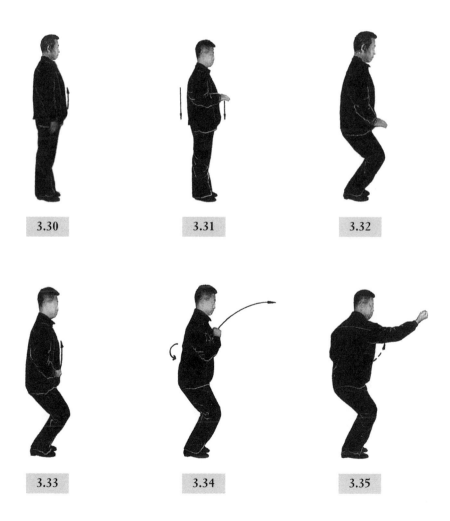

3.30          3.31          3.32

3.33          3.34          3.35

iii. In drilling the fist, it must twist outward. The jing is horizontal, yet not observed as horizontal. This is what is meant by "starting out horizontal, yet not observed as horizontal." Eyes follow the small finger curvature.

iv. When issuing the punch, lower torso must face forward, back must be erect. Power of the punch originates from the shoulder, which in turn pushes the elbow, which in turn pushes the hand. The upper body is both forward-facing and side-facing.

v. In this out-drilling of the right fist, because no stepping is involved, it is therefore more difficult to gather power. In practice, begin by pursuing smooth flow and body extension, and gradually try to issue power from the Yao.

6) Yuan Di Zuo Ying Zhuo: Left fist, still in contact with the chest center, drills upward until it reaches the top of the right elbow curvature (picture 3.36). Without pausing, left foot steps forward, right toes follow by pivoting outward slightly, thus forming the stance for Post Standing Meditation of San Ti Shi. Simultaneously, left fist drills forward along the right forearm; when the two fists meet, both fists turn inward to form San Yuan Zhang. Left palm turns forward and downward to height of the heart, palm facing down; right palm pulls back as it turns downward and inward, with elbow maintaining contact with the ribs, resting at the right side of the navel, palm facing down. Eyes look to the front of the left palm. The On-Spot Left Eagle Grasp, also known as the *Zuo San Ti Shi* (左三体式; Left Three Body Stance), is formed (pictures 3.37 and 3.38).

PRINCIPLES

   i. In On-Spot Eagle Grasp, we do not rely on the back foot's spring-ing forward momentum to gather power; rather, this is a highly skilled technique that relies on merely shifting the body weight slightly to gather power on the spot. Of course we should practice all opening stances, but there are some who would single out this particular opening stance for practice. There are others who would skip practicing this opening for the sake of saving time and sim-ply practice the Three Body Stance. The difference in gain or loss between these two groups is great.

  ii. When stepping out with the left foot and pivoting the right foot, they must meet the Zhuang Bu requirement that the front heel is in line with the back foot ankle bone.

 iii. One must fully appreciate the "rise and drop," "drill and turn" spe-cial techniques and holistic power.

The movements shown in figures 3.30 to 3.38 are the preparation movement of all Shang-style Xingyiquan (with a few exceptions). It is referred to as "Qi Shou Ying Zhuo." The *Wu Xing Quan* (五行拳; Five Element Fist) and *Lian Huan Quan* (连环拳; Linking Fist) described in this book both use it as the preparation movement.

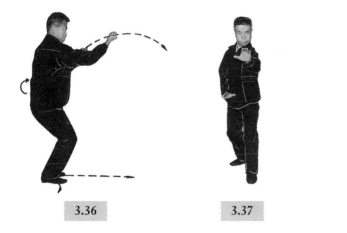

3.36                     3.37                     3.38

## 2: *Jin Bu You Ying Zhuo* (進步右鷹捉; Advance–Stepping Right Eagle Grasp)

1) *Che Ban Bu Hui Shou* (撤半步回收; Retreat Half-a-Step Wrap-In): Continue from the previous movement. Left palm becomes a fist. With elbow dropped and maintaining contact with the ribs, left forearm pulls back as the fist turns outward, so that the fist is facing upward and resting at the left side of the navel. At the same time, the right palm also changes into a fist, turning outward as it pulls back slightly, resting at the right side of the navel. While the left fist is pulling back, left foot retreats simultaneously, to stay close (or press tight?) to the right foot ankle bone, toes and knee point forward, right knee should stay close to the inside of the left knee. Eyes look forward (picture 3.39).

PRINCIPLES

i. When forming the fist, fold the fingers in order, starting with the small finger; fist must be held solid, yet without exaggerated force. When pulling back, both the fist and the forearm must twist and turn and use power from the waist region.

ii. Retreating the left foot and pulling back the fists must be executed in synchronization with coordinated force and power. Body must not rise; maintain the original height.

2) *Ti Bu Zuo Zuan* (提步左钻; Lift Step Left Drill): Left fist turns inward as it drills upward along the chest center line until it reaches under the chin (picture 3.40). Without pausing, right leg bends at the knee to press on the heel; left foot tang forward while staying close to the ground; as soon as the left foot lands, right foot follows immediately with a quick forward lift step, pressing against the top of the inside ankle bone of the left foot. This is the *You Ti Bu* (右提步; right lift step). At the same time the left foot tang forward, left fist drills upward then outward from under the chin as it twists outward, stopping at a height not exceeding the brows; the fist faces diagonally outward, with the small finger curvature pointing upward; eyes look to the left fist (picture 3.41).

PRINCIPLES

i. When the left fist is drilling upward along the chest center line, it must follow the "elbow attached to the rib, hand attached to the heart" principle; do not hold the breath, or use exaggerated force.

ii. The left fist's forward drilling and the left foot's forward tang must be executed at the same time, achieving the upper- and lower-body synchronization. Shoulders must be dropped, elbows are tugged in. Power should originate from the waist region, which in turn pushes the elbow, which in turn pushes the palm. The upper body is facing partly forward and partly to the side, exploiting the power of Long Zhe Shen.

iii. In the right lift step, when the right foot inside ankle bone is pressing on top of the left foot's inside ankle bone, right toes should point upward while the foot is flat. In all lift steps, either left or right, both feet must follow the same principles.

iv. In the lift step, body balance must be maintained; do not lean to the left or to the right.

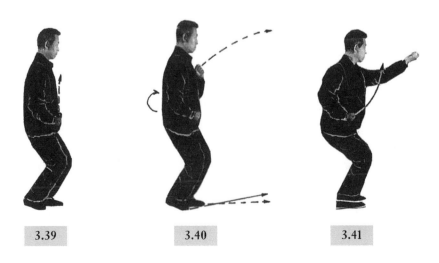

|   3.39   |   3.40   |   3.41   |

3) *Shang Bu You Ying Zhuo* (上步右鹰捉; Advance-Stepping Right Eagle Grasp): Right fist maintains contact with the chest center as it drills upward until it reaches the left elbow curvature (picture 3.42); without pausing, left foot presses on the heel, right foot tang forward; left foot follows immediately with a half forward step to form the *You San Ti Shi* (右三体式; Right Three Body Stance). Simultaneously, right fist drills forward along the left elbow. When the two fists meet, they both turn inward and change into palms. Right palm reaches forward, then downward, to stop at the heart level; palm is facing downward. Left palm turns downward and pulls back while maintaining contact with the ribs, stopping at the left side of the navel; palm is facing down. Eyes look to the front of the right palm (picture 3.43).

PRINCIPLES

i. When turning the right palm downward, shoulders must drop, elbow is tucked in. Utilize power from the waist region, achieving *San Jian* (三尖) alignment. Apply the *San Cui* (三催) principle and extend the *San Xing* (三星) to enable the power to reach root joints. The pulling back of the left palm and the drilling forward of the right palm must be coordinated in speed and power; both palms should exploit the power of twist and turn with extend and pull.

3.42                                 3.43

ii. The left foot's pressing on the heel, right foot's forward tang and landing must be executed at the same time the right palm is dropped downward; only then have you achieved the "hand and foot arrive in synchronization" requirement of the technique. The forward drilling of the fist and the downward pressing of the palm must be in a curved path, as in the turning of waves. Movements must be expansive yet natural in order to achieve upper and lower body coordination. Cultivate speed and power from natural and synchronized movements; only then is one able to issue solid, hard power. Body must not rise throughout the movement.

### 3: *Jin Bu Zuo Ying Zhuo* (進步左鷹捉; Advance-Stepping Left Eagle Grasp)

1) *Che Ban Bu Hui Shou* (撤半步回收; Retreat Half-a-Step Wrap-In): Right palm changes into a fist, then, while maintaining contact with the ribs near the abdomen, pulls downward and inward, twisting outward at the same time, to rest at right side of the navel; fist is facing upward. Simultaneously, right foot retreats, while staying close to the ground, to be by the left foot inside ankle bone; toes point forward. Also at the same time, left palm changes into a fist and twists outward as it pulls back slightly to rest at the left side of the navel; fist is facing upward. Eyes look forward (picture 3.44).

PRINCIPLE
Same as for step 1 of movement 2 (Advance-Stepping Right Eagle Grasp), only reversing the left and the right.

2) *Ti Bu You Zuan* (提步右钻; Lift Step Right Drill): Right fist turns inward as it drills upward along the chest center line up to under the chin (picture 3.45). Without pausing, left leg bends at the knee and presses the foot on the heel; right foot tang forward while staying close to the ground; as soon as the right foot lands, left foot follows immediately with a quick forward lift step, to press the ankle bone against top of the right foot inside ankle bone. This is the *Zuo Ti Bu* (左提步; left lift step). At the same time the right foot steps forward, right fist drills

3.44

upward from under the chin, then forward from the mouth, resting at a height not exceeding the brows; fist faces diagonally outward, with the small finger curvature facing upward. Left fist remains firmly at the left side of the navel, mirroring the sinking power of the right fist. Eyes look toward the right fist (picture 3.46).

PRINCIPLE

The same as for step 2 of movement 2 (Advance-Stepping Right Eagle Grasp), only reversing the left and the right.

3) *Shang Bu Zuo Ying Zhuo* (上步左鷹捉; Advance-Stepping Left Eagle Grasp): Left fist maintains contact with the chest center as it drills upward until it reaches the right elbow curvature (picture 3.47). Without pausing, right foot presses on the heel, left foot tang forward and lands, right foot follows immediately with a half forward step to form the Zhuang Bu. Simultaneously, left fist drills upward and forward; when the two fists meet, they both turn inward and change into palms. Left palm drills forward then downward, stopping at the heart level; palm is facing downward. Right palm turns inward as it pulls back to the right side of navel while maintaining contact with ribs; palm is facing downward. Eyes look to the front of the left fist (picture 3.48).

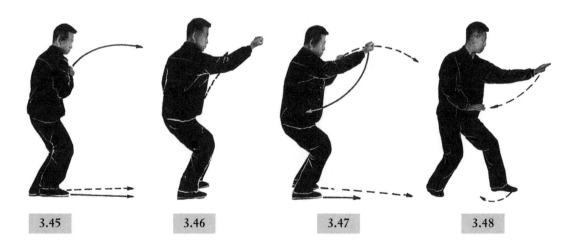

| 3.45 | 3.46 | 3.47 | 3.48 |

PRINCIPLE

The same as for step 3 of movement 2 (Advance-Stepping Right Eagle Grasp), only reversing the left and the right.

Practice the left and the right stances repeatedly; the number of repetitions depends on the size of the practice area. Use the *Zhuo Ying Zhuo Hui Shen Shi* (左鹰捉回身势; Left Eagle Grasp Turning Body Stance) as an example for how to turn around and practice in the other direction.

## 4: Ying Zhuo Hui Shen Shi (鹰捉回身势; Eagle Grasp Turn-around Stance)

1) *Kou Jiao Shou Quan* (扣脚收拳; Hook-in-Foot and Fist-Back): Both palms change to fists at the same time. Without shifting the body weight, left foot pivots on the heel to turn the toes inward, so that both feet are hooked in. Simultaneously, left fist pulls back as it twists outward at the same time to rest at left side of the navel; fist is now facing upward. Right fist also twists outward as it pulls back slightly to rest at the right side of the navel. The two fists are now symmetrically aligned. Eyes look toward the left (picture 3.49).

**3.49**

PRINCIPLES

i. When pulling back the left fist, use the elbow to pull the palm. The pulling back of the fist and the pivoting movements of the foot must be coordinated and synchronous.

ii. Contract the body when twisting the fists; movements and use of force must be in complete coordination.

2) *Zhuan Shen Shou Jiao* (转身收脚; Turn Around and Retreat Foot): Do not pause from the previous movement. Upper body turns to the right, and body weight shifts to the left foot; right foot pivots on the ball to turn the heel inward and retreats, staying close to the ground, to the inside ankle bone of the left foot. Eyes look forward (picture 3.50).

PRINCIPLES

i. When shifting the body weight, keep the body straight; do not lean forward or backward; do not stand up or protrude the hip.

ii. When the right foot retreats, the toes of the right foot and the right knee point forward; the left knee points inward, touching the inside of the right knee; the two feet must be very close together.

**3.50**

### 5: *Jin Bu Zuo Ying Zhuo* (進步左鷹捉; **Advance-Stepping Left Eagle Grasp)**

Movements and principles are the same as for movement 3: *Jin Bu Zuo Ying Zhuo* (進步左鷹捉; Advance-Stepping Left Eagle Grasp) (pictures 3.51–3.54).

| 3.51 | 3.52 | 3.53 | 3.54 |

The movement below can be practiced in left or right stance interchangeably. Practice up to *Ying Zhuo Qi Shi* (鷹捉起势; Eagle Grasp Preparation Stance); you may then wrap up after turning around and finishing the left stance (picture 3.55). If you must wrap up in the middle of a practice, you may do so only after finishing the left stance.

3.55

## 6: *Ying Zhuo Shou Shi* (鹰捉收势; **Eagle Grasp Closing Stance)**

Movements and principles are the same as for the Step 16: Closing Stance of San Ti Shi (pictures 3.56 to 3.61).

3.56    3.57    3.58

3.59    3.60    3.61

# Wu Xing Quan
## (五行拳; Five Element Fist)

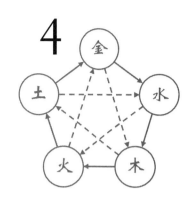

The creation of Wu Xing Quan is based on the Yin Yang theory in the Internal Classics; its application follows the principles of generating, controlling, restricting, and transforming. The Xingyiquan Classics state: "The shape of *Pi Quan* (劈拳; Chopping Fist) is like an ax and its nature is of metal; the shape of *Zuan Quan* (钻拳; Drilling Fist) is like electricity or lightning and its nature is of water; the shape of *Beng Quan* (崩拳; Smashing Fist) is like an arrow and its nature is of wood; the shape of *Pao Quan* (炮拳; Cannon Fist) is like a cannon and its nature is of fire; the shape of *Heng Quan* (横拳; Crossing Fist) is like a mud ball and its nature is of earth." Since we are following the Five Element Theory to practice Xingyiquan, we have to pay attention to the principles of generating, controlling, restricting, and transforming.

Wu Xing Quan is the foundation of Xingyiquan. It emphasizes the functions of dispelling diseases, cultivating health, and transforming one's constitution. Furthermore, its main purpose is to train in the basic techniques and solidify a foundation in Xingyiquan. So when we practice Wu Xing Quan, we need to follow the order of generating—metal generates water; water generates wood; wood generates fire; fire generates earth—so that the training process can be more efficient. If we don't follow this order, problems will arise. For example, Pi Quan belongs to water and Beng Quan belongs to wood; it is inappropriate to do Pi Quan immediately before Beng Quan. Zuan Quan belongs to water and Pao Quan belongs to fire; it is inappropriate to do Pao Quan right after Zuan Quan. The former is a case of metal controlling wood, and the latter is a case of water controlling fire, and as the Internal Classics say, "Wood is chopped down when it encounters metal; fire is extinguished when it encounters water." When we practice Wu Xing Quan, our purpose is to promote and gain instead of controlling or resisting. If we follow the order of controlling, it not only violates the theory of generating but also reduces the training effect. When teaching Wu Xing Quan, Shang Yun-Xiang emphasized following the order of Pi, Zuan, Beng, Pao, and Heng. This is one of the features of Shang-style Xingyiquan.

Shang-style Xingyiquan is unique in its moves and technique executions. Among them, its Pi Quan and Zuan Quan show the most differences from other styles. The Xingyiquan Classics state, "The shape of *Pi Quan* (劈拳) is like an ax and its nature is of metal." Since it is named as a *quan* (拳; fist), it should not be shown as a *zhang* (掌; palm). If we are trying to execute the technique of *pi* (劈; chopping, splitting), then it should have the shape of an ax and it must carry the energy and force of an ax. Some people consider Ying *Zhuo* (鷹捉; Eagle Grasp) to be Pi Quan, which obviously is a mistake. The Pi Quan and Ying Zhuo that Master Shang taught look similar, except that the former uses the fist and the latter uses the palm. As a matter of fact, there is a huge distinction between them in their essence. In Ying Zhuo, we use the palm and issue power from the end joint [the wrist]. When we execute Pi Quan, we use the forearm and issue power from the middle joint [the elbow joint]. That is why people say that the execution of Pi Quan is always accompanied by an elbow strike. The most valuable trait of using energy in this way is that it does not use the protruding point of a joint to strike or issue power. The chopping force/energy originates from the forearm, between the fist and the elbow. This theory and approach extend the scope of routines that most people follow when practicing martial arts. Because of this unique feature, Pi Quan and Zuan Quan in Shang-style Xingyiquan have special applications and significance; these have become part of the essence of Xingyiquan in general.

The Xingyiquan Classics state, "The shape of Zuan Quan is like electricity or lightning. Its nature is of water, which is connected to the kidneys." The execution of Zuan Quan involves both shape and intent.

It needs to cover the practical applications of the techniques and enhance health at the same time. Missing one of them will result in the loss of the true value of Zuan Quan. The Zuan Quan that Master Shang taught has the shape of lightning in such movements as *Shuai Bei* (甩臂; Throwing Out the Arms Freely) and *Lou Zhang* (搂掌; Turning Back the Palm Quickly). In addition, the *Dou Yao* (抖腰; Shaking the Lumbar Region) movement directly enhances the functioning of the kidneys. Due to its emphasis on shape and intent, it is very effective in both training in Gong Fu and cultivating health.

From the descriptions of Pi Quan and Zuan Quan above, we now have a glimpse of the characteristics of Shang-style Wu Xing Quan. We can say that each and every quan has its own *jing* (劲; force/energy). Sometimes, a single quan can have several completely different jing. When it comes to stepping, the most striking features are *Jia Jian Tui* (夹剪腿; Tongs Leg) and *Huai Chong Bu* (槐虫步; Inchworm Stepping). They can be done with a wide variety of footwork, which includes advance stepping, backward stepping, diagonal stepping, padding stepping, half-stepping, hooked stepping, and lifting stepping. As for the issuance of power, Master Shang's belief was that "70 percent of success in fighting relies on leg techniques." One attacks in advance or in retreat, using a tang step or deng step. All techniques rely heavily on footwork.

When teaching Wu Xing Quan, Master Shang seldom talked about the forms. Instead, he focused on cultivating internal strength, searching for the right jing, and exerting the essence and spirits. The Xingyiquan Classics state, "All techniques for striking the fourteen places on the body involve the use of qi from Dantian." (In fact, according to the Xingyiquan Classics, there is one more strike, which is aimed at the floating rib. Therefore, there should be fifteen striking areas.) The Xingyiquan Classics point out that "The yao is the core." Following the requirements of each technique in Wu Xing Quan, we need to reach the goal of having "the upper and lower body follow each other" and "internal and external aspects integrated into one." Not only do we need to develop the natural and harmonious holistic power, but we also have to be able to exert the spirits and power coming from the internal and external five elements. Only when we accomplish this can we say that we have grasped the essence of Wu Xing.

The Xingyiquan Classics state, "Wu Xing and Wu Jing (五精; Five Essence) are Five Tigers." "Wu Xing, in their nature, are five gates. Although no one is guarding them, the defense mechanism is there." "As long as ends of the four limbs are at the right positions, the five elements will function well." "Wherever and whenever the five elements are combined, as long as you bring up your courage, you will always succeed." If we train this way, we will feel our essence enhanced and our spirits and courage boosted very quickly. This is crucial in learning to fight. Master Shang said, "Our inside has to be lifted up." This means that we need to extract the essence and spirits, including the five elements inside of our bodies. "When the heart moves, it goes like a flying sword; when the liver moves, it goes like flame; when the lungs move, they turn into thunder; when the spleen moves, the kidneys become more powerful." Using this mindset and energy to execute the techniques, the confidence and power to defeat one's enemies will be strengthened.

There is one more thing that needs to be pointed out. The most striking feature of Shang-style Xingyiquan is its quick, fierce, hard, and solid energy when issuing power. This type of energy is fostered by pursuing what *Quan Jing* describes:

*Qi ru feng, luo ru jian, da dao hai xian man;*
*Qi ru jian, luo ru feng, zhui feng gan yue bu ang song.*

起 如 风, 落 如 箭, 打 倒 还 嫌 慢;
起 如 箭, 落 如 风, 追 风 赶 月 不 放 松.

Rise up like the wind, drop like an arrow; the opponent is beaten on
    the ground, yet it is still not fast enough;
Rise like an arrow, drop like the wind; chase the wind and catch up
    with the moon, there is no letting go.

The speed and power in those movements will be obtained not by putting forth all your strength at a time or using clumsy force but by doing the techniques in a relaxed and natural manner. You have to be able to relax first, and then you will be able to strike long, throw far, land solidly, and issue fast. Only when all of these requirements are met can the *Gang Jing* (刚劲; Hard Energy) be developed. Once you have the hard energy in *Bao Fa Jing* (爆发劲; Explosive Power), then you are able to *Fa Ren* (发人; issue explosive power on someone). This style of training needs to be established as soon as you start training in Wu Xing Quan. That is why we say that if we have the correct understanding about Wu Xing Quan and learn it very well, we will be able to find the true essence of Xingyiquan.For this reason, we need to explore the subtleties of Wu Xing Quan.

Chinese medicine treats diseases by applying the Yin Yang and Five Element theories. We can practice Wu Xing Quan to get rid of diseases and enhance our health. If the liver is not strong enough, we should practice Zuan Quan to cultivate kidney water, which will nurture the liver. Then, we should practice more of Beng Quan to release the liver wood. What we are applying is the principle of generating in the Five Element theory. On the other hand, if the liver energy is excessive, which means that the liver fire is too strong, then we should apply the principle of controlling by practicing more Pi Quan, using metal to control wood. After that, we should practice more Beng Quan to release the excessive energy in the liver. Practicing with such a purpose is more effective than just doing Beng Quan for no reason. In order to dispel diseases and enhance your health, you might want to give it a try.

# The Method and Requirements of Wu Xing Quan

The way of holding the fist to issue power is the essence of doing Wu Xing Quan. Therefore, we should understand the method and its requirements.

## THE WAY OF HOLDING THE FIST

Curl the fingers one at a time, starting with the pinky. Form a solid fist, but try not to use clumsy force. Bend the thumb downward to press the index finger and middle finger. The focus of power falls on the root joints of the index finger and middle finger.

## UP-FACING FIST

The fist that was drilled out or thrown out with crossing energy has to be twisted outward as much as possible. The palm side of the fist has to face upward; even better, the outside of the pinky finger can be turned to face upward. By doing so, when punching, the fist and the arm that are in the front would look like they are moving straight forward, but in fact there is a crossing/twisting energy. This is what the Xingyiquan Classics require: "when issuing a crossing punch, no crossing shape is seen." This fist-holding technique is used in Pi Quan, Zuan Quan, and Heng Quan.

## VERTICAL (STANDING) FIST

The fist that is thrown out needs to have the Hukou facing up. Also, the fist has to be extended forward as much as possible. By doing so, the fist becomes bigger and the power of pushing forward and punching downward will be increased. The Xingyiquan Classics state, "Once we clearly put the *San Xing* (三星; Three Stars) in the right positions, our power will become stronger." This means that you need to extend your shoulder joint, elbow joint, and wrist joint. They should form a straight line, so that you will see the alignment when looking at the arm from the front. After the San Xing positions are clear, the power issued from the shoulder will be pushed to the elbow, and the power in the elbow will be pushed to the hand. This type of *San Cui Jing* (三催劲; Three Pushing Energy/Force) is holistic, and it can easily be sent to the end of the limb. Due to the extension of the arm and the fist, the power becomes stronger, even if it is extended for only one more inch. That is why we say that we will have "one more force." We need to follow this rule when we are doing the chopping movement in Pi Quan, Beng Quan, and Pao Quan.

We use different names to distinguish the variations of the advancing footwork. We call it *"Jin Bu"* (进步; Forward Stepping) when both feet step forward—when we advance two steps in total. We call it "Shang Bu" (上步; Advance Stepping) if only one foot steps forward. With both kinds of footwork, we need to be sure that when we step forward, we always have Tang Jing and Deng Jing to create the springing power to move forward quickly and strongly.

In order to memorize the guidelines of practicing Wu Xing Quan, some people have made songs for each fist. Unfortunately, most of them are too shallow in meaning or they miss the real concepts. To help learners of Shang-style Xingyiquan grasp the substance and applications, I have revised the songs and put them at the beginning of each section, before the explanations of the movements in each fist.

# Pi Quan (劈拳; Chopping Fist)

The Xingyiquan Classics state, "The shape of Pi Quan is like an ax. It belongs to metal, connects with the lungs, and goes out through the nose. The manifestation of it in our bodies is the skin and hair." It is the very first technique in Wu Xing Quan. Since its shape is like an ax, we need to form the shape of an ax, so that we can train to have the energy of an ax. Pi Quan uses the fist and forearm as the leverage for issuing power. The combination of the two is considered the blade of the ax. Because we use the elbow to issue power, people say that "Pi Quan strikes with the elbow." This is a unique technique in Xingyiquan and was treasured by our ancestors in the field. However, many practitioners use Ying Zhuo instead of Pi Quan, which is a very serious mistake. There are two types of fists in Pi Quan. See figures 4.1 and 4.2.

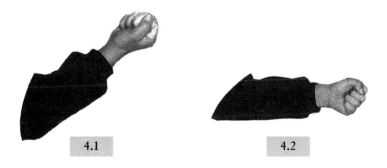

4.1          4.2

The song of Pi Quan:

*Pi quan si fu xing shu jin,*
*Sheng zuan ke beng miao jue lun.*
*Ti wei pi mao bi tong fei,*
*Qian bi fa jing jing nai shen.*

劈拳似斧性属金,
生钻克崩妙绝伦.
体为皮毛鼻通肺,
前臂发劲劲乃神.

Pi Quan is like an ax and of has the property of metal,
It generates Zuan Quan and controls Beng Quan; this is wonderfully
     designed.
The energy goes through the skin and hair, and it benefits the nose
     and the lungs,
It uses the forearm to issue power, and the force is thus strong and
     miraculous.

## THE SPECIFIC WAYS OF TRAINING IN PI QUAN (劈拳; CHOPPING FIST)

### 1. *Yu Bei Shi* (预备式; **Preparation Stance**)

This is the same as movement 1: On-Spot Left Eagle Grasp of Ying
Zhuo (Eagle Grasp). Refer to movement 1 of Ying Zhuo (page 68) for
movement descriptions and principles. Movement descriptions begin
from the position in picture 4.3.

4.3

### 2. *Jin Bu You Pi Quan* (进步右劈拳; Forward–Stepping Right Chopping Fist)

1) Retreat Half-a-Step Wrap-In: Continuing from Eagle Grasp, left palm changes into a fist; with the elbow dropped and maintaining contact with the ribs, the left forearm turns outward as it pulls back to rest at the left side of the navel; fist is facing upward. Simultaneously, right palm also changes into a fist and turns outward as it pulls back slightly to rest at right side of navel. While the fists are pulling back, left foot retreats to be close by the ankle bone of the right foot, with toes and knee pointing forward. Right knee stays tight to the inside of left knee. Eyes look forward (picture 4.4).

4.4

PRINCIPLES

   i. When changing palms to fists, do not use clumsy force. When pulling back the fists and forearms, they must twist, by utilizing yao power, as if to tear something apart.

   ii. When retreating with the left foot and pulling back the fists, the fists must be synchronous and with coordinated power. Body must not rise.

2) Lift Step Left Drill: The left fist twists inward as it drills upward along the chest line of the center until it reaches under the chin (picture 4.5). Without pausing, the right leg bends at the knee and deng backward; the left foot tang forward while staying close to the ground; as soon as the left foot lands, the right foot follows immediately and comes to rest against the inside ankle bone of the left foot and form the right lift step. At the same time that the left foot tang forward, left fist twists outward as it drills forward from under the chin to a height not exceeding the brows; the fist is facing diagonally outward with the curve of the small finger facing upward. The right fist remains tightly by the right side of the navel, reflecting the sinking power of the left fist. Eyes look to the left fist (picture 4.6).

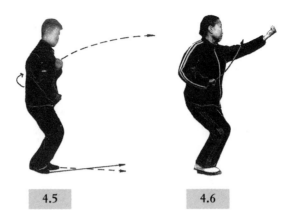

4.5                           4.6

PRINCIPLES

   i. When the left fist is drilling upward along the center line of the chest from the abdomen, it must remain in firm contact with the chest; do not hold the breath.

  ii. The left fist's forward drilling and the left foot's forward stepping must be synchronous; the body rotates 45° to the right, so that it faces partly forward and partly sideways. Shoulders and elbows must be dropped; utilize yao power to drill the left fist outward, fulfilling the requirement of having the yao pushing the shoulder, shoulder pushing the elbow, and elbow pushing the palm.

 iii. In forming the right lift step, the two feet must be tightly together; center of body weight must be maintained.

   3) Advance-Stepping Right Chopping Fist: The right fist maintains close contact with the center chest as it drills upward until it reaches the top of the left elbow joint (picture 4.7). Without pausing, the left foot deng backward, the right foot tang forward and lands, and the left foot follows immediately with a forward half-step to form a Zhuang Bu. Simultaneously, the right fist drills forward along the left forearm; when the two fists meet, both twist at the same time. The right fist chops forward and downward, with the curve of the thumb facing upward and the forearm at the level of the heart. At the same time,

the left fist maintains contact with the ribs as it pulls downward and backward to the left side of the navel; the fist is facing upward. Eyes look to the front of the right fist (picture 4.8).

4.7                    4.8

PRINCIPLES

i. When the right fist chops downward, the shoulders and elbow must drop. Utilize yao power and achieve San Jian alignment. Apply San Cui principle and extend San Xing to enable power to permeate the forearm. The pulling back of the left fist and the forward chopping of the right fist must be coordinated in speed and power.

ii. The left foot's backward deng, the right foot's forward tang, and the landing must be completed at the same time that the right fist chops downward; only then have you achieved the "hand and foot arrive in synchronization" technique requirement. Cultivate speed and power from natural and synchronized movements; only then is one able to issue solid, hard power. The body must not rise throughout the movement.

### 3. *Jin Bu Zuo Pi Quan* (进步左劈拳; Forward–Stepping Left Chopping Fist)

1) Retreat Half-a-Step Wrap-In: The left fist does not move. The right fist maintains contact with the ribs near the abdomen as it twists outward and pulls downward and inward to rest at the right side of the navel; the fist is facing upward. Simultaneously, the right foot stays close to the ground while retreating to touch inside ankle bone of the left foot; toes point forward. Eyes look forward (picture 4.9).

PRINCIPLE

Same as for step 1 of movement 2 above, only reversing the left and the right.

**4.9**

2) Lift Step Right Drill: The right fist twists inward so that the curve of the thumb is in contact with the body, then drills upward along the center line of the chest until it reaches under the chin (picture 4.10). Without stopping, the left leg bends at the knee and deng backward; the right foot tang forward while staying close to the ground; as soon as the right foot lands, the left foot follows immediately with a quick forward lift step, with the ankle bone of the left foot pressing against the top of the inside ankle bone of the right foot. At the same time that the right foot steps forward, the right fist drills upward from under the chin, then outward from the mouth to a height not exceeding the brows; the fist is facing diagonally outward; the curve of the small finger is facing upward. The left fist remains firmly at the left side of the navel, mirroring the sinking power of the right fist. Eyes look to the right fist (picture 4.11).

PRINCIPLE

Same as for step 2 of movement 2 above, only reverse the left and right.

3) Advance-Stepping Left Chopping Fist: The left fist maintains contact with the chest center as it drills upward to top of the left elbow curvature (picture 4.12). Without stopping, the right foot deng backward, the left foot tang forward, and the right foot follows immediately with a forward half-step to form a Zhuang Bu. Simultaneously, the left fist drills forward along the right forearm; when the two fists meet, both fists twist at the same time. The left fist chops forward, then downward, so the forearm is at the level of the heart, with the curve of the thumb facing upward. At the same time, the right fist maintains contact with the ribs as it pulls downward and backward to the right side of the navel, with the fist facing upward. Eyes look to the front of the left fist (picture 4.13).

PRINCIPLE

Same as for step 3 of movement 2 above, only reverse the left and right.

Practice by repeating the left and right stances; the number of repetitions depends on the size of the practice area. For now, practice up to the Left Chopping Fist, then turn around (with movement 4 below) and practice in the other direction.

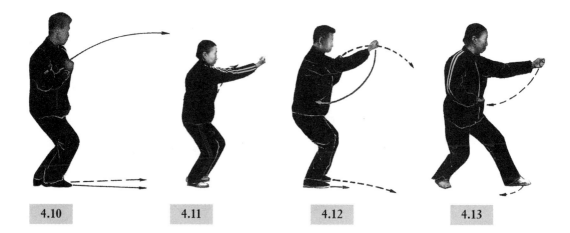

4.10     4.11     4.12     4.13

## 4. *Pi Quan Hui Shen Shi* (劈拳回身势; Chopping Fist Turn Around Stance)

1) Hook-in Stepping Wrap-up Fist: Without shifting the body weight, the left foot pivots on the heel and hooks the toes inward so that the toes of both feet are pointing at each other. Simultaneously, the left fist pulls back by bending the arm and comes to rest at the left side of the navel; the fist is facing upward, mirroring the right fist. Eyes look to the left (picture 4.14).

2) Turn Around and Retreat Foot: The upper body turns to the right as body weight shifts to the left foot. The right foot stays close to the ground as it pivots on the ball to turn the heel inward and retreats to the inside ankle bone of the left foot; toes point forward. Eyes look forward (picture 4.15).

PRINCIPLES

i. When pulling back the left fist, utilize yao power to pull from the elbow; twist the fist as you pull.

ii. When shifting the body weight, keep the body straight; do not stand up, or stick out the hip.

iii. After the right foot retreats, the right toes and right knee point forward; the left knee hooks inward to touch the inside of the right knee joint; the two legs must be tightly together.

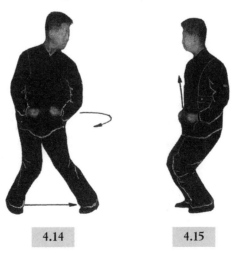

4.14          4.15

## 5. *Jin Bu Zuo Pi Quan* (进步左劈拳; Forward–Stepping Left Chopping Fist)

The descriptions and principles are the same as for movement 3 above, only facing the opposite direction (pictures 4.16 to 4.19).

After this movement, repeat the left and right stances to the starting position, then turn around and follow with Left Chopping Fist (picture 4.20) and wrap up [with the Closing Stance below]. If you must wrap up in the middle of a practice, you may do so only after finishing the Left Chopping Fist.

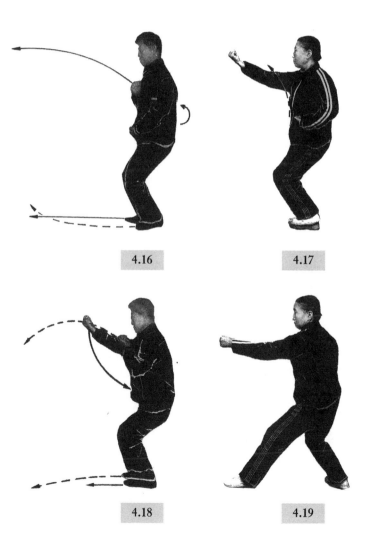

4.16     4.17

4.18     4.19

### 6. *Pi Quan Shou Shi* (劈拳收势; Chopping Fist Closing Stance)

The descriptions and principles are the same as for Step 16: Closing Stance of San Ti Shi (picture 4.20).

**4.20**

# Zuan Quan (钻拳; Drilling Fist)

The Xingyiquan Classics state, "The shape of Zuan Quan is like electricity or lightning, and it has the property of water. Its energy is connected with kidneys. Its manifestation is through the ears and the bones." Zuan Quan is the second technique in Wu Xing Quan. In ancient times, electricity meant lightning in a thunderstorm. The phrase "like electricity or lightning" does not refer to the speed, but to the shape. Since we say that Zuan Quan "is like lightning and is connected with kidneys," the way we execute it needs to have the shape of lightning. Zuan Quan is helpful to kidney function and the lumbar region. Its execution in Shang-style is very different from other styles. Before each punch, the front hand is hooked and issues the *Lu Jing* (捋劲; roll back energy) to come back to the chest level. Then, the same hand swings outward, forward, and inward to come back to the chest area with the *Bao Guo Jing* (包裹劲; wrapping energy). The whole series of movements form the shape of lightning. The hooking in and swinging outward movements require turning and shaking the waist, which extends the waist and strengthens the kidney function. Practicing this way, the shape and meaning of the movements will fulfill the requirements stated in the Xingyiquan Classics. From the fighting perspective, when we hook the front hand, we focus on the use of the wrist. This is a technique that defends and attacks at the same time. When the hand comes back and the elbow bends in front the chest, the focus is on the forearm. This is to gather energy to issue power. We can also issue power with the forearm when the hand comes back. In addition, when the hand swings outward and hooks inward, the focus is on the Hukou. We use the momentum to issue power from Hukou. The entire series of movements can be broken down into three parts, and they can also be integrated into one. This forms the unique wrapping energy, which cannot be found in other fists.

Some people mistakenly consider the *jie* (截; intercept energy) in Xingyiquan's *Ba Zi Gong* (八字功; the Eight Character Method Gong Fu) as Zuan Quan, and the guo (裹; wrapping energy) as Heng Quan. This is because they do Zuan Quan without showing the shape of lightning and thus missing the wrapping energy. In fact, the Ba Zi Gong is a set of movements that encompasses the following eight techniques: *zhan* (斩; chop), *jie* (截; intercept), *guo* (裹; wrap), *kua* (胯; groin strike), *tiao* (挑; lift up), *ding* (顶; push against), *yun* (云; swing overhead), *ling* (领; lead). It is not the combination of *Wu Xing Quan* and animal form, because it is a *gong* (功; internal power training) instead of a *quan* (拳; fist, boxing technique). If we analyze the energy characteristic in Heng Quan and Zuan Quan, we will find that the concept [that jie is Zuan Quan and that guo is Heng Quan] is not correct either. For example, the purpose of an inward piercing palm is to issue the crossing power. If the major technique is to throw an outward crossing punch, then we should not say that it has the wrapping energy. Besides, the technique of "crossing punch is not seen as a crossing movement" is to intercept the attack from the opponent. Therefore, the energy for Heng Quan should be jie instead of guo. As for Zuan Quan, the hooking downward movement is to prepare for the upward drilling punch. It does not show the energy of jie. Its shape of lightning and the movements of hooking hands inward and swinging outward show the technique of "wrap and conceal," which is exactly the energy of guo. The guo energy in Zuan Quan makes up the inward power issuing technique and makes Xingyiquan more comprehensive. The Xingyiquan of the Dai family of Shan Xi province has listed Zuan Quan as one of the "the Three Extraordinary Quan and Staff." This shows how unique Zuan Quan is when it comes to techniques. If we just practice with one hook followed by one drill, we definitely will miss its special traits.

Since Shang-style Zuan Quan has this extra movement with the shape of lightning, there are more variations in the hand posture. When the front hand is coming back with an inward hook, the hand shape is called *Diao Shou* (刁手; Hooked Hand) (picture 4.21). When the hand swings outward, forward, and comes back inward in front of the chest, the hand shape is called *Lou Zhang* (搂掌; Rolling Inward Palm) (picture 4.22).

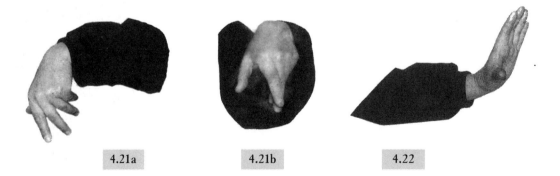

4.21a                4.21b                4.22

The song for Zuan Quan:

*Zuan quan si dian xing shu shui,*
*Sheng beng ke pao ruo shan lei,*
*Zai ti wei gu er tong shen,*
*Lou bi dou wan yao jing cui.*

钻拳似电性属水,
生崩克炮若闪雷,
在体为骨耳通肾,
搂臂抖腕腰劲催.

Zuan Quan is like lightning and has the property of water,
It generates Beng Quan, controls Pao Quan, and moves as fast as
    lightning and thunder,
It promotes kidney function and benefits the bones and ears.
When rolling the arm in a curve to the front of the chest, shake the
    waist region to issue power.

# THE SPECIFIC WAYS OF TRAINING IN ZUAN QUAN (钻拳; DRILLING FIST)

## 1. *Yu Bei Shi* (预备式; Preparation Stance)

This is the same as movement 1: On-Spot Left Eagle Grasp of Ying Zhuo (Eagle Grasp). Refer to movement 1 of Ying Zhuo (page 68) for movement descriptions and principles. Movement descriptions begin from the position in picture 4.23.

4.23

## 2. *Jin Bu You* Zuan Quan (进步右钻拳; **Forward-Stepping Right Drilling Fist)**

1) *Che Ban Bu Zho Diao Gui* (撤半步左刁桂; Retreat Half-a-Step Left Hook-in Palm): The left forearm twists outward so the palm faces upward. Right palm changes into a fist, twists outward, and pulls back slightly to the right side of the navel; the fist faces upward (picture 4.24). Without pausing, the *yao* twists slightly to the left; the left foot stays close to the ground as it retreats to have the heel touching inside of the ankle of the right foot; the toes point forward. Simultaneously, the left palm turns into a hooked hand as the left elbow coils rightward and inward to rest in front of the chest; the four fingers are pointing downward; the forearm bends horizontally in front of the chest, at one fist's distance from the body. Eyes look to the hooked hand (picture 4.25).

PRINCIPLES

   i. The hooking in of the palm and the retreating of the left foot must be coordinated.

   ii. When hooking in the palm, the shoulders must be sunk, and the elbows must drop. Focus on the wrist and utilize the *yao* power.

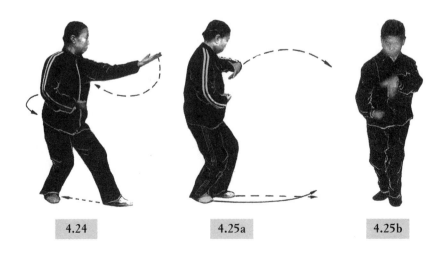

4.24                           4.25a                         4.25b

2) *Ti Bu Zuo Lou Zhang* (提步左搂掌; Lift Step Left Hook-in Palm): The left arm twists under as it wraps downward and to the left, while the hooked hand changes into an open palm and the wrist twists to throw the palm under and then outward to become a stand-up palm resting in front of the head. The Hukou of the palm is higher than the eye level. Simultaneously, the right leg bends at the knee and deng backward, and the left foot stays close to the ground as it tang forward; as soon as the left foot lands, the right foot follows immediately with a quick forward lift step, to press the ankle bone against the top of the inside ankle bone of the left foot. Eyes look to the palm in the front (picture 4.26).

PRINCIPLES

    i. When throwing the left palm downward then forward, focus on Hukou, which must be completely open. Apply San Cui principle by using yao power to push the shoulder, which in turn pushes the elbow, which in turn pushes the palm. Apply wrist and throwing power to complete the movement in one breath.

    ii. The forward stepping and the throwing of the left palm must be coordinated in movement and in power. The body must not shift to the left or to the right. The yao must face forward; back must be erect. The upper body faces partly forward and partly sideways. The right fist stays close to the body with a sinking power.

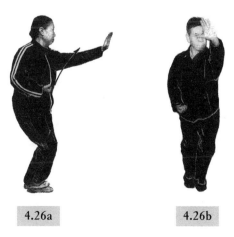

4.26a            4.26b

3) *Shang Bu You* Zuan *Quan* (上步右钻拳; Advance-Stepping Right Drilling Fist): The right fist maintains contact with the body as it twists outward and drills upward until it reaches the inside of the left elbow joint (picture 4.27). Without pausing, the left leg bends at the knee and deng backward, the right foot then stays close to the ground to tang forward, and the left foot follows immediately with a half-step forward to form a Zhuang Bu. Simultaneously, the right fist drills forward along the left forearm to no higher than brow height. When the right fist reaches the top of the left palm, the left palm changes into a fist, twists outward, and pulls back to the left side of the navel, maintaining contact with the ribs as it pulls back; the fist is facing upward. Eyes look to the fist in the front (picture 4.28).

PRINCIPLES

i. The right fist's drilling forward, the left palm's changing into a fist and pulling back, and the forward stepping must all be synchronized and coordinated in movement and power.

ii. The front fist, front foot, and the tip of the nose must be aligned.

iii. When the two hands pull against each other, power must originate from yao. Incorporate drilling and grinding energies in the forward drilling of the right fist.

4.27                    4.28

### 3. *Jin Bu Zuo* **Zuan Quan** (进步左钻拳; **Forward-Stepping Left Drilling Fist)**

1) Retreat Half-a-Step Right Hook-in Palm: The right fist changes into an upward-facing open palm (picture 4.28). Without stopping, the right foot stays close to the ground as it retreats to have the heel touching the inside ankle of the left foot, with the toes pointing forward. Simultaneously, the *yao* twists slightly to the right, and the right palm changes into a hooked hand as the right arm wraps leftward, then inward, to rest in front of the chest; the four fingers are pointing down; and the forearm bends horizontally in front of the chest, at one fist's distance from the body. The shoulders must be sunk, hence the elbows are dropped. Eyes look to the hooked hand (picture 4.29).

PRINCIPLE

This is the same as step 1 of movement 2 above, only reverse the left and the right.

2) Lift Step Right Hook-in Palm: The right arm turns under as it coils downward and to the right, while the hooked hand changes into an open palm and the wrist twists to throw the palm under and then outward to become a stand-up palm resting in front of the head. The

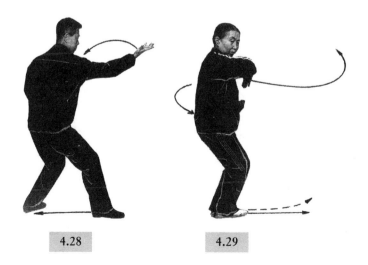

4.28         4.29

Hukou of the palm is higher than eye level. Simultaneously, the left leg
bends at the knee and deng backward, and the right foot stays close to
the ground as it tang forward; as soon as the right foot lands, the left
foot follows immediately to press the ankle bone against the top of the
inside ankle bone of right foot, thus forming a left lift step. Eyes look
to the palm in the front (picture 4.30).

**4.30**

PRINCIPLE

This is the same as step 2 of movement 2 above, only reverse the left and
the right.

3) Advance-Stepping Left Drilling Fist: The left fist maintains contact with the body as it twists outward and drills upward until it reaches
the inside of the left elbow joint (picture 4.31). Without stopping, the
right leg bends at the knee and deng backward, the left foot then stays
close to the ground to tang forward, and the right foot follows immediately with a half-step forward to form a Zhuang Bu. Simultaneously, the
left fist drills forward along the right forearm to no higher than brow
height. When the left fist reaches the top of the right palm, the right
palm changes into a fist, twists outward, and pulls back to the right side
of the navel, maintaining contact with the ribs as it pulls back; the fist
is facing upward. Eyes look toward the fist in the front (picture 4.32).

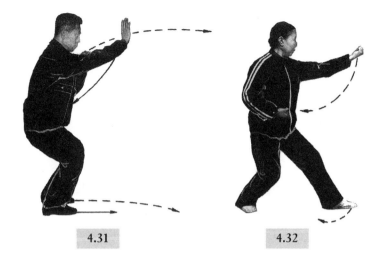

4.31                    4.32

PRINCIPLE

This is the same as step 3 of movement 2 above, only reverse the left and right.

Practice by repeating the left and right Drilling Fists. The number of repetitions depends on size of the practice area. You can turn around after either the left or right Drilling Fist. For now, we'll use turning around after a Left Drilling Fist as an example.

## 4. *Zuan Quan Hui Shen Shi* (钻拳回身势; Drilling Fist Turn Around Stance)

1) Hook-in Stepping Wrap-up Fist: Without shifting the body weight, the left foot pivots on the heel and hooks the toes inward so that both feet are hooked in. Simultaneously, the left arm bends downward to pull the fist back to the left side of the navel; the fist is facing upward to mirror the right fist. Eyes look to the left (picture 4.33).

2) Retreat-Stepping Hook-In Palm: The upper body turns to the right as the body weight shifts to the left foot; the right foot pivots on the ball, turns the heel inward, and stays close to the ground as it retreats to the inside ankle bone of the left foot; the toes are pointing forward. Simultaneously, the right fist changes into a hooked hand with four fingers pointing downward; the forearm is lifted, and the

elbow bent, so that the forearm is horizontal in front of the right chest at one fist's distance from the body. Eyes look to the hooked hand (picture 4.34).

PRINCIPLES

    i. Use the elbow to pull back the left fist; utilize *yao* power in hooking the hand.

   ii. When hooking in the toes of the left foot and shifting the body weight, maintain the same body height, do not rise or stick out the hip.

  iii. Each movement—turning around, the foot retreating, and the palms changing to hooked hands, and so forth—must be executed with clarity and in coordination with one another.

4.33                                    4.34

## 5. *Jin Bu Zuo Zuan Quan* (进步左钻拳; **Forward–Stepping Left Drilling Fist)**

Descriptions and principles are the same as steps 2 and 3 of movement 3 above (pictures 4.35 through 4.37), only facing the opposite direction.

Practice the left and right stances repeatedly. When you arrive at the starting position, turn around and wrap up after the Left Drilling Fist.

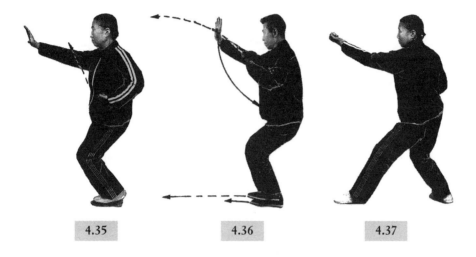

| 4.35 | 4.36 | 4.37 |

## 6. Zuan *Quan Shou Shi* (钻拳收势; **Drilling Fist Closing Stance)**

Descriptions and principles are the same as Step 16: Closing Stance of San Ti Shi (page 64) (picture 4.38).

4.38

# Beng Quan (崩拳; Smashing Fist)

The Xingyiquan Classics state, "The shape of Beng Quan is like an arrow, and it has the property of wood." "The energy of Beng Quan is connected with liver. The manifestation of liver is eyes and tendon." It is the third fist of Wu Xing Quan. "The shape is like an arrow" indicates that its energy is both straight and fast. It goes straight forward, takes the shortest path, and the hand moves very quickly. In addition, following the guiding rule of "Step into the mid-door of the opponent, even the immortal hand cannot defend himself," each step of Beng Quan advances to the mid-point between the opponent's legs. This is the shortest path, and the power is tremendous. With the addition of the power from *Zhan Shen Zong Li* (沾身纵力; You issue power spontaneously upon attack), Beng Quan is so effective in both short- and long-range fighting that many people consider it the main feature of Xingyiquan. Both Grandmasters Guo Yun-Shen and Shang Yun-Xiang are famous for Beng Quan, making this fist even more important.

When doing Beng Quan, the front foot moves forward while the back foot follows with just a small step. That is why it is called "Half-a-Step Beng Quan." Although the front foot only advances by half a step, the impact can be as big as with a full step. The power is tremendous, because it takes people by surprise. This power comes from the training of the techniques, such as "In fighting, we express our intent with foot work; the timing of the attack is determined by the readiness of the back foot to pounce forward," "When fighting, we rely 70 percent on the use of legs and 30 percent on hands," and "The intent of moving forward is as strong as the wind sweeping over the ground." Without the foot techniques, Beng Quan would lose half of its power.

In Beng Quan, the hands take turns to throw the punches while the front foot is advancing. It does not rely on speed, like a machine gun, to defeat the opponent. Instead, it requires each punch to create the absolute impact. It follows that a rule stated in the Xingyiquan Classics says, "There is no empty punch. It's nothing spectacular if the thrown punch does not hit the target" and "As soon as you pull the trigger, the target must be down." These statements highlight the fact that each Beng Quan punch thrown must have its impact, and this includes the energies of twisting, wrapping, extending, and pulling, as well as the force of Three Pushes. The power is holistic and tremendous. After understanding the concept of "attacking the Three Joints of the opponents without being seen" and practicing it for a long time, your Gong Fu will become better and the punch you throw will hit the target each time. Practicing Beng Quan without this mindset will make the training futile.

Some people say that the groin strike in Ba Zi Gong Fa refers to Beng Quan. This is inappropriate, because Ba Zi Gong is for internal power cultivation, not boxing techniques. If we examine the force generated by the groin strike, we will find that it comes from the Snake Form, not from Beng Quan.

The Beng Quan in Shang-style requires issuing straight force. The waist moves forward in the same way an arrow travels, so that the body can dash forward. The fists are twisted and wrapped inward. They support and hold up each other. Every punch you throw has to be fast, hard, fierce, and solid, and the power it sends out is as tremendous as roaring thunder. The way that the front foot steps forward firmly and the back foot presses against the ground when advancing is just like "the wind that sweeps the ground." The force is big and the distance of each step is very far. All of these features form the unique traits of Shang-style Xingyiquan.

The song of Beng Quan:

*Beng quan si jian shu mu xing,*
*Sheng pao ke heng ban bu gong,*
*Zai ti wei jin gan zhu mu,*
*Xun meng gang shi quan bu kong.*

崩拳似箭属木性,
生炮克横半步功,
在体为筋肝主目,
迅猛刚实拳不空.

Beng Quan is like an arrow and has the property of wood.

It generates Pao Quan and controls Heng Quan.

Although it moves only half a step at a time, its power cannot be
    underestimated.

In the human body, wood is manifested by sinew, refers to liver,
    and is revealed through the eyes. Beng Quan is a fist that is fast,
    fierce, hard, and solid, which never misses the target.

## THE SPECIFIC WAYS OF TRAINING IN *BENG QUAN* (崩拳; SMASHING FIST)

### 1. *Yu Bei Shi* (预备式; Preparation Stance)

This is the same as movement 1: On-Spot Left Eagle Grasp of Ying
Zhuo (Eagle Grasp). Refer to movement 1 of Ying Zhuo (page 68) for
movement descriptions and principles. Movement descriptions begin
from the position in picture 4.39.

4.39

## 2. *Ao Bu You Beng Quan* (拗步右崩拳; *Ao Bu* **Right Smashing Fist)**

1) Start from Left Eagle Grasp. The body does not move; both forearms twist and turn outward while both hands form fists. The left fist's Hukou faces upward; shoulders and elbows are dropped, forearm is straight at the heart level. Right fist faces upward; right fist and forearm are at right side of the navel. Eyes look to the front of the left fist (picture 4.40).

2) Continue from the preceding step. The body twists slightly to the left as body weight shifts slightly forward. The right fist twists outward; it maintains contact with the body while drilling upward until it reaches the inside of the left elbow joint; the curve of the small finger is facing upward. Eyes look to the front of the left fist (picture 4.41).

PRINCIPLES

i. To shift body weight forward, use kua to push the knee, and bend the knee forward. The body should twist slightly to the left. Make sure the body maintains its erectness; do not lean.

ii. When the right fist drills up to the left elbow joint, elbow must not part from the rib, hand must not part from the heart to maintain a wrap-in energy.

**4.40**                    **4.41**

3) Do not pause. The right leg bends at the knee and deng backward, and the left leg bends at the knee and stays close to the ground as it tang forward and lands. The right foot follows immediately with a forward step (the right knee presses against inside of left knee; the toes of the right foot must be behind the left heel; the two feet should be at a 45° angle). At the same time, the left foot tang forward, and the right fist maintains contact with the left forearm as it twists inward and smashes forward; the Hukou is facing upward; the fist is at heart level. Simultaneously, the left fist maintains contact with the ribs as it twists outward and pulls back to press against left side of the navel; fist is facing upward. Eyes look to the front of the right fist (picture 4.42).

PRINCIPLES

i. Smash the fist forward by utilizing the yao power. Have the yao push the shoulder, shoulder push the elbow, and elbow push the hand with spiraling energy. Smash straight forward while twisting, with explosive power. Shoulders must be sunk; elbows must drop. The right arm must exhibit San Xing and achieve San Jian. Pulling back the left fist and smashing forward the right fist must be coordinated, with a twist-and-tear energy and unified power.

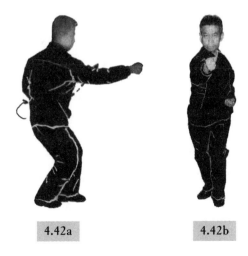

4.42a                    4.42b

ii. The left foot's forward tang must borrow momentum from the right foot's backward deng; utilize yao to push kua, kua to push the knee, the knee to push the foot. The forward tang must be swift, with the power of a whirling wind; the landing must be with a stomping energy.

iii. Twisting the body to smash the fist forward must fully exploit the function of a Dragon Folding the Body. Qi must be pushed, and the forward smash must be far reaching. Right fist's forward smash and left foot's forward tang must be coordinated and simultaneous. The head must lift upward, the shoulders must be sunk, and the elbows must drop. The two legs must press tight against each other with both knees bending forward to achieve a holistic power.

### 3. *Shun Bu Zuo Beng Quan* (順步左崩拳; *Shun Bu* Left Smashing Fist)

1) The body turns slightly to the right; the left fist maintains contact with the body as it twists outward and drills upward to inside of the right elbow joint; the curve of the small finger is facing upward. Eyes look forward (picture 4.43).

**4.43.**

PRINCIPLE

This step is the same as step 2 of movement 2 above, only the left and right fists are reversed.

2) Do not pause. The right leg bends at the knee and deng backward, and the left foot stays close to the ground to tang forward and lands. The right foot follows immediately with a forward step (the right knee presses tightly against inside of left knee; the toes of the right foot must remain behind the left heel; the two feet are at a 45° angle). At the same time, the left foot tang forward, and the left fist maintains contact with top of the right forearm as it twists inward and smashes forward; the Hukou is facing upward; the fist is at heart level. Simultaneously, the right fist maintains contact with the ribs as it twists outward and pulls back to the right side of the navel; the fist is facing upward. Eyes look to the front of the left fist (picture 4.44).

PRINCIPLE

This step is the same as step 3 of movement 2 above, only the left and right fists are reversed.

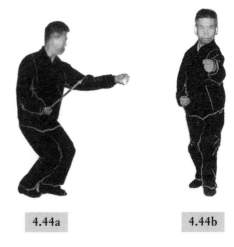

4.44a                    4.44b

## 4. *Ao Bu You Beng Quan* (拗步右崩拳; *Ao Bu* **Right Smashing Fist**)

Descriptions and principles of this movement are the same as for steps 2 and 3 of movement 2 above (pictures 4.45 and 4.46).

Practice by repeating the left and right Smashing Fist sequences. The number of repetitions can be determined by the size of the practice area. Turn around either after the left or the right Smashing Fist. But in the last Smashing Fist, before turning around, keep a larger distance between the follow-up step and the front foot to facilitate turning around with a hooked-in step. Using the right Smashing Fist as an example, the right follow-up step should be about a one-foot distance from the left foot heel (picture 4.47).

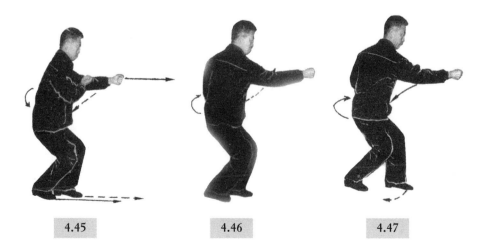

4.45          4.46          4.47

**5.** *Beng Quan Hui Shen* (崩拳回身; **Smashing Fist Turn Around**)
(狸猫倒上树; **Leopard Cat Turns Around to Climb Up The Tree**)

1) Without shifting the body weight, the body turns to the right; the left foot pivots on the heel and turns inward so that two feet point at each other. Simultaneously, with the left fist remaining in position as the body is turning, the right fist maintains contact with the ribs as it twists outward and pulls back to the right side of the navel; the fist is facing upward; the two fists are now mirroring each other. Eyes look to the left (picture 4.48).

PRINCIPLES

    i. The right fist's pulling back and the left foot's hooking inward must be coordinated and synchronous.

    ii. When hooking in the left foot, the upper body must not lean forward or backward; the hip must not protrude.

2) Do not pause. The body weight shifts to the left leg; the body turns immediately 90° to the right by twisting the yao. The right leg lifts upward by bending the knee with toes swung outward. Without pausing, borrowing the momentum of the yao-twist and the turning of the body, the right knee swings outward as right foot kicks forcefully forward with the heel. Simultaneously, the right fist maintains contact with the body as it drills upward and outward from under the chin.

4.48

The left fist remains in the same position. Eyes look to the front of the right fist (picture 4.49).

PRINCIPLES

i. The right foot's outward kick must borrow the momentum from the yao-twist and the turning of the body.

ii. The right outward kick and the right fist's forward drill must be swift, outward-reaching, and coordinated. Height of the kick should be higher than the knee but no higher than the waist. The foot must be horizontal; issue power from the heel. The right foot, right fist, and the tip of the nose must be aligned.

iii. Body must not lean sideways when kicking and drilling the fist outward. The left foot must be rooted with the leg bent slightly.

3) Do not pause. The body twists to the right; the right foot stomps forward with the toes pointing outward on landing. The left knee presses against inside of the right knee joint. Simultaneously, the left fist maintains contact with the right arm as it drills upward. When the two fists meet, both fists change to palms. The left palm drops forward then downward, and simultaneously, the right palm maintains contact with the ribs as it turns inward and pulls back to the right side of the navel; the palm is facing downward. Eyes look to the front of the left hand (picture 4.50).

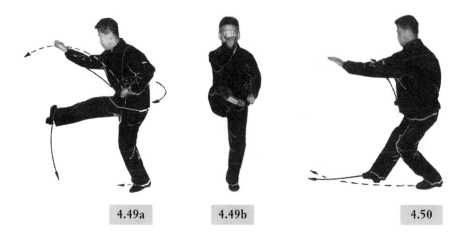

4.49a            4.49b                    4.50

PRINCIPLES

   i. The right foot's landing, the left palm's dropping forward and downward, and the left palm's pulling back must all be coordinated; the power must be swift, forceful, and holistic.

   ii. After the right foot lands, the two legs must press tightly against each other; the body weight must be centered and firm. The upper body twists to the right so that the body faces partly forward and partly sideways. The left arm must be extended. Issue power by twisting the yao.

   iii. This turning around smashing fist was originally named "Leopard Cat Turns around to Climb Up the Tree." If the right foot stomps forward with a distance, then the left foot could follow with a forward step. If the right foot lands by borrowing the body's twisting momentum, then it is possible to issue power on the same spot without a follow-up step. But the right foot's landing and the left palm's forward drop must be coordinated and synchronous.

## 6. *Ao Bu You Beng Quan* (拗步右崩拳; *Ao Bu* Right Smashing Fist)

1) The right foot moves forward by half a step; the left foot follows immediately with a lift step, pressing against the ankle bone right foot. Simultaneously, both palms change to fists; the left fist twists outward to become a standup fist; the right fist maintains contact with the body as it twists outward and drills upward—with the fist facing upward—to press against inside of the left elbow joint. Eyes look to the front of the left fist (picture 4.51).

PRINCIPLES

   i. Stepping forward with the right foot and changing palms to fists must be coordinated.

   ii. Drill the fist upward only when ready to smash it outward. The elbow must stay in contact the ribs, and the fist must stay close to the heart to wrap inward.

2) Do not pause. The right leg bends at the knee and deng backward, and the left foot stays close to the ground as it tang forward and lands. The right foot follows immediately with a forward step to form a Smashing Fist Stance. Simultaneously, the right fist stays in contact with top of the left arm as it drills and smashes forward; the Hukou is facing upward; the fist is at the height of the center of the chest. The left fist stays in contact with the ribs as it twists and pulls back to press on the left of the navel; fist is facing upward. Eyes look to the front of the right fist (picture 4.52).

## PRINCIPLES

i. This step is the same as step 3 of movement 2 above.

ii. Practice by repeating the left and right Smashing Fist movements until you reach the starting position and turn around, finish the first Ao Bu Right Smashing Fist (picture 4.53) then proceed to the closing movement, but not before completing *Tui Bu Zuo Beng Quan* (退步左崩拳; Backward-Stepping Left Smashing Fist).

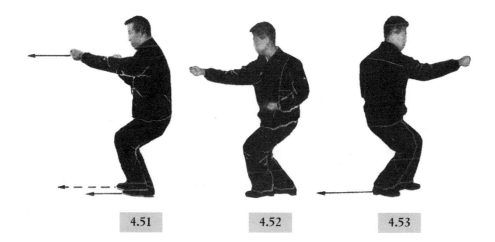

|     |     |     |
| 4.51 | 4.52 | 4.53 |

### 7. *Tui Bu Zuo Beng Quan* (退步左崩拳; **Backward-Stepping Left Smashing Fist)**

1) The fists do not move. The body weight shifts backward. The right foot, with toes still pointing outward, takes one big step directly backward to form a Bow Stance (a transitional stance). Eyes look to the front of the right fist (picture 4.54).

PRINCIPLE

To practice swift and far retreat stepping and also be able to issue power while retreating, the retreat stepping must be far and agile.

2) Without pausing, the body weight shifts backward as left foot stays close to the ground and immediately takes a backward step to the inside of the right foot, to form a left lift step. Simultaneously, the upper body twists slightly to the right; left fist maintains contact with the body as it drills upward to inside of the right elbow joint; the curve of the small finger is facing upward. Eyes look to the front of the right fist (picture 4.55).

PRINCIPLE

The Xingyiquan Classics state: "Attack when advancing; also attack when retreating." This means to attack while retreating and also to gather power and wait to issue; hence the left forearm must wrap in front of the chest with power.

3) Without pausing, continue to shift body weight backward. The left foot stomps backward with left knee pressing against the right knee so that the two feet are locked in a firm stance. Simultaneously, the left fist stays in contact with top of the right arm as it twists, drills, and smashes forward; the Hukou is facing upward; shoulders are sunk; elbows drop; apply San Cui to display San Xing. The fist is at center chest height. When the two fists meet, the right fist stays in contact with the ribs as it twists outward and pulls back to press tight against right side of navel; fist is facing upward. This is the Retreat-Stepping Smashing Fist Stance. Eyes look to the front of the left fist (picture 4.56).

PRINCIPLES

i. There should not be any pause between the steps in this movement. In smashing the left fist forward, the back must be erect, shoulders must be extended, and energy is pushed to the elbow. In pulling back the right fist, the elbow must wrap in, and yao must twist; it must also be coordinated and synchronous with the left foot's retreat-stepping.

ii. When the left foot lands on the retreating step, there should be a bouncing-back deng energy in the foot. Borrow the yao power to enhance the left fist's forward smashing speed and forcefulness, thereby applying the "also attack when retreating" principle.

iii. The two legs must lock tightly together; left foot should deng backward. Twist yao and elongate the back; shoulders sink and elbows drop. The head must lift upward to allow qi to sink to Dantian. All parts of the body are coiled to issue a holistic power. Do not lean to the left or to the right.

4.54                    4.55                    4.56

4.57

### 8. *Beng Quan Shou Shi* (崩拳收势; Smashing Fist Closing Stance)

Fists and body do not move. Left foot takes one step directly forward. Eyes look to the front of the left fist (picture 4.57). The closing movement that follows is identical to that of the Three Body Stance.

# Pao Quan (炮拳; Cannon Fist)

The Xingyiquan Classics state, "The shape of Pao Quan is like a cannon, and it has the property of fire. It connects with the heart and is manifested through the tongue. In the human body, it is related to blood and vessels." When doing Pao Quan, we move in a zigzag.

Some people say that the *ding* (顶; push against) energy in Xingyi Ba Zi Gong techniques refers to Pao Quan; this is not accurate. The ding movement in Ba Zi Gong is a technique to train internal force and is not relevant to Pao Quan at all. Some people interpret the hand on the top in Pao Quan as using force to block or push upward against a punch on the head. If this were the case, we violate the concept of "offence within a defense" by using brute force to fight against the incoming attack. In fact, the upper hand in Pao Quan does not use any upward pushing energy. It uses a combination of twisting, rolling, brushing away, and deflecting energies to break the attacking force. That is why we say that Pao Quan is not related to ding energy at all.

In the traditional Qigong, we work hard to seek "the harmony between heart and kidneys" and have "water and fire reinforce each other." Practicing Pao Quan can help us reach the goal.

Although the footwork in Shang-style Xingyiquan moves in a zigzag, each step still has the force coming from the front foot grabbing the ground firmly, and back foot pressing the ground to pounce forward. The upper fist has the energies of twisting, rolling, brushing away, and deflecting, while the fist at the center of the chest is twisting and wrapping inward to gather energy. At the same time, you shake the *yao* to issue power. Therefore, it has its own feature and energy path.

The song in Pao Quan:

*Pao quan si pao xing shu huo,*
*Sheng heng ke pi ao bu huo,*
*Ti wei xue mai xin zhu she,*
*Ning zhuan huo ji wu bi luo.*

炮拳似炮性属火,
生横克劈拗步活,
体为血脉心主舌,
拧转火机物必落.

Pao Quan is like a cannon and has the property of fire.
It generates Heng Quan, controls Pi Quan, and the footwork is very
    agile.
In the human body, it relates to blood vessels and the heart, which
    are manifested through the tongue.
When fighting with Pao Quan, it is like pulling the trigger of a gun
    and the target shall fall!

## THE SPECIFIC WAYS OF TRAINING IN PAO QUAN

### 1. *Yu Bei Shi* (预备式; **Preparation Stance**)

This is the same as movement 1: On-Spot Left Eagle Grasp of *Ying Zhuo* (Eagle Grasp). Refer to movement 1 of *Ying Zhuo* (page 68) for movement descriptions and principles. Movement descriptions begin from the position in picture 4.58.

**4.58**

### 2. *Ti Bu Shuang Pao Quan* (提步双炮拳; Lift-Stepping Double Cannon Fist)

**4.59**

1) The left palm does not change. The right palm reaches outward to be parallel with the left palm; the thumbs of the two palms touch each other. Simultaneously, the left foot tang straight forward by one step; the right foot follows immediately by lifting upward to press against inside of the left foot's ankle bone, thus forming a right lift step. Eyes look to the front of the hands (picture 4.59).

PRINCIPLES

   i. The right palm's reaching forward must borrow the momentum from the right foot's backward deng and the left foot's forward tang. Its completion must be synchronous with that of the right lift step so as to coordinate the upper and lower parts of the body.

  ii. In probing the palm, the shoulders must be sunk and the back must be extended. The left foot's forward tang must be far; the lift step must be firm. The body must not lean or lift.

2) Do not pause. The right foot gathers energy from the lift step and tang forward by another big step. Left foot follows immediately with a forward lift step, pressing against inside of ankle bone of the right foot. Simultaneously, both hands form fists and twist outward as they maintain contact with the ribs and pull back to both sides of the navel; the fists are facing upward, mirroring each other. This is the Lift-Stepping Double-Cannon Fist. Eyes look to the left front (picture 4.50).

PRINCIPLES

   i. When the right foot gathers energy from the lift step to tang forward, the stepping must be agile, long, and firm.

  ii. When forming the left lift step, changing palms to fists, and pulling the fists back to the navel, the energy is that of contracting the yao as if to tear apart. Completion of the lift step must be synchronous with the pulling back of the fists. The two legs must press against each other. The body must not lean forward or sideways.

**4.50**

### 3. *Ao Bu You Pao Quan* 拗步右炮拳 (*Ao Bu* **Right Cannon Fist**)

1) Continue from the preceding movement. The body twists slightly to the right. The left fist twists outward as it drills upward along the center line of the body to under the chin. Simultaneously, the right fist twists outward as it drills upward to press on the inside of the left elbow joint. Both fists' Hukou are facing forward. Eyes look to the left front (picture 4.51).

PRINCIPLE

When the fists are drilling upward, twist and wrap them inward tight to gather power.

2) Do not pause. The yao twists to the left; the right leg bends at the knee to deng backward; the left foot tang forward by one big step 45° to the left; the right foot follows immediately with a big forward half-step to press the right knee against back of the left knee; the body weight is on the right foot; the Left Cannon Fist Stance is thus formed. At the same time the the feet are going forward, the left fist drills forward and upward to the front of the head, then continues to twist outward and pull back to the left temple. The wrist and back of the fist press tightly against the left temple; the fist is facing outward. The right fist twists inward and drills forward from the chest; the Hukou is facing upward.

4.51

Shoulders are sunk; elbow is dropped; display San Xing; the right fist is at center chest height. Eyes look to the left front (picture 4.52).

PRINCIPLES

   i. Both fists gather energy by the twist and wrap-in movement in the preceding step; then issue power by twisting in reverse. The left fist borrows momentum from the body's left-twist and forward movement to pull back to the left temple. The right fist borrows the spiraling momentum of the reverse twist to drill forward.

  ii. The left foot's forward tang, the left fist's drilling pullback, and right fist's forward drill must all be coordinated. Yao is the governor. Power issuance must be swift and forceful, yet natural and smooth at the same time.

 iii. Steps in Cannon Fist are bigger than steps in Smashing Fist, about one foot's length. Legs must press tightly against each other. Body must not lean. The hip and the forehead must not protrude. The right fist, the toes of the left foot, and the tip of the nose must be aligned to achieve San Jian alignment.

4.52

## 4. *Ao Bu Zuo Pao Quan* (拗步左炮拳; *Ao Bu* Left Cannon Fist)

1) The upper body turns to the right by 90°. As it turns, the left fist drops forward to be level with the right fist and both fists swing to the right by 90° along with the body. The right fist twists inward as it swings to form a hooked fist. Both fists are facing downward with the Hukou facing each other; they are one fist's width apart from each other. Eyes look to the fists (picture 4.53).

PRINCIPLE

The body's turning and the fists' swinging to the right must be coordinated.

2) Do not pause. The left foot takes one big forward step 90° to the right to past the right foot. The right foot follows immediately with a forward lift step, pressing against the inside of the ankle bone of the left foot. Simultaneously, the upper body twists to the left, and both fists maintain contact with the ribs as they twist outward and pull back to both sides of the navel; contract the yao and hold the fists tightly. This is the Single-Stand Double Cannon Fist. Eyes look to the right front (picture 4.54).

PRINCIPLE

The left foot's forward step and the right foot's lift step must be coordinated with the body's twist and fists' pullback.

4.53          4.54

3) Do not pause. The feet do not move. The upper body twists slightly to the left. The right fist maintains contact with the body as it twists outward while drilling upward along the center line of the body to the front of the chin. The left fist maintains contact with the body as it twists outward and drills upward to inside of the right elbow joint. Both fists are facing outward, with Hukou facing forward. Eyes look to the right front (picture 4.55).

PRINCIPLE

Both arms must twist and wrap inward to gather power.

4) Do not pause. The right foot tang forward by one big step and lands; the left foot follows immediately with a big half-step to press left knee against back of the right knee. The feet are about one foot's distance apart, with the body weight on the left leg. Simultaneously, the yao twists to the right as the right fist drills upward to the front of the head, then continues to twist outward and pull back to the right temple; the wrist and back of the fist presses tightly against the temple; the fist is facing outward. Also simultaneously, the left fist twists inward as it drills outward from the chest; the Hukou is facing upward. Shoulders are sunk; elbow is dropped; display San Xing; the left fist is at center chest height. Eyes look to the right front (picture 4.56).

PRINCIPLE

This is the same as for step 2 of movement 3 above; only the left and right are reversed.

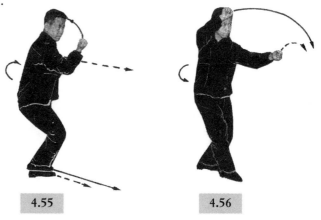

4.55                              4.56

## 5. *Ao Bu You Pao Quan* (拗步右炮拳; *Ao Bu* Right Cannon Fist)

The movement description and principles are the same as for movement 4 above, only the left and right are reversed (pictures 4.57 through 4.60).

Practice by repeating the left and right fist movements. Number of repetitions is determined by the size of the practice area. Turn around after either the left or the right Cannon Fist movement. For now, we'll use the right Cannon Fist as an example. Turn around to the right to repeat the movements.

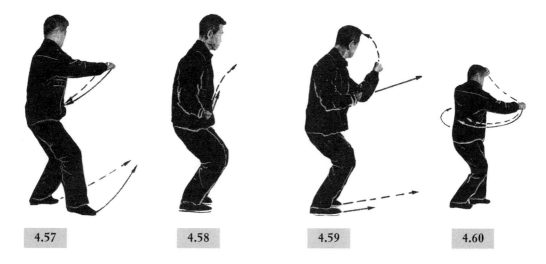

| 4.57 | 4.58 | 4.59 | 4.60 |

## 6. *Pao Quan Huei Shen Shi* (炮拳回身势; Cannon Fist Turn Around Stance)

1) The right fist turns inward to become a hooked fist. At the same time, the left fist drops from front of the head to level with the right fist. The Hukou of the two fists now face each other at center chest height. Shoulders are sunk; elbows drop. Eyes look to the fists. Without pausing, the yao turns toward the back on the right. Along with the body's movement, fists also swing backward horizontally. Eyes follow the hand movement, looking at the fists (picture 4.61).

PRINCIPLE

Utilize the yao power to swing the fists to the right, and do not shift the body weight.

2) Do not pause. Borrowing the yao-twisting momentum, the body pivots on the right foot and continues to turn to the right as left foot maintains contact with the ground and hooks in over the toes of the right foot. Simultaneously, both fists maintain contact with the ribs as they twist outward and pull back to both sides of the navel; fists are facing upward. Eyes look to the right front. At this point, the body has turned around by about 180° (picture 4.62).

PRINCIPLES

  i. When turning around with a hooked-in step, the pivoting right foot must not move. The left foot borrows the yao-twisting momentum to do the hook-in step; it must be swift, agile, and firm.

  ii. Lift the rectum. Keep the knees together and the kua concave. The hip must not protrude. Body must not lean.

4.61                              4.62

## 7. *Ao Bu Zuo Pao Quan* (拗步左炮拳; *Ao Bu* **Left Cannon Fist**)

1) Do not pause. Shift the body weight to the left foot. The right foot borrows the momentum from shifting the body weight to pivot on the heel and point toes toward the right front. Simultaneously, the right fist maintains contact with the center chest as it twists outward while drilling upward to the front of the chin. Also simultaneously, the left fist maintains contact with the body as it twists outward while drilling upward toward inside of the right elbow and pressing tight. Both fists are facing outward with Hukou facing forward. Eyes look to the right front (picture 4.63).

PRINCIPLE

Both forearms must wrap tight to gather power. Hip must not protrude when shifting body weight.

2) Do not pause; proceed to the left Cannon Fist. The descriptions and principles are the same as that of step 4 of movement 4 above, only reverse the direction (picture 4.64).

Practice by repeating the left and right Cannon Fist movements until arriving at the starting point. You must complete the right Cannon Fist before proceeding to the Closing Stance. If you turn around from the left Cannon Fist, then follow with the right Cannon Fist before proceeding to the Closing Stance.

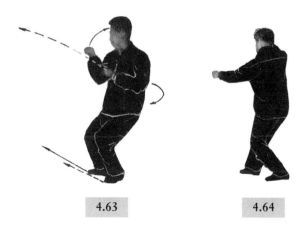

4.63          4.64

## 8. *Pao Quan Shou Shi* (炮拳收势; **Cannon Fist Closing Stance**)

This movement is to follow the right Cannon Fist (picture 4.65).

1) The right fist does not move. The left fist drops to under the right elbow joint; the fist is facing downward. Eyes look to the front of the right fist (picture 4.66).

PRINCIPLE

The left fist drops naturally, with the elbow bent. The left elbow must maintain contact with the ribs.

2) Do not pause. The body twists to the right to face forward. The left foot tang forward by half a step to form a Zhuang Bu. Simultaneously, the left fist maintains contact with the right forearm as it twists while drilling forward; shoulders must be sunk; elbows must drop; Hukou is facing upward; fist is at center chest height. Also simultaneously, the right fist twists outward and pulls back to the right side of the navel while maintaining contact with the ribs. Eyes look to the left front (picture 4.67).

PRINCIPLE

The left fist must borrow the body-twisting momentum to drill outward. The outward drill must be coordinated with the left foot's forward tang.

The remainder of the Closing Stance is the same as the Eagle Grasp Closing Stance (page 80).

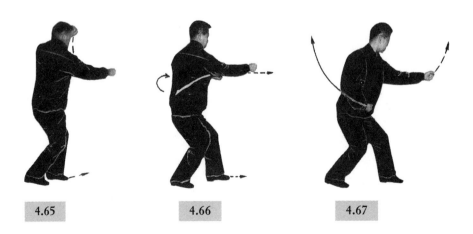

4.65                4.66                4.67

# *Heng Quan* (橫拳; **Crossing Fist**)

The Xingyiquan Classics state, "The shape of Heng Quan is like the ball of a slingshot, and it has the property of earth. Its energy is connected with spleen, the energy of which is manifested through the mouth. In the human body, it is revealed through muscles." It is the fifth fist of Wu Xing Quan. It moves forward in a zigzag.

Many people do not understand why we say that the shape of Heng Quan is like the ball of a slingshot. This is something we should clarify. Actually, the "image mimicking" and "meaning interpretation" used in Wu Xing Quan shows very close proximity to the techniques executed. For example, in Heng Quan, the "ball" refers to the projectile used in the traditional martial arts slingshot. It was used by the Immortal Slingshot Li Wu described in the novels and Shi San Mei in the Legend of Iron Bow. This slingshot is made from a regular bow that has been modified. The ends of the bow are cut shorter and the string replaced with bamboo plates at each end; the bamboo plates are connected with a bowl held in the middle with a strand of silk thread. The bowl is used for holding the bullet and is placed right in front of the riser of the bow. People who are not so skillful would hit the bullet on the riser. However, those who know how to use the horizontal power in the bow would shoot the bullet straight forward without hitting the riser. Using the way that a slingshot works to describe the crossing energy in Heng Quan fits very well with the statement "When using Heng Quan to strike, one cannot see the punch go across." Besides, it is appropriate to say that the shape of Heng Quan is like a bullet in a slingshot.

It is also interesting to ask why we say that the nature of Heng Quan belongs to earth. The way we execute Heng Quan relies on twisting the yao, one arm touching the ribs. One arm contracts the muscle while the other relaxes to massage the liver, spleen, and stomach. All the movements can strengthen the function of the spleen, which is why we say that it is connected with spleen. According to the Five Element Theory, the spleen belongs to earth. The bullet in the slingshot is made of earth

and hair, the nature of which also belongs to earth. This is why we say
that the nature of Heng Quan belongs to earth. In addition, there is a
saying in the Five Element Theory: "All things are born from the earth."
Indeed, Heng Quan can generate other fists. For example, San Ti Shi is
the Mother Form of Xingyiquan. The fist with drilling energy added
before San Ti Shi transforms into Ying Zhuo is Heng Quan.

The Xingyiquan Classics state, "When the fist goes upward, it is a
drilling punch; when it goes downward, the palm needs to turn over."
And "When a fist goes upward, it carries a crossing energy; when it
comes down, the force goes forward." This drilling upward fist is actually a crossing punch. Because it does not go out underneath the front
arm, it thus looks like a drilling punch instead of a crossing punch. In the
Mother Form of Ying Zhuo, Heng Quan comes before other fists. That's
why we say that Heng Quan generates other fists. In Heng Quan, there
is a combination of straight and crossing energies. In addition, it can be
used for both defense and offense. The energies are mingled harmoni-
ously. Therefore, it is easy to apply it in a dynamic way. Due to these
features, people say, "When fighting against Heng Quan, it is very hard
to defend yourself." Many Xingyiquan practitioners use Heng Quan to
start when fighting opponents because it hides attacking energy inside,
has the function of both defense and offense, and is easy to change into
other techniques.

When teaching Heng Quan, Master Shang emphasized the concept
"When using Heng Quan to strike, one cannot see the punch go across."
If people can see the crossing energy in your punch, it means that you are
using arm power and the force comes from the middle and end joints.
Doing it in this way will lose the true essence of Xingyiquan. Instead,
Heng Quan uses the power from the yao. It has to fulfill the requirement
"Nothing can be seen when using the fist to strike the Three Joints of the
opponent." The difference between these two is huge. The Xingyiquan
Classics state, "However good your techniques may be, if you cannot get
the essence of the art, all you do is in vain." This is something that we
must believe and make clear.

The song of Heng Quan:

*Heng Quan si dan xing shu tu,*
*Sheng Pi ke Zuan xing bu lou,*
*Ti wei ji rou pi zhu kou,*
*Chu shou nan zhao miao nan shu.*

横拳似弹性属土
生劈克钻形不露,
体为肌肉脾主口,
出手难招妙难书.

Heng Quan looks like the bullet of a slingshot and its property belongs to earth.

It generates Pi Quan and controls Zuan Quan.

When using Heng Quan, you cannot see the crossing movement.

It connects with the spleen, is manifested through the mouth, and governs the function of muscles.

The difficulty of defending against the Heng Quan is beyond description.

## THE SPECIFIC WAYS OF TRAINING IN HENG QUAN

### 1. *Yu Bei Shi* (预备式; Preparation Stance)

This is the same as movement 1: On-Spot Left Eagle Grasp of Ying Zhuo (Eagle Grasp). Refer to movement 1 of Ying Zhuo (page 68) for movement descriptions and principles. Movement descriptions begin from the position in picture 4.68.

4.68

### 2. *Ti Bu Shuang Pao Quan* (提步双炮拳; **Lift-Stepping Double Cannon Fist)**

This is the same as movement 2 of Cannon Fist (page 124) (pictures 4.69 and 4.70).

4.69                    4.70

### 3. *Ao Bu You Heng Quan* (拗步右横拳; *Ao Bu* **Right Crossing Fist)**

1) The stance does not change. The left fist twists and pierces outward toward the left front; the fist is facing outward at shoulder height. The right fist does not move. Eyes look to the left fist (picture 4.71).

PRINCIPLE

When the left fist pierces outward, the shoulders must not rise; the body must not lean. The movement must be relaxed and natural.

2) Do not pause. The stance does not change. The right elbow maintains contact with the ribs as the right fist twists inward and pierces upward to under the left elbow; the fist is facing downward. Eyes look to the left fist (picture 4.72).

PRINCIPLE

The right elbow must not detach from the ribs; the fist must not detach from the heart [it should stay close to the chest]. Gather energies, preparing to advance.

3) Do not pause. The left foot takes one big forward step 45° to the left. Right foot follows immediately with half a step. Two feet are now about one foot's length apart; the right knee presses against inside of left knee joint, forming the Left Crossing Fist Stance. Simultaneously, the right fist maintains contact with the underside of the left elbow as it twists and drills outward; shoulders must sink; elbow must drop; the fist is facing upward at shoulder height. When the two fists meet, the left fist maintains contact with the ribs as it twists outward while pulling back to press against left side of the navel; the fist is facing upward. Eyes look to the front of the right fist (picture 4.73).

PRINCIPLES

i. Steps 1 through 3 are continuous movements; do not pause between them. The body must not rise during the movements.

ii. The left foot's forward tang, the right fist's outward drill, and the left fist's pulling back must all be coordinated and synchronous. Forward tang and forward fist drill must be accompanied by yao power. In Au Bu, even though the feet and the hands are not in the same direction, the energy must still be smooth. The front fist, front foot, and the tip of the nose must be aligned. The movement must be natural, yet swift and forceful. When drilling the right fist outward, incorporate a horizontal power, yet it should not be observed as horizontal.

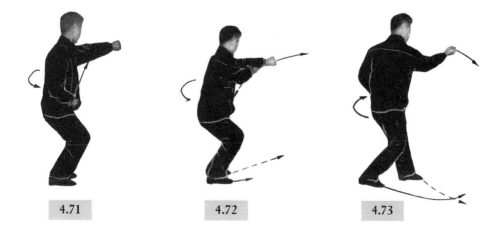

4.71　　　4.72　　　4.73

iii. The right foot's following forward step must be natural; the two feet must be firm. The two legs must stay close to each other. Shoulders must be sunk; elbows must drop. Twist the *yao,* yet keep the arms forward-facing. Body must not lean. Head must lift upward. The entire body must be holistically coordinated.

### 4. *Ao Bu Zuo Heng Quan* (拗步左横拳; *Ao Bu* Left Crossing Fist)

1) The body turns to the right; the right fist moves with the body. The left foot takes one big step forward to land diagonally in front of the right foot. Right foot follows immediately by lifting the foot to press against the inside ankle bone of the left foot thus forming a right lift step. Eyes look to the right fist (picture 4.74).

PRINCIPLE

In twisting the body to advance diagonally, it is important to press the knees together and concave the kua. Furthermore, the feet must incorporate forward tang and backward deng energy. Stepping must be firm. Body must be erect.

2) Continue from the preceding step. The stance does not change. The body turns slightly to the right. The left fist twists inward as it pierces upward to under the right elbow; the fist is facing downward. Eyes look to the right fist (picture 4.75).

4.74          4.75

PRINCIPLE

This is the same as step 2 of movement 3 above, only the left and right are reversed.

3) Do not pause. The body twists to the right; the right foot takes one big step diagonally forward to the right. The left foot follows immediately with a half-step forward. The two feet are about one foot's length apart. The left knee presses against back of the right knee joint. Simultaneously, the left fist maintains contact with the arm as it twists outward while punching forward from under the right elbow. Shoulders must be sunk; elbow must drop; the fist is facing upward at shoulder height. When the left fist meets the right fist, the right fist then maintains contact with the ribs as it twists outward and pulls back to press tightly against the right side of the navel. The fist is facing upward. Eyes look to the front of the left fist (picture 4.76).

PRINCIPLE

This is the same of step 3 of movement 3, only the left and right are reversed.

4.76

**5. *Ao Bu You Heng Quan* (拗步右横拳; *Ao Bu* Right Crossing Fist)**

The movement is the same as movement 4, only the left and right are reversed (pictures 4.77 through 4.79).

Practice the left and right movements repeatedly in the forward direction. The number of repetitions is determined by the size of the practice area. You may turn around either after the left or the right Crossing Fist. For the moment, we shall use turning around after the *Ao Bu* Right Crossing Fist as an example for continuing in the other direction.

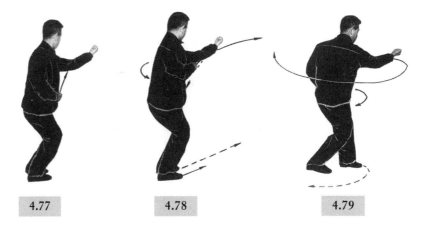

4.77                4.78                   4.79

## 6. *Heng Quan Huei Shen Shi* (横拳回身势; **Crossing Fist Turn Around Stance**)

1) The body turns around to the right by pivoting on the right foot, while left foot maintains contact with the ground to take a hooked-in step toward the outside of the toes of the right foot. The right fist follows the body to turn around. Eyes look to the right fist (picture 4.80).

PRINCIPLES

  i. The left foot must borrow the yao-twisting momentum to take the hook-in step. The right foot must be grounded and not move. The hook-in step must be agile and solid.

  ii. Lift the rectum. Press the knees together. The kua must be concave. The hip must not protrude. The body must not lean.

   2) Do not pause. Shift body weight to the left foot. Right foot then steps forward to press against the ankle bone of the left foot to form a right lift step. Simultaneously, the left fist maintains contact with the ribs as it twists inward and pierces upward to under the right elbow joint; the fist is facing downward. Eyes look to the right fist (picture 4.81).

PRINCIPLE

When shifting the body weight after the turn-around, the hip must not protrude. The left fist and forearm must twist and maintain contact with the ribs to gather power.

4.80                    4.81

### 7. *Ao Bu Zuo Heng Quan* (拗步左横拳; *Ao Bu* Left Crossing Fist)

Do not pause. The body turns to the right as the right foot takes one big diagonal forward step to the right. The left foot follows immediately with a half-step forward; press the left knee tightly against the back of the right knee. The two legs press tightly against each other. Simultaneously, the left fist maintains contact with the underside of the right arm as it twists outward and punches forward; the fist is facing upward. Shoulders must be sunk; elbow must drop; fist is at shoulder height. When the two fists meet, the right fist maintains contact with the ribs as it twists outward and pulls back to press against right side of the navel; the fist is facing upward. Eyes look to the front of the left fist (picture 4.82).

PRINCIPLE

This is the same as step 3 of movement 4; only facing the opposite direction.

Practice by repeating the left and right Crossing Fist movements. Turn around when reaching the starting point to close. Stepping is identical to that of Cannon Fist. If you complete the Left Crossing Fist and turn around, then proceed to *Ao Bu* Right Crossing Fist, follow with the Closing Stance.

4.82

## 8. *Heng Quan Shou Shi* (横拳收势; Crossing Fist Closing Stance)

This movement is to follow *Ao Bu* Right Crossing Fist (picture 4.83).

The left fist maintains contact with the ribs as it twists inward and pierces upward to under the right elbow joint; the fist is facing downward (picture 4.84). Without pausing, the body turns to the right as the left foot takes a big half-step to form a Zhuang Bu. Simultaneously, the left fist maintains contact with the underside of the right arm, twists outward to become a standup fist and punches forward. Shoulders must be sunk; elbows must drop. The fist is at center chest height. When the two fists meet, right fist maintains contact with the ribs as it twists outward and pulls back to press against right side of the navel; the fist is facing upward. Eyes look forward (picture 4.85).

The remainder of the Closing Stance is the same as the Eagle Grasp Closing Stance (page 80).

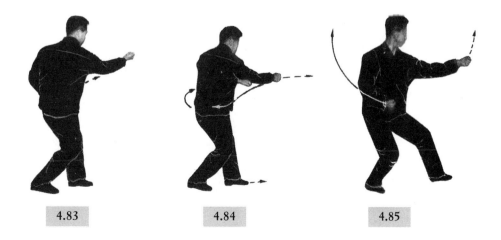

4.83　　　　4.84　　　　4.85

# Jin Tui Lian Huan Quan (进退连环拳; Forward and Backward Linking Fist)

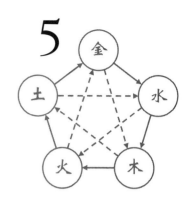

## The Meanings and Functions of Jin Tui Lian Huan Quan in the Form

Xingyiquan is rich in content, practical in use, simple in appearance, and concise in structure. In Wu Xing Quan and Shi Er Xing (Twelve Animal Form), we repeat a single technique over and over again to cultivate internal strength, and we search for the right type of force to apply in real combative situations. Subsequently, in order to develop the ability to apply these techniques and issue power in a dynamic fashion, we must establish routines that train us to execute the individual movements together. In training, routines are complementary to the practice of single techniques. Routines are more like a performing art, with an artistic and aesthetic effect. But if we are only interested in learning routines, instead of practicing the real Gong Fu to search for the right energies, we will lose the essence of the art.

The purpose of repeating a certain technique over and over is to grasp its essence and realize its special energy, thereby increasing the internal force and solidifying the foundation of Gong Fu. Once you are able to find the right energy and apply it to different movements with strong internal power, your combative skills will be enhanced. This is the reason we practice the forms. Each of several traditional Xingyiquan forms has its own distinctive traits and special purpose. Therefore,

145

when we practice a form, we must completely understand its techniques and features; we must find its unique type of energy. Practicing forms can train us to integrate spirit with courage, vital energy with force. It also increases our stamina and ability to understand and apply the techniques. When many people practice the same forms together and observe one another, they increase their understanding of the execution of the techniques, and their skill level is inproved. Many traditional forms were created by the old masters this way. They have been well recognized for ages and passed down to us. Lian Huan Quan (Linking Fist), which uses Wu Xing (Five Elements) as the foundation, is the very first traditional routine in Xingyiquan. In addition, there are *Liu He* (六合; Six Harmonies), *Ba Shi* (八式; Eight Movements), *Shi Er Hong Chui* (十二洪锤; Twelve Big Fists), and *Za Shi Chui* (杂式锤; Miscellaneous Fists). In Wu Xing, there is a two-person fighting form, *Wu Xing Pao* (Five Element Cannon Boxing); likewise, in Shi Er Xing, there is *An Shen Pao* (Secure Body Cannon Boxing). Within Shi Er Xing, some techniques, such as Monkey Fist, Rooster Form, and Swallow Fist, are categorized as forms because of the varieties of their movements. The forms mentioned above are the traditional ones. Nowadays, many people create their own forms for demonstration, competion, and teaching. It is understandable that these people do not know much about this tradition. However, it's important that they tell their students that they created those new forms. It would be a serious moral issue if they pretended that those forms had been passed down from their teachers and misled the younger generation of practitioners.

Jin Tui Lian Huan Quan, which is a widely practiced and highly recognized traditional form, uses Wu Xing Quan as its foundation. It includes forward- and backward-moving footwork. Its structure is good, its rhythm is clear, and its power is tremendous. But the features of movements vary from style to style. Master Shang demanded that his students fulfill requirements described in the Xingyiquan Classics, such as "Whether you are advancing or retreating, you are always attacking. If you don't understand when to advance or retreat, or when to attack, then it is a waste of time even if you have practiced for many years." The footwork has to be agile and the power issued has to be hard and solid. In the first three fists of the form, although the stepping is different, each punch has to be fast, strong, hard, and solid so that it will show the power of "attack while advancing or retreating." This forms a special feature in power issuance.

The two techniques in the form, *Bai He Liang Chi* (白鹤亮翅; White Crane Spreads Out Its Wings) and *Yi Ma San Jian* (一马三践; One Horse with Three Stomps, or 一马三箭; One Horse with Three Arrows) are very good examples of using energy in different ways. When teaching the first technique, Master Shang emphasized that the crane is spreading out its wings instead of pulling in its wings. Therefore, we need to use the power coming from shaking our yao and extending our arms. The energy has to go upward and outward to create the power. In the second technique, there are three steps in a row, all of which have the left foot in front and the right foot following. Each step is long, firm, and continuous, just like a horse galloping. It's why we call the footwork "One Horse with Three Stomps." In addition, with these three steps, we throw two palms and one punch. We use hand techniques and issue power three times, just like shooting three arrows. It's why, if we focus on the hand technique, we call it "One Horse with Three Arrows." When we are taking the three steps, however, we need to cultivate the holistic power and the speed of a galloping horse. This is the special feature of Shang-style Jin Tui Lian Huan Quan that we need to know.

In Jin Tui Lian Huan Quan, we comprehend the techniques and energies of Wu Xing Quan thoroughly by practicing the linked movements. Especially in Beng Quan and Zuan Quan, we need to embody the phrase "the body looks like the bow and the fist punches like an arrow." Furthermore, if we want to show spirits in doing the entire form, we need to emphasize each technique and find the right rhythm first.

The song for the Shang-style Jin Tui Lian Huan Quan:

*Lian huan yi qi xian shen wei,*
*tui da ying jin ba di cui:*
*ao shun bu dai zhong men qu,*
*yi ma san jian si ben lei.*

连环一气显神威,
退打硬进把敌摧:
拗顺不贷中门取,
一马三箭似奔雷.

Link into one unit to express the tremendous power,

attack while retreating or advancing to destroy the enemy;

Whether the footwork is Ao Bu or Shun Bu, you cut into the middoor of the opponent;

One horse with three arrows in one shot, at the speed of the roaring thunder.

# Explanations of the Movements in Jin Tui Lian Huan Quan

## NAMES OF THE MOVEMENTS IN JIN TUI LIAN HUAN QUAN

1) *Yu Bei Shi* (预备式; Preparation Stance)

2) *Shang Bu You Beng Quan* (上步右崩拳; Advance-Stepping Right Smashing Fist)

3) *Tui Bu Zuo Beng Quan* (退步左崩拳; Backward-Stepping Left Smashing Fist) / *Qing Long Chu Shui* (青龍出水; Blue Dragon Exiting from Water)

4) *Shun Bu You Beng Quan* (顺步右崩拳; *Shun Bu* Right Smashing Fist) / *Hei Hu Chu Dong* (黑虎出洞; Black Tiger Exiting from Cave)

5) *Tui Bu Bai He Liang Chi* (退步白鹤亮翅; Backward-Stepping White Crane Opening Its Wings)

6) *Shang Bu Zuo Pao Quan* (上步左炮拳; Advance-Stepping Left Cannon Fist)

7) *Tui Bu Zuo Ying Zhuo* (退步左鹰捉; Backward-Stepping Left Eagle Grasp)

8) *Che BuYan Shou* (撤步掩手; Retreat-Stepping Covering Hands)

9) *Yi Ma San Jian* (一馬三箭; One Horse with Three Arrows) (在脚为一马三践; in footwork, it's called "One Horse with Three Stomps")

    a) *Shang Bu Tuo Xing Cheng Zhang* (上步鮀形撑掌; Advance-Stepping *Tuo Xing* Extending Palm)

    b) *Au Bu You Zuan Quan* (拗步右钻拳; *Au Bu* Right Drilling Fist)

    c) *Jin Bu Li Mao Shang Shu* (进步狸猫上树; Forward-Stepping Leopard Cat Climbs Up the Tree)

10) *Jin Bu You Beng Quan* (进步右崩拳; Forward-Stepping Right Smashing Fist)

11) *Hui Shen Li Mao Dao Shang Shu* (回身狸猫倒上树; Leopard Cat Turns Around to Climb Up the Tree)

12) *Shou Shi* (收势; Closing Stance)

## THE SPECIFIC WAYS OF TRAINING IN JIN TUI LIAN HUAN QUAN

### 1. *Yu Bei Shi* (预备式; Preparation Stance) (Same as On–Spot Left Eagle Grasp)

The movement is the same as movement 1: On-Spot Left Eagle Grasp of Ying Zhuo (Eagle Grasp). Refer to movement 1 of *Ying Zhuo* (page 68) for movement descriptions and principles (picture 5.1).

5.1

### 2. *Shang Bu You Beng Quan* (上步右崩拳; Advance-Stepping Right Smashing Fist) (Same as *Ao Bu* Right Smashing Fist)

Both hands simultaneously form fists; the left fist's Hukou is facing upward; the right fist is facing upward with the forearm staying close to the right abdomen. The upper body twists slightly to the left as the right fist maintains contact with the abdomen and the rib and twists outward and drills upward until it reaches top of the left elbow joint; the Hukou is facing forward (picture 5.2). Without pausing, right leg bends at the knee and deng backward, while left leg bends at the knee and tang forward, then lands; the right foot follows with a forward step to land behind and inside of the left foot; the right knee presses on the back of the left knee joint; the body weight is primarily on the left foot. Simultaneously, the right fist maintains contact with the left forearm as it twists inward and smashes outward; the fist is at heart level, with the Hukou facing upward. Also simultaneously, the left fist twists outward as it pulls back to the left side of the navel, with the fist facing upward. Eyes look to the front of the right fist (picture 5.3).

5.2          5.3

PRINCIPLES

i. Twisting the right fist upward and outward is to gather power to issue; it is important to incorporate drilling, turning, twisting, wrapping, and sinking energies. Movement must be relaxed and natural, without exaggerated force.

ii. Power for the right fist's punch originates in the feet and is issued from the yao, borrowing the momentum from the right foot's backward deng and the left foot's forward tang. But it's essential to apply the "to fight you must utilize upper body" technique by twisting the body slightly to the left, thus applying the principle "shape the body like a bow" to gather power, then the principle "punch like a fast arrow" to issue the power. Furthermore, utilize the yao power in Dragon Folds the Body to throw a long punch and make qi go far and strong.

iii. When the right fist drills forward along the left forearm, there should be a spiraling, explosive energy. This is complemented and supported by the twisting and pulling back of the left fist. Apply the San Cui principle and extend San Xing.

iv. The left foot starts out being in front, then steps forward again; although it advances by only half a step, it's important to cultivate the "leg attack is 70 percent" tang power; furthermore, the leg and the fist must arrive at the same time in order to achieve a holistic coordination and power.

### 3. *Tui Bu Zuo Beng Quan* (退步左崩拳; Backward-Stepping Left Smashing Fist) / *Qing Long Chu Shui* (青龍出水; Blue Dragon Emerging from Water)

The fists and the left foot do not move. Contract the body and step back with the right foot to form a left Bow Stance (picture 5.4). Without pausing, the left foot steps backward along the inside of the right foot to press on the right foot's inside ankle bone, with the toes lifted upward, to form a left lift step. Simultaneously, the left fist twists outward as it drills upward toward the top of the right elbow joint; the Hukou is facing forward (picture 5.5). Without pausing, the left foot continues to retreat by about half a step, landing at about one foot's distance behind the right foot; the toes are pointing forward; the body weight is centered between the two legs; the left knee presses against back of the right knee joint; the legs are tightly together. Right foot does not move, maintaining the same direction as before the retreat (forming about a 45° angle with the left foot). Simultaneously, the left fist twists inward as it smashes forward along the top of the right forearm; the Hukou is facing upward; the fist is at the center chest height. Also simultaneously, the right fist twists outward as it pulls back to the right side of the navel; the fist is facing upward. Eyes look to the front of the left fist (picture 5.6).

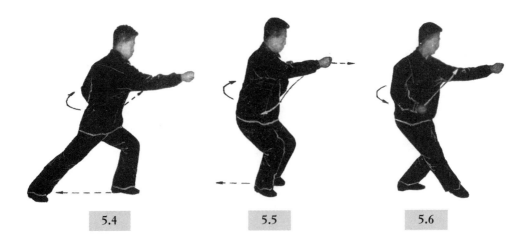

5.4                    5.5                    5.6

PRINCIPLES

i. When the right foot retreats, the stepping must be naturally long as to follow the "advance be long, and retreat must also be long" principle. Borrow the momentum of the right foot retreat in the left foot retreat to form the left lift step. Xingyiquan applies *Mo Jing* (摩经; massage channel) to gather energy in order to increase the advancing power. Applying Mo Jing in retreat also works to gather energy to increase the retreating power. The lift step is a momentary stance that enables the two lower legs to massage each other. Because the form movements are fast, it is easy to ignore the details. The Mo Jing principle is specifically pointed out here so that the lift step is executed in its completeness.

ii. The left fist's drilling up to the right elbow joint and the left foot's pressing against right foot's ankle bone are two mirroring massages of the upper and lower body; both are used to gather energy and wait to issue. Hence, the left fist's forward smash and left foot's retreat must be connected and the *yao* must be loosened, so that the left foot's retreating energy is directed to the left fist's forward smash; thus, even though the foot is retreating, power is directed to the forward attack, fully illustrating the essence and magnificence of the "attack in advance; also attack in retreat" principle. Apply the San Cui principle and extend San Xing.

iii. Because this is an Au Bu forward punch in retreat, the knees must bend and press tightly against each other to ensure firm stepping and a solid stance and to gather holistic energy so that the smash is swift and powerful.

### 4. *Shun Bu You Beng Quan* (顺步右崩拳; *Shun Bu* Right Smashing Fist)/*Hei Hu Chu Dong* (黑虎出洞; Black Tiger Exiting from Cave)

The left fist does not move. The right fist maintains contact with the ribs and abdomen as it twists outward and drills up to the top of the left elbow joint; the Hukou is facing forward (picture 5.7). The right foot then moves to have toes point forward, the knee bends, and the foot tang forward by one step. The left foot follows immediately with deng backward then one step forward, and it lands behind inside of the right foot to form a right Smashing Fist Stance. Simultaneously, the right fist maintains contact with the top of the left forearm as it twists inward and smashes forward; the Hukou is facing upward; the fist is at the heart level. Also simultaneously, the left fist twists outward as it pulls back to the left side of the navel; the fist is facing upward. Eyes look to the front of the right fist (picture 5.8).

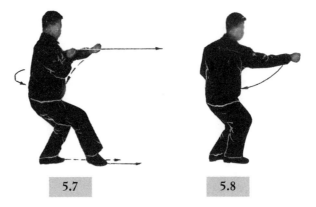

5.7          5.8

PRINCIPLES

i. It is easy to lose the yao power in a Shun Bu Smashing Fist. Hence, after the right fist's forward smash, the upper body and the front leg must maintain the pose that faces partly forward and partly sideways. The left knee must press tightly against back of the right knee joint; the two legs must press tightly against each other.

ii. The right foot's forward tang, left foot's backward deng, and the right fist's forward smash must all be coordinated so that the foot and fist arrive simultaneously. Gather power by twisting yao forward and leftward to facilitate the right fist's smash. Apply the San Cui principle and extend San Xing.

iii. Up to this movement of the linking fist, we have three smashing fists. Each has its own distinct stepping. There is forward stepping, backward stepping, Au Bu, and Shun Bu. These three fists are the representatives of Linking Fist and are also named "forward-backward," as they are the core movements for cultivating the ability to issue power in forward- and backward-stepping. Therefore, it's important to be agile and forward facing, powerful, and solid. Each punch must mimic a mini-cannon, fully displaying the magnificence and technique of "punch like a cannon, body folds like a dragon."

### 5. *Tui Bu Bai He Liang Chi* (退步白鹤亮翅; Backward–Stepping White Crane Opening Its Wings)

The right arm twists inward as it pulls downward, while the left arm twists inward and downward so that the two wrists cross each other in front of the abdomen; right arm is over left arm, with both arms slightly bent and the Hukou facing inward (picture 5.9). Without pausing, both arms rise upward, above the head, then spread to both sides of the body, by utilizing the power from expanding the body and shaking the yao. Simultaneously, the left foot takes one step backward to form a right Bow Stance. The eyes look to the right fist (picture 5.10). Without pausing, after both arms have issued power above the head, both arms fold downward in an egg-shape curve to rest by the two sides of the navel; the forearms must press tight against the abdomen with both fists facing upward. Simultaneously, the right foot steps back to rest by the inside ankle of the left foot. Eyes look forward to the right (picture 5.11).

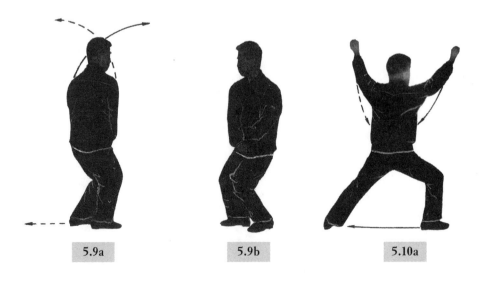

5.9a                5.9b                5.10a

PRINCIPLES

i. There should be sealing and wrapping-in energy when pulling back the two arms to the abdomen. When the arms cross each other, it is to gather power for the upward expansion.

ii. As the two arms are rising upward, focus on the fists and wrists with outward and upward expansion energy. This is what is referred to as issuing power by "opening the wings." When the arms are folding back to the abdomen, they must follow an egg-shape curve—wider at the top, narrower at the bottom—with emphasis on the top, though the arms must not be parted too widely at the top, lest power be dispersed.

iii. Because this is an "opening the wings" movement, not a "closing the wings" movement, when the arms are folding downward to the abdomen, do not stomp the feet or smash the wrist. Rather, it is important to tuck in the arms, sink the *yao,* contract the body so that after issuing power in the upward expansion, the energy in the body does not disperse and is prepared for the next movement.

5.10b                    5.11a                    5.11b

### 6. *Shang Bu Zuo Pao Quan* (上步左炮拳; **Advance-Stepping Left Cannon Fist)**

The right fist twists outward as it drills upward, passing the chest, then forward to the front of the mouth; the Hukou is facing forward. Simultaneously, the left fist also twists outward and drills upward until it reaches the right elbow joint; the Hukou is facing forward (picture 5.12). Without pausing, the right forearm rotates inward as the right hand moves upward so that the back of the right wrist is touching the right temple. Simultaneously, the yao twists to the right, while the left fist twists inward as it punches outward; the fist is at heart level; the Hukou is facing upward. Also simultaneously, right leg bends at the knee and tang directly forward by one big step; the left leg follows immediately by bending at the knee and deng backward, then taking one half-step forward, keeping one foot's distance from the right foot. Body weight rests primarily on the left leg. Eyes look to the front of the left fist (picture 5.13).

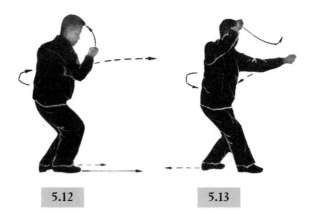

5.12                                    5.13

PRINCIPLES

i. When drilling the right and left fists upward and outward, it is important to observe the rule "elbow does not part from the rib; hand does not part from the chest." Wrap in to gather energy, yet do not use exaggerated force. This is precisely the "Tiger Holding the Head" principle.

ii. When twisting the right forearm inward and pulling it upward, it's important to keep the shoulders sunk and elbow dropped; do not lift the forearm. When the right fist borrows the forearm's twisting energy to pull upward to the right temple, it must not be too high or too low, lest it blocks the vision.

iii. When twisting the yao to the right, it is important to observe the requirement that the upper body "face partly forward and partly to the side"; straighten the lower back region and extend the entire back so that the punch is far-reaching and filled with forward energy.

iv. The right forearm's twist and uplift, the left fist's twist and forward punch, and the right foot's forward tang all utilize the yao-twisting power. Furthermore, all three elements of the movement must be coordinated and must complement one another; the hands and the foot must arrive at the same time so as to achieve a holistic power.

v. After the left foot follows the right foot's advance, the left knee must press tightly against the back of the right knee joint; the two legs must press tightly against each other so as to achieve a firm and well-rooted stance.

### 7. *Tui Bu Zuo Ying Zhuo* (退步左鷹捉; **Backward–Stepping Left Eagle Grasp)**

To continue from the preceding movement: the body turns slightly to the left; the left foot takes one backward step to form a right Bow Stance. Simultaneously, the left fist twists outward as it pulls back to the left of the navel; the fist is facing upward. Also simultaneously, the right fist twists outward as it presses forward and downward, with the fist facing upward; the power must permeate through inside of the right forearm. Eyes look to the front of the right fist (picture 5.14). Without pausing, utilizing the left foot's retreating momentum, the right foot takes one backward step to have the ankle bone of the right foot pressing on top of the ankle bone of the left foot, forming a right lift step. Simultaneously, the left fist twists outward as it drills upward to the inside of the right elbow joint, maintaining contact with the left rib (picture 5.15). Without pausing, the left foot deng backward, and the right foot borrows the deng momentum to take one step backward; the left foot follows immediately by retreating slightly to form a left-foot-in-front Three Body Stance. Simultaneously, the left fist maintains contact with top of the right forearm as it twists inward and drills forward, then changes into an open palm to press downward, forming an Eagle Grasp Stance. Also simultaneously, the right fist pulls back to the right side of the navel, while maintaining contact with the body; the fist is facing upward. (In terms of movement and power issuance, this stance is identical to the Backward-Stepping Eagle Grasp, except that the right hand is a fist, not an open palm.) Eyes look to the front of the left palm (picture 5.16).

PRINCIPLES

i. When retreating with the left foot, make the stepping long and agile; once you form the right Bow Stance, do not pause: the right foot borrows the retreating momentum and follows immediately with another retreating step. In the retreating process, it's important to do Mo Jing (hence the right lift step)—yet do not pause at the lift step, gather energy, borrow left foot's forward deng momentum to step backward. The backward-step landing must be fast and firm; furthermore, it should cause the left foot to retreat slightly, with both feet landing and firmly grabbing the ground almost at the same time. When the right foot lands, it should also press forward at the same time to enhance the power in the left fist's forward press.

ii. After the left fist's upward drilling to the right elbow joint and preparing to strike forward with a backward step, it's important not to bend the yao, raise the shoulders, use exaggerated force, or hold the breath.

iii. The left palm's pressing downward and the landing of both feet must be coordinated; both issue power by right-twisting the yao. Pay attention in order to cultivate the magnificence of the "attack even in retreat" principle.

| 5.14 | 5.15 | 5.16 |

### 8. *Che Bu Yan Shou* (撤步掩 手; **Retreat-Stepping Covering Hands)**

The left foot takes one half-step backward to land in front of the inside ankle bone of the right foot; the toes are pointing forward. Simultaneously, the yao twists rightward as the left hand changes into a Tuo Xing [see Chapter 2] palm (picture 5.17) and, by twisting the forearm outward, pulls backward in a curved path to be hidden in front of the chest. Palm is facing upward; the Hukou is facing forward. Eyes look to the left palm (picture 5.18).

PRINCIPLES

i. When pulling back the left palm, it is important to twist outward as you pull; utilize power from yao to exploit twisting, wrapping-in, and dropping techniques; furthermore, borrow energy from wrist-twisting to deliver power to the back of the palm.

ii. Pulling back of the Tuo Xing palm and the left foot landing must be coordinated and completed in one breath.

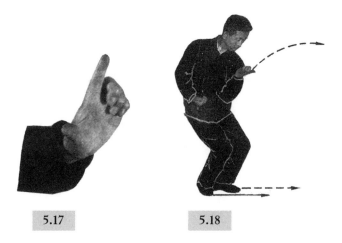

5.17          5.18

## 9. *Yi Ma San Jian* (一馬三箭; **One Horse with Three Arrows**) (在脚为一马三践; **in Footwork, One Horse with Three Stomps**)

1) *Shang Bu Tuo Xing Cheng Zhang* (上步鮀形撑掌; Advance-Stepping *Tuo Xing* [see Chapter 2] Extending Palm): The yao twists slightly to the left; utilize the power from the yao-twist and from backward deng of the right foot. The left foot tang forward by one big step. The right foot follows immediately with another forward step to land behind the left foot. Simultaneously, the left hand's Tuo Xing palm becomes a stand-up palm as it twists and extends forward; the palm is facing forward; the palm's height does not exceed the brows; power must reach the palm. Eyes look to the palm in front (picture 5.19).

**5.19**

PRINCIPLES

   i. The left foot's forward tang must be swift and forceful, while the right foot's forward stepping must be light and agile.

  ii. The left foot's landing and the left palm's forward pushing must be coordinated. Shoulders must be sunk; elbows must be dropped; upper body must face partly forward and partly sideways to allow power to permeate to the forearm.

  2) *Au Bu You Zuan Quan* (拗步右钻拳; Au Bu Right Drilling Fist): Do not pause. The right fist maintains contact with the ribs as it twists outward and drills upward until it reaches the inside of the left elbow joint (picture 5.20). Without pausing, the yao twists further to the left;

utilize the power from the yao-twist and from the right foot's backward deng; the left foot tang forward by another big step, the right foot follows immediately with another forward step to land behind the left foot. Simultaneously, the left hand's Tuo Xing palm remains unchanged while the right fist drills forward, maintaining contact with the left forearm; when the two hands meet, the left palm changes into a fist as it twists outward and pulls back to the left of the navel; the fist is facing upward; the right fist continues to drill directly forward with the fist facing upward at a height not exceeding the brows. Eyes look to the fist in the front (picture 5.21).

5.20                                 5.21

PRINCIPLES

i. When the right fist is drilling toward the left elbow joint, the shoulders must be sunk and the elbows must drop so as to gather energy and wait to issue.

ii. The left foot's forward tang and the right foot's following forward step must be swift and forceful, yet agile; this step must link with the preceding step (上步鮀形撑掌) as one single movement, without any pause between them.

iii. The right fist's drilling forward, the left foot's landing, and the left fist's pulling back to the left navel must all be coordinated to achieve a unified power.

3) *Jin Bu Li Mao Shang Shu* (进步狸猫上树; Forward-Stepping Leopard Cat Climbs Up the Tree): Do not pause. Gather momentum by bending the knees, leaning the upper body forward, and having the right foot deng backward. The left foot tang forward by yet another big step; the right foot follows immediately with another forward step, passing inside of the left foot, and then the knee bends and kicks upward, with toes pointing outward as if to intercept an attack; the height of the kick does not exceed the kua. Simultaneously, the left fist, facing upward and maintaining contact with the rib, twists outward as it drills toward the inside of the right elbow joint, ending with the Hukou facing forward (picture 5.22). Without pausing, the yao twists to the right, the body weight shifts forward, and the right foot kicks forward with inside of the foot and lands with the toes still pointing outward. The left foot follows immediately with half a step forward, toes pointing forward, leaving one foot's distance between the two feet. Left knee presses against inside of right knee joint; the two upper legs press tightly against each other. The body weight rests primarily on the left foot. Simultaneously, the left fist drills outward while maintaining contact with the top of the right forearm. When the two fists meet, both fists change into Three Round Palm [refer to Chapter 3]. The left palm continues to twist and drill forward, then drops downward to chest height with the palm facing downward. The right palm traces the left arm as it twists downward and inward to pull back to the right

side of the navel; the palm is also facing downward; the forearm is in firm contact with the right abdomen. Eyes look to the front of the left palm (picture 5.23).

5.22          5.23

PRINCIPLES

i. From step 1 to step 3 of this movement, the left foot is always in the front; the forward tang must be long and swift, and it must be linked as a single movement, without pause—hence the movement is named "One Horse with Three Stomps" when referring to the footwork. The Xingyiquan Classics say "punch like a galloping horse, attack without pause." The three stomps of the foot, "three arrows" of the hand, two palm strikes, one fist strike, and one kick must be fast, powerful, and continuous, with the energy of a racing horse, completed as one single movement. The fact that this form is named "Linking Fist" refers to exactly its continuous nature. But speed does not mean sloppiness; each step must be fast yet precise; each attack must be swift and powerful.

ii. The left palm's pressing forward, the right palm's pulling back, and the right foot's kicking forward must all rely on the momentum of the left foot's deng and the power from the yao-twist. Left and right are of equal importance; hand and foot must arrive at the same time to ensure coherence between the upper and lower bodies.

iii. For the right leg in the Leopard Cat Climbing Up the Tree step, when going up, the power is intercepted with a kick; when landing, the power is intercepted by stepping on the opponent. These two intercepting attacks are linked, yet with different intent. Bend the left knee to carry the main body weight and to provide the root of the right foot's power; it is important to stand firm and be well rooted. Do not raise the shoulders; let qi sink down to Dantian.

## 10. *Jin Bu You Beng Quan* (进步右崩拳; **Forward-Stepping Right Smashing Fist)**

The left leg bends at the knee and deng backward; the right leg bends at the knee and tang forward by one step; the left foot follows immediately to press against the inside ankle bone of the right foot to form a left lift step. Simultaneously, both palms change to fists by folding the fingers in order, starting with the small finger; left fist's Hukou is pointing upward while right fist is facing upward. Eyes look to the front of the left fist (picture 5.24). Without pausing, the right fist maintains contact with the rib as it twists outward and drills upward to the inside of the left elbow joint (picture 5.25). Without pausing, the right foot deng backward, the yao twists to the left, the left foot tang forward by one big step, the right foot follows immediately with one forward step to land behind the inside of the left foot, forming a (slightly bigger) Smashing Fist Step. Simultaneously, the right fist maintains contact with the top of the left forearm as it twists inward and smashes forward; the Hukou is facing upward and the fist is at heart level. At the same time, the left fist maintains contact with top of the right forearm as it twists outward and pulls back to the left of the navel; the fist is facing upward. Eyes look to the front of the right fist (picture 5.26).

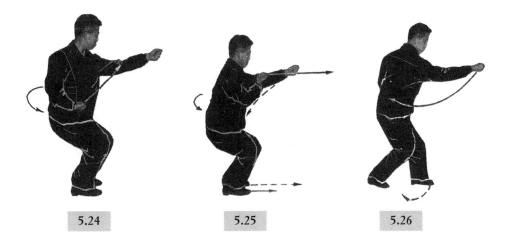

5.24          5.25          5.26

PRINCIPLES

i. Pay attention to align the yao in the forward direction and bend the knee before tang forward with the right foot so to avoid raising the upper body and dispersing the energy.

ii. The right fist's drilling up to the left elbow joint is to gather energy; but pay attention not to raise the shoulders; smash the fist forward with the yao power.

iii. The left foot relies on the "massaging channel" in the lift step to enhance the forward tang power. Landing of the left foot and the smashing forward of the right fist must be coordinated. To facilitate the turning around with a hooked-in step, the right foot's following advance step should be smaller.

## 11. *Hui Shen Li Mao Dao Shang Shu* (回身狸猫倒上树; **Leopard Cat Turns Around to Climb Up the Tree)**

1) Utilize the power from twisting the yao rightward, left foot pivots on the heel; hook the toes inward so that the toes of both feet are pointing at each other at the same angle. Simultaneously, the right fist twists outward as the elbow pulls it back to the right side of the navel; the fist is facing upward; the body weight remains on the right leg. Eyes look to the left-front direction (picture 5.27).

2) Do not pause. Borrow the momentum of the body turning around to the right, shift the body weight to the left foot and bend the left leg slightly; the right leg maintains contact with the inside of the left leg as it bends at the knee to lift upward and forward with the toes pointing upward, then swing them outward as right foot kicks forward; the foot is horizontal and no higher than the kua; the bottom of the foot is facing forward. Simultaneously, the right fist maintains contact with the rib and the center of the chest as it twists and drills outward from under the chin; the Hukou is facing diagonally forward and no higher than the brow. Eyes look to the front of the right fist (picture 5.28).

3) Immediately following, the left leg bends at the knee and deng backward, and the body weight shifts forward. As the upper body twists to the right, the right foot stomps forward diagonally, with the toes pointing outward, and lands with the foot in the same position; the left foot follows immediately with a half-step forward, with the toes pointing forward, leaving about one foot's distance between the two feet. The left knee presses against inside of right knee joint; the body weight is on the left foot. Simultaneously, the left fist maintains contact with the ribs and the center of the chest as it twists outward and drills upward to the inside of the right elbow joint, and then continues to drill forward along the right forearm. As the two fists meet, both fists change to open palms, the left palm twists inward and drops forward, then downward, to center chest height; the palm is facing downward. The right palm maintains contact with the left arm as it twists inward and pulls back to the right side of the navel. Eyes look to the front of the left palm (picture 5.29).

PRINCIPLES

i. Hook in the left foot and pull back the right fist with power from the yao. The fist and foot must be coordinated.

ii. The upward kick in this movement is different from that described in Forward-Stepping Leopard Cat Climbs Up the Tree (step 3 of

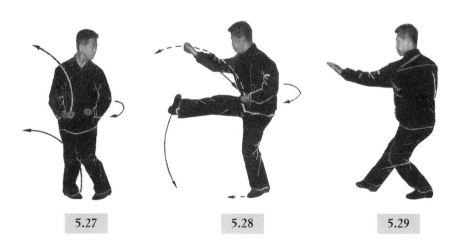

5.27            5.28            5.29

movement 9 above). In step 3 of movement 9, the kick borrows power from the forward stepping to aim the kick at the opponent's knee and kua areas, then follow with downward stomp. Utilize the momentum of the body's turning around, apply the outward-swing knee and foot and the heel-kicking energy to intercept the opponent's attacking foot; follow with an attacking forward landing. Hence, in the right foot's uplift and kick, the knee incorporates both outward swinging and forward pressing energies, while the foot incorporates intercepting kicking and stomping energies. This is the only kicking technique to be repetitively practiced when turning around in Beng Quan. When practicing this form, it is important to fully appreciate its application. The Xingyiquan Classics say, "A punch has many targets and methods; yet a leg kick has limited targets." Xingyi emphasizes the strengths of "advancing and stomping," "hands and feet arriving simultaneously," and "cultivating internal strength to issue power efficiently." It does not propose using the kick to fight. Hence, in Xingyi forms, aside from this intercepting kick, there is only one other forward-intercept kicking technique in the Eight-Form Fist.

iii. The right foot's intercepting kick and its stomp are of two different energies, but in practice, they are combined as one, completed in the same breath. The left palm's pressing forward, the right palm's pulling back, and the right foot's intercepting kick and landing must all be coordinated; utilize power from the waist-twisting.

The above describes the former half of the Forward and Backward Linking Fist and turn around. To continue with the second half, twist the waist slightly to the left, the left foot deng backward, the right foot takes a small half-step forward, the left foot follows forward to form a left lift step; the two palms change to fists, proceed to Forward-Stepping Right Smashing Fist, follow with Backward-Stepping Left Smashing Fist, and so forth, in the order described above. The movements in the first and second halves are the same, only in the opposite direction.

When finished with the second half, turn around with Leopard Cat Turns Around to Climb Up the Tree, then proceed to Advance-Stepping Right Smashing Fist; follow with Backward-Stepping Left Smashing Fist (picture 5.30), then proceed to the Closing Stance.

5.30

## 12. *Shou Shi* (收势; **Closing Stance**)

Following the previous movement, the fists and the right foot do not move—only the left foot moves. It takes one step forward to form a left Chopping Fist Stance, which is the Closing Stance step 1 (picture 5.31). (The remaining steps are omitted; refer to San Ti Shi [page 55].

5.31

# Traditional Xingyi Weapons

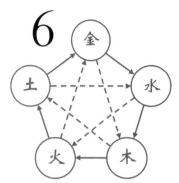

**6**

## Features of Traditional Xingyi Weapons

People say that within *Xingyi Men* (形意门; Xingyi system), initially martial artists fought with only boxing techniques, without weapons. However, Ji Ji-Ke (姬际可), who created the boxing style that was the predecessor of Xingyiquan, was a master in weapons, particularly in big spears, though the spear he used was different from the Xingyi spear created later on.

The sophistication in Xingyiquan theories and training approaches has been obtained through experimentation, realization, and refinement. By the same token, the techniques in Xingyi weaponry have been developed by combining the mastery of various weapons and the understanding of the energy paths in Xingyiquan. This integration has taken place gradually, and the weapon forms have been created in the same manner as well.

The most striking feature and the biggest strength of traditional Xingyi weapons is the integration of *quan* (拳; fist, boxing) and *xie* (械; weapon) techniques. There is a saying in the martial arts world that the "weapon is the extension of the arm." This statement describes the nature of Xingyi weapons very well, as boxing techniques are the foundation of weapon techniques. The latter arises from the existence of the former. The only difference is that each weapon has its own nature and applications, and we need to learn the ways of handling them. Unlike other boxing styles, which have separate forms for quan and weapons, in Xingyi the weapons and quan reinforce each other. Because of this, the training of both becomes easier and more efficient.

Because the foundation of Xingyi weapons lies in quan, the way of practicing them is different from the way other weapons are practiced. It is not appropriate to practice with Xingyi weapons by following the rules of other weapons. Based on the concept "Boxing and weapon are fused into one," the ways to manipulate Xingyi weapons have their own special style. The following will help us see the general picture of this style.

## AS IN QUAN, XINGYI WEAPONS HAVE SPECIAL TYPES OF JING

The way of issuing power and the application of techniques in Xingyi weapons are the same as those in Xingyiquan. However, they are quite different from those in other boxing styles. There are many fundamental exercises to train to exert jing from the body and hands to the weapons in each single technique and to achieve proficiency in the entire form. Besides *Wu Xing Dao* (broadsword), *jian* (sword), *gun* (staff), and *qiang* (spear), there are some other fundamental forms to serve this purpose. The forms of Wu Xing Lian Huan Dao, jian, gun, and qian are the integration of the five elements, which are put into movements for application training. Despite the connected movements in these weapon forms, each single technique in quan is still highly emphasized. For example, in *Pi Dao* (劈刀; chopping broadsword), most styles would keep the arm straight and chop downward. They use the power issuing method of *qi* (起; starting), *sui* (随; following) and *zhui* (追; chasing). But, in Shang-style Xingyi Pi Dao, the way we issue power is just like that in Pi Quan. We use San Cui jing, in which the yao pushes the shoulder, the shoulder pushes the elbow, and the elbow pushes the wrist. We do not keep the arm straight and swing it in a big circle to chop down. Instead, we bend the arm when chopping down with the energies of *pi* (劈; chopping), *tui* (推; pushing), and *cuo* (错; grinding). Not only do we issue power from the yao, but we also emphasize the synchronization of foot and hand movements. This is a very special feature of the *Jing Fa* (劲法; method of using energy/force) used in Shang-style Xingyi weapons.

Another example is *Beng Dao* (崩刀; smashing broadsword). Generally, people issue power by vibrating the arm and shaking the wrist. Xingyi Beng Dao is different. It is the same as in Beng Quan, which uses San Cui jing to issue power from the yao. Furthermore, the hands and the feet must arrive at the same time. In applying the technique, there are *Tui Jing* (推劲; pushing energy/force), *Cuo Jing* (错劲; grinding energy/force), and *Ci Jing* (刺劲; jabbing or stabbing energy/force). Even more, the San Xing have to be extended to the utmost. If you cannot find this type of jing, then you should not call it Beng Dao, because the strength of Beng Dao is missing. Xingyi Jian techniques basically are the same as those in Dao except that Jian uses both sides of the blade to fight; and it misses the *Chan Tou Guo Nao* (缠头裹脑; wrap around the head with the broadsword) technique.

In the long weapons, the techniques for *gun* and *qiang* are quite different. The general method of using a *gun* is described as "*Gun* strikes by momentum" and "*Gun* strikes in huge range." When fighting with a *gun,* we use the momentum from circling the *gun* to attack. The focus of power falls on the tip of the staff. As in quan, Xingyi Gun uses San Cui jing. The yao is the axis, the supporting point, and the source of power. We use it as leverage to issue power. The movements are not showy in appearance. They focus more on taking shortcuts and finding ease in high-speed and quick interchanges between the hard and solid energies. The purpose of using the waist to create shocking power is not to just hurt the enemies at the surface level. We want to severely damage their tendons and bones. For example, in Pi Gun, we do not move the staff around in big circles before chopping down. Instead, we use the yao as the leverage to issue power, having the arms support each other; the hands and the feet arrive simultaneously and apply *tui* (推; pushing), *za* (砸; smashing), and *chuo* (戳; poking, jabbing) energies in all the strikes.

Xingyi Qiang method is different from that most people use for spear. There is a common saying: "Circling spear is the mother technique." Many people who practice with a spear call this basic technique *lan* (拦;

parry), *na* (拿; grasp), and *zha* (扎; stab, jab). Some people propose that the front hand holds the spear still to aim at the target, and that one should "completely rely on the stirring power from the back arm to break the attacking energy." Xingyi Qiang calls the basic set of techniques differently. They are named *beng* (崩; smash), *kou* (扣; hook), and *zha* (扎; stab, jab). They have different meanings from *lan, na,* and *zha.* Xingyi Qiang is just like quan, which emphasizes the energies of *qi* (起; rising), *luo* (落; falling), *zuan* (钻; drilling), and *fan* (翻; turning over). The yao is the source of power. The two hands support and reinforce each other. After knowing all these traits, we can see that the energies in beng and kou are completely different from those found in just parrying and sticking to the enemy's spear. They include both defense and offense techniques. That is why Xingyi Qiang is a lot more powerful. People say that Xingyiquan is derived from the spear. Regardless of the relationship between them, there is no denying that the boxing and weapon techniques in Xingyi are an integrative unit. Though despite their integration, since each weapon has its own nature and applications, we need to train by practicing internal strength and seeking the right energy/force for each.

## Simultaneous Defense and Offense

Xingyi weapons have their own unique traits. Shang-style Xingyi weapons have even more so. Due to its emphasis on using the jing developed in quan, it is easier to take care of both defense and offense at the same time.

Something needs to be made clear first. The "defense" we are talking about here is different from what people normally think. It does not mean simply stopping the enemy's attack. Instead, it means that, while blocking the attacking force, we issue power to counterattack as well. We can even say that the offense is the defense. This strategy directly involves the use of Xingyiquan jing and techniques, which is also a secret passed down by many generations of masters: if we only learn the techniques without knowing how to find the right jing, there is no way we are able to use this strategy.

For example, in Pi Dao, when the enemy finds an opportunity to stab at my head and chest, I bend my arm to hold the dao to meet with the incoming blade. I issue power as soon as my blade touches his or hers. By doing so, the enemy's weapon would be pushed to the side when it encounters the jing from my blade. Furthermore, if I add my arm power to it, my dao would hit the enemy's body immediately. This example shows why we do not have to fend off the attack first before fighting back. This is the shortest and the simplest way to take care of defense and offense simultaneously. The applications of this concept in jian and gun are similar, except that the shape and part of the weapon we use are different, and thus the techniques of handling them are not the same.

Qiang is different from dao, jian, and gun. In the Circling Qiang technique, whether it is *Wai Beng* (外崩; smashing outward) or *Li Kou* (里扣; hooking inward), as soon as the enemy's spear touches mine, I issue power. This effect of "issuing full power upon contact" is exactly the same as what we have in Xingyiquan. As long as we can find the right jing, the enemy's spearhead will be pushed down. Even better, you can knock the weapon out of the enemy's hand. Some older grandmasters—for example, Master Shang—could knock the spears out of the opponents' hands immediately upon contact. This is the combined product of jing and *fa* (法; method, technique). At the surface level, it is called "defense," but this defense can render the opponent powerless against your attack. That is why "defense is also offense." This technique is obviously a lot more powerful and effective than just blocking the opponent's spear without any counterattack.

## WEAPONS IN SYNC WITH STEPPING

In Xingyiquan, we describe the footwork as "moving like an inchworm" [i.e., when the front part of the body moves, the back part of the body follows immediately] and "attack as in walking" [i.e., when a person walks, as soon as the front foot moves forward, the back foot will catch up]. When practicing with weapons, we follow the same rules. The front foot moves forward by utilizing the momentum created by the back foot pressing downward. The stepping and the weapon must move in sync, with their energies following each other; body and weapon are fused into one. The goal is to train the holistic power. "Only when hands and feet arrive at the same time can we call it the authentic technique." This statement also stands true when doing quan. The power of the weapon increases with the synchronization of stepping and body movement. This constitutes one of the features of Xingyi weapons.

When it comes to short weapons, Shang-style Xingyi differs from others in that we could use one or both hands to hold the weapon. For the single broadsword [i.e., using one hand], the rule is that "the proficiency of single broadsword is judged by the coordination of the non-weapon hand." The emphasis is on how the empty hand coordinates with the weapon hand and on how well it assists and complements the weapon hand in defense and offense.

When the footwork does not involve a following step, all of the following Xingyi single broadsword techniques use a single hand to make the movements flexible and fast: vertical or horizontal strike, turning around, intercepting at a short distance, or attacking at a longer distance, *liao* (撩; lift up in a curve), *gua* (挂; stab in a curve, leading with the tip of the broadsword), *yun* (云; circle the broadsword around above the head), *dian* (点; point the tip of the broadsword at the target), *tiao* (挑; use the tip of the broadsword to lift up), *zha* (扎; jab, stab), *mo* (抹; slice), and *dai* (带; carry). They all need to rely on the wrist power and coordination from the empty hand. When we are using the strategy of "defend and attack simultaneously," we have to use both hands so that it is strong enough to break the attacking energy. This also enables us to issue explosive power upon meeting the opponent's weapon. These approaches constitute a very special set of fighting techniques in Shang-style Xingyi weapons. That is why there is a saying that says, "Single hand is flexible and easy to change, so we use it on ordinary occasions; double hands are firm, solid, and powerful, so we use them at critical moments." This method of applying short weapons is also a secret of old masters. There is no question that it is one of the most prominent features of Xingyi.

## Traditional Xingyi Weapons and Forms

Xingyi hand forms and weapons are integrated. Whether it is a single- or double-handed, a long or short weapon, it is always true that hand forms were created earlier than weapon forms. For example, after Lian Huan Quan was established, Lian Huan Dao, Jian, Gun, and Qiang then came into existence. By the same token, Liu He Dao, Jian, Gun, and Qiang were created after Liu He Quan. Some weapons forms use the jargon in Xingyi techniques when there are no corresponding hand forms. Since they do not follow the principle of "hand forms and weapons are integrated," they cannot be considered as traditional routines. No matter how many people are practicing them, we should be able to differentiate one from the other based on their jing, origins, methods, and the features of the movements. For example, there is *Qi Quan* (七拳; Seven Fists) in Xingyiquan. It is also called *Qi Yao* (七曜; Seven Suns) or *Qi Xing* (七星; Seven Stars). However, there is no such hand form as "Qi Xing Quan." Therefore, there will not be any weapon named after "Qi Xing." It would be ridiculous for someone to say that "Qi Xing Jian" form belongs to Xingyi Men. As another example, Xingyi Zhuang Gong San Ti Shi is also call San Cai Shi, but there is never a fist called San Cai Quan. There are many people who practice San Cai Jian, because some people need it, and it has become a convention. Master Shang specialized in Xingyi and passed down many techniques that were rarely known. However, he never talked about practicing and teaching San Cai weapons, because he knew that they were not the traditional Xingyi routines.

Some older masters mentioned that *Za Shi Chui* (杂式锤; Miscellaneous Hammers) was created by linking the twelve animal techniques by a person who had never been officially taken as a disciple. He did it in exchange for learning the essence of Wu Xing Quan from an old master. Although this form has a lot of repetition and the movements are stiff, because people like to have a form that includes the twelve animal techniques, it has been accepted and passed down and is considered a traditional routine. Things like this can happen. However, true Xingyiquan practitioners will never let the fancy-looking superficial material from other styles affect the purity and authenticity of Xingyi techniques. Instead, they will learn from their strengths. In order to promote good tradition and avoid confusion, we should solve the problem of the imbalance between demand and supply. Since there are not many people who know about Xingyi weapons and the art has not been spread wide enough, some people seek teaching materials by borrowing from here and there, which impedes the promotion of this art. Concern about this is what motivated us to write the section on Xingyi weapons.

Traditional Xingyi weapons were created by famous old masters and have been enriched during the process of transmission. In Shan Xi province, the Dai family passed down the mysterious *San Gun* (三棍; Three Staffs), which refers to *Beng Gun* (Smashing Staff), *Pao Gun* (Cannon Staff), and *Fan Bei Gun* (Turning Around Staff). Furthermore, Liou He weapons were widely practiced. These techniques have become richer and richer in content with time. So far, we have never seen any Xingyi weapon created by the He Nan branch. We can infer that those weapons were all developed by Li Luo-Neng and his talented students in He Bei. Those teachers who taught in Shan Xi, such as Song Shi-Rong and Che Yi-Zhai, and those who taught in He Bei, such as Guo Yun-Shen and Liu Qi-Lan, together with Li Cun-Yi, who integrated the He Bei and Shan Xi branches, have enriched and added innovations to the weapon art. Master Shang inherited Master Li's skills and Master Guo Yun-Shen's spectacular techniques—such as "Half-a-Step Beng Quan," "Strike with Dantian Qi," and "Big Pole"—and became a great master of his generation. He devoted his entire life to mastering the art of Xingyiquan. When it came to practicing martial arts, Master Shang always said that nothing could be as fulfilling as practicing Xingyiquan. It is so deep in content and resourceful in techniques. Due to his devotion and mastery, the techniques he passed down have very unique features.

Within the most commonly seen weapons, like broadsword, sword, staff, and spear, there are individual pi, zuan, beng, pao, and heng fundamental exercises; hand forms such as Wu Xing, Lian Huan, Liu He, and *Shi Er Xing* (Twelve Animal Forms); and weapon forms such as *Ba Shi* (Eight Techniques) and *Shi Er Hong Chui* (Twelve Big Hammers). Furthermore, there are Unicorn Horn Dao and Phoenix Wing Tang. In addition, Master Shang passed down the weapons themselves, such as Double Broadsword, Double Canes, Double Hammers, Iron Chopsticks, and Long Staff. All these weapon forms not only reflect the principle "hand form and weapon integrated," but they also have their own styles and unique skill sets. This reflects the old masters' serious attitude in seeking the essence and probing into the subtleties of the art. They have left us with the invaluable information to help us broaden our minds, upgrade our skill levels, and enhance our abilities to differentiate gold from sand.

# Xingyi Lian Huan Dao (形意连环刀; Xingyi Linking Broadsword)

## NAMES OF THE MOVEMENTS IN XINGYI LIAN HUAN DAO

1) *Yu Bei Shi* (预备式; Preparation Stance)

2) *Ge Dao Tui Zhang* (格刀推掌; Parry *Dao* Push Palm)

3) *San Ti Shi Cang Dao* (三体式藏刀; *San Ti Shi* Hidden *Dao*)

4) *Jin Bu Beng Dao* (进步崩刀; Forward-Stepping Smashing *Dao*)

5) *Tui Bu Fan Beng Dao* (退步反崩刀; Backward-Stepping Reverse-Smashing *Dao*)

6) *Xie Jin Bu Pi Dao* (斜进步劈刀; Diagonal Forward-Stepping Chopping *Dao*)

7) *Fan Shen San Ti Shi Cang Dao* (反身三体式藏刀; Turn-Around *San Ti Shi* Hidden *Dao*)

8) *Jin Bu Ci Dao* (进步刺刀; Forward-Stepping Stabbing *Dao*)

9) *Fan Shen Ti Xi Pi Dao* (翻身提膝劈刀; Twist-and-Turn Lift-Knee Chopping *Dao*)

10) *Jin Bu Pao Dao* (进步炮刀; Forward-Stepping Cannon *Dao*)

11) *Tui Bu Ti Xi Guo Nao Dao* (退步提膝裹脑刀; Backward-Stepping Knee-Lifting Wrapping-Overhead *Dao*)

12) *Jin Bu Zuan Dao* (进步钻刀; Forward-Stepping Drilling *Dao*)

13) *Deng Jiao Zhan Pi Dao* (蹬脚斩劈刀; Heel-Kicking Sweeping *Dao*)/ *Li Mao Shang Shu Dao* (狸猫上树刀; Leopard Cat Climbing Up the Tree *Dao*)

    a) *Deng Jiao Heng Zhan Dao* (蹬脚横斩刀; Heel-Kicking Cross-Slicing *Dao*)

    b) *Luo Bu Xie Pi Dao* (落步斜劈刀; Landing Diagonal Chopping *Dao*)

14) *Jin Bu Beng Dao* (进步崩刀; Forward-Stepping Smashing *Dao*)

15) *Che Bu Ning Shen Fan Pi Dao* (撤步拧身反劈刀; Retreat-Stepping Twist-Body Reverse-Chopping *Dao*)

16) *Zhuan Sheng Shang Bu Pi Dao* (转身上步劈刀; Turn-Around Advance-Stepping Chopping *Dao*)

17) *Tui Bu Shi Dao* (退步拖刀; Backward-Stepping Dragging *Dao*)

18) *Zhuan Sheng Jie Kang* (转身截砍; Turn-Around Intercept and Chop)

19) *Dao Bu Heng Pai Zhang* (倒步横拍掌; Exchange-Stepping Cross-Slapping Palm)

20) *Jin Bu Ci Dao* (进步刺刀; Forward-Stepping Stabbing *Dao*)

21) *Hui Shen Deng Jiao Zhang Pi Dao* (回身蹬脚斩劈刀; Turn-Around with Heel-Kick Sweeping *Dao*)/*Hui Shen Li Mao Dao Shang Shu Dao* (回身狸猫倒上树刀; Leopard Cat Turns Around to Climb Up the Tree *Dao*)

22) *Jin Bu Beng Dao* (进步崩刀; Forward-Stepping Smashing *Dao*)

23) *Bai Ko Bu Zuan Shen Sao Dao* (摆扣步转身扫刀; *Bai-, Kou-Bu* Turn-Around Sweeping *Dao*)

24) *Shou Shi* (收势; Closing Stance)

# Explanations for the Movements in Xingyi Lian Huan Dao (形意连环刀; Xingyi Linking Dao)

## 1. *Yu Bei Shi* (预备式; **Preparation Stance**)

Stand up straight with feet together; shoulders and elbows are dropped; head is erect; tip of the tongue touches the upper palate; qi is sunk to Dantian; eyes look forward. The left hand holds the dao by having thumb and Hukou wrapped around the dao guard, the index finger and middle finger grab the dao handle, the ring finger and small finger support the dao from underneath the guard so that the dao bei is pressed against the left forearm, the tip of dao is pointing upward, and the dao blade is facing the front and leaning against left side of the body. The right palm drops down naturally with fingers closed, resting by the right kua (picture 6.1).

6.1

## 2. *Ge Dao Tui Zhang* (格刀推掌; **Parry *Dao* Push Palm**)

1) Bend both legs slightly and shift the body weight forward as body turns slightly to the right. The right foot takes one big step forward, with toes turning diagonally to the left to form a Kou Bu. Simultaneously, the left hand, holding the dao, turns leftward, forward, then inward to draw a half curve at left-front of the body, then drops to the front of the chest by bending the arm. The dao guard is grabbed under the wrist at center chest height. Also simultaneously, the right palm lifts upward to press by the right side of the yao; the palm is facing upward. Eyes look to the left (picture 6.2).

PRINCIPLE

The left arm's outward swing, while grabbing the dao guard, and the right foot's forward stepping must borrow the yao power. The hand and foot movement must be coordinated and completed in the same breath.

6.2

2) Do not pause. Shift the body weight to the right foot. The body twists to the left. The left foot steps past, inside of the right foot, then takes one big step forward. Simultaneously, the left hand hooks the dao downward and brushes it toward the left, and—with the body twisting and left foot stepping—rests the dao by the left kua. The dao tip is pointing upward; the dao blade is facing forward. Also simultaneously, the right hand changes into a standup palm and pushes forward; the palm is facing leftward. Shoulders must be sunk; elbow must drop. Right forearm is at center chest level. Eyes look to the hand in front (picture 6.3).

PRINCIPLES

    i. Throughout the movement, let the yao lead the hands. Brushing the dao, pushing the hand forward, and left foot's forward stepping must all be coordinated; the power must be holistic.

    ii. In brushing the dao, the power is centered at the handle and the guard. In pushing the palm forward, the power is centered at the outside of the small finger.

6.3

### 3. *San Ti Shi Cang Dao* (三体式藏刀; *San Ti Shi* **Hidden** *Dao*)

1) The yao turns slightly to the right so body faces forward. Simultaneously, the left hand lifts the dao forward and upward to the height of the right arm. The right hand takes hold of the dao (picture 6.4). The left wrist turns inward and changes into a standup palm at inside of the right wrist. Simultaneously, the body weight shifts forward as the left foot takes one big step forward to form a left Bow Stance. Eyes look to the front of the dao handle (picture 6.5).

2) Do not pause. The body weight shifts to the left foot. The right leg bends at the knee and presses the kneecap against back of left knee. Simultaneously, the left hand *lv* [see glossary] the dao and becomes a standup palm to push forward, while the right hand pulls the dao downward and backward behind the right kua. The tip of the dao is pointing forward. Eyes look to the left front (picture 6.6).

3) Do not pause. The body weight shifts backward. The right foot takes one step backward. The left foot follows immediately by lifting upward with the bent knee to form a single-foot stand. Simultaneously, the left palm turns downward and inward as it comes back to pierce upward and press on center chest. The right hand turns the wrist outward and backward and lifta the dao upward so that the dao bei is pressed against back of the head; the tip of the dao is pointing downward. Eyes look forward (picture 6.7).

4) Do not pause. The left foot lands forward to form a Zhuang Bu. The right hand wraps the dao around the left shoulder to the front of the chest, then pulls it downward and backward behind the right side of the body. Simultaneously, the left hand *lv* the dao bei along the inside of the right arm with the back of the palm, which then changes to a standup palm and pushes forward, thus forming the San Ti Shi Hidden Dao Stance. Eyes look forward (picture 6.8).

PRINCIPLES

i. This is the opening stance of Xingyi dao application. All steps of the movement must be executed as one continuous sequence, without pausing between steps. Wrapping the dao around the head must be natural and coordinated. Do not raise the shoulders or lower the head.

ii. The body weight shifts, knee lift, foot landing, and hand movements must all be coordinated, complete, and synchronous.

6.4

6.5

6.6

6.7a

6.7b

6.8

### 4. *Jin Bu Beng Dao* (进步崩刀; **Forward-Stepping Smashing** *Dao*)

1) Shift the body weight forward as the left foot takes a half-step forward to form a left Bow Stance (a transitional stepping). Simultaneously, the right hand stabs the dao forward, with the blade facing downward and the tip of the dao at shoulder height. The left hand holds onto the back end of the dao handle. Eyes look forward (picture 6.9).

2) Do not pause. The body weight shifts forward as the right foot brushes the inside of the left foot before taking one big step forward. The left foot follows immediately to press against the inside of the right foot to form a left lift step. Simultaneously, the two hands turn their wrists to pull the dao upright by having the right hand pulling the handle upward while the left hand pushes the handle forward. The dao bei rests by front of the right shoulder; both elbows hug the ribs; both hands press against right side of the abdomen. Eyes look forward (picture 6.10).

3) Do not pause. Left foot tang forward and lands. Right foot follows immediately with a quick step to land behind the inside of the left foot to form a Smashing Fist Stance. Simultaneously, the two hands push, grind, and smash the dao forward by having the left hand pulling the handle while the right hand is pushing the handle. The blade of the dao is facing downward; the dao lies horizontally at center chest height. Eyes look to the front of the dao (picture 6.11).

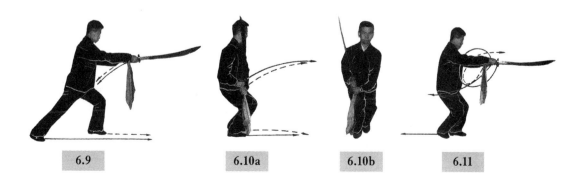

| 6.9 | 6.10a | 6.10b | 6.11 |

PRINCIPLES

i. In picture 6.9, stabbing the dao forward is merely a transitional movement. Pull back the dao and immediately tang forward; foot and hands must be coordinated. When smashing the dao forward, borrow power from the upper body and the backward deng momentum to enhance the speed and forcefulness of the smash.

ii. Incorporate pushing, grinding, and stabbing energy in the smashing dao.

## 5. *Tui Bu Fan Beng Dao* (退步反崩刀; **Backward-Stepping Reverse-Smashing** *Dao*)

1) Shift the body weight backward as right foot takes one big step backward to form a left Bow Stance (a transitional step). Simultaneously, the left hand pulls downward then backward, then twists the wrist so the back of the hand presses against the chest of the center. At the same time, the right hand gua the dao downward, backward, upward, then forward on the right side of the body. When the dao passes in front of the chest, the left hand *lv* the dao bei along the right arm and changes into a standup palm to push forward. Simultaneously, the right hand pulls the dao downward and backward to the right kua. Eyes look to the front of the left hand (picture 6.12).

2) Continue to shift the body weight backward to the right leg as left foot steps backward and lifts to rest by the inside of the right ankle to form a left lift step. Simultaneously, the right wrist turns outward so that the dao rotates backward, upward, then up to above the right shoulder; the dao blade is facing upward; the tip of the dao is pointing forward. The left palm sinks downward slightly. Eyes look forward (picture 6.13).

3) Continue to shift the body weight backward as the left foot lands quickly backward in a straight line to form a Backward-Stepping Smashing Fist Stance. Simultaneously, the right hand pushes, drills, and reverse-stabs [the dao blade is facing upward] the dao forward; the dao blade is facing upward at head level. The left palm pulls downward and backward to the inside of the right forearm. Eyes look to the front of the dao (picture 6.14).

PRINCIPLES

  i. The retreating steps must be long. Maneuvering the dao by twisting and throwing the wrist must be free and flexible. The lift step must be agile, yet firm.

  ii. The quick landing of the left foot, reverse stabbing of the right hand, and pulling back of the left palm must all be coordinated. Power must be holistic.

  iii. In the reverse stabbing, utilize left foot's landing and deng momentum, and the yao power, so that energy permeates to the dao.

6.12                                   6.13                                   6.14

### 6. *Xie Jin Bu Pi Dao* (斜进步劈刀; **Diagonal Forward-Stepping Chopping** *Dao*)

The left foot steps past the inside of the right foot to take a diagonal step forward to the right. The right hand gua the dao downward, backward, then upward and forward, passing the left side of the body, to the front of the left shoulder. Simultaneously, the left wrist turns inward so that the palm pierces downward to the front of the left abdomen. Eyes look to the diagonal front (picture 6.15).

The right foot tang quickly forward by one big step to the right diagonal front. The left foot follows immediately with a half-step forward to form a Chopping Fist Stance. The right hand chops the dao forward and downward; the dao blade is level at center chest height. Simultaneously, the left arm swings backward and upward to have the palm facing upward over left side of the head; the fingers point in the direction of the dao. Eyes look to the front of the dao (picture 6.16).

PRINCIPLES

i. *Gai Bu* (盖步) refers to the left foot stepping past the inside of the right foot in the right diagonal direction to the front of the right foot. The Gai Bu, the right hand's gua dao, and the left palm's downward pierce must all be coordinated.

ii. The right foot's forward tang and the dao's forward chop must also be synchronized as one movement; be swift and complete.

6.15                    6.16

## 7. *Fan Shen San Ti Shi Cang Dao* (反身三体式藏刀; **Turn-Around** *San Ti Shi* **Hidden** *Dao*)

1) The toes of the right foot hook inward. The body weight shifts to the right foot as the body turns around to the left; the left foot lifts upward to form a single-foot stand pose. Simultaneously, the right wrist turns outward to wrap the dao backward and upward around the head so the dao bei is against the back; the tip of the dao points downward. With the turning around, left hand drops downward, then continue to turn the wrist inward so the palm is in contact with the body as it pierces up to the center chest; palm is facing outward. Eyes look forward (picture 6.17).

2) Do not pause. The left foot lands forward to form a San Ti Shi. The right hand wraps the dao around the left shoulder, passing the center of the chest, to pull it downward and to the right to rest by the right kua. As the dao is passing the center of the chest, the left palm *lv* the dao bei along inside of the right arm, then becomes a standup palm to push forward; the palm is facing to the right at center chest height. Eyes look forward (picture 6.18).

PRINCIPLES

   i. This is the turn-around-lift-knee-and-wrap-around-the-head movement. It must be expansive, natural, swift, and agile. Do not raise the shoulders or lower the head.

   ii. The foot landing, the pulling of the dao, and the pushing of the palm must all be complete and with power.

| 6.17 | 6.18 |

### 8. *Jin Bu Ci Dao* (进步刺刀; **Forward-Stepping Stabbing** *Dao*)

1) The left foot lifts upward. The right wrist turns outward to wrap the dao backward, then upward, around the head and the left shoulder, and to the front of the chest. Simultaneously, the left wrist turns downward and inward so the left hand brushes the inside of the right arm, then along the dao bei, and becomes a standup palm to push forward; the palm is facing to the right at center chest height. Simultaneously, the right hand pulls the dao from the front of the chest downward and to the right, to the right kua. The left foot tang forward by one big step. The right foot follows immediately forward to form a right lift step. Eyes look forward (picture 6.19).

2) Do not pause. The right foot tang forward by one step to form a Zhuang Bu. Simultaneously, the right hand stabs the dao forward with force; the dao is at shoulder height; the dao bei is facing diagonally to the right. As the dao is stabbing forward, the left palm presses backward to rest on the inside of the right forearm. Eyes look to the front of the *dao* (picture 6.20).

PRINCIPLES

   i. Lifting the foot, pulling the dao backward, and pushing the palm forward must all be coordinated.

   ii. Stabbing the dao forward, the left palm's pressing backward and the right foot's landing must be synchronous, swift, and forceful, with power permeating to the tip of the dao.

|  |  |
|:---:|:---:|
| 6.19 | 6.20 |

## 9. *Fan Shen Ti Xi Pi Dao* (翻身提膝劈刀; **Twist-and-Turn Lift-Knee Chopping *Dao*)**

The right foot toes hook inward. The body weight shifts to the right leg, and the body turns around to the left. The left foot lifts upward swiftly to form a single-foot stand. Simultaneously, the right hand turns the wrist outward as it lifts the dao upward from behind, with the tip pointing downward, then chops the dao forward and downward over the right shoulder; the front part of the dao is level with the kua. Simultaneously, the left palm maintains contact with the body as it swings, from below, to the left and upward to over the head on the left. Eyes look to the tip of the dao (picture 6.21).

PRINCIPLES

i. The movements of chopping the dao forward and swinging the palm upward are in opposite directions. The two arms support each other. The movement must be fast, firm, and powerful.

ii. Utilize the momentum of the knee-lift, yao-twist, and the left palm's upward swing to enhance the power in chopping the dao and to aid the firmness of the single-foot stand.

6.21

**10.** *Jin Bu Pao Dao* (进步炮刀; **Forward–Stepping Cannon Dao**)

1) The left foot lands in the front. The right hand turns the wrist outward to lift the dao upward, in a curve, to the left front of the head. Simultaneously, the left palm drops downward to the inside of the right wrist. Eyes look to the front of the dao (picture 6.22).

2) Do not pause. The right foot tang forward by one big step, past the left foot. The left foot follows immediately with a half-step forward to form a Cannon Fist Stance. Simultaneously, the right hand swings the *dao* downward then forward. The left hand moves in coordination with the right hand to rest on the inside of the right forearm. The dao blade is facing upward with the tip slightly lower. Eyes look to the front of the dao (picture 6.23).

PRINCIPLES

   i. Swinging the dao upward and the following forward-stepping cannon dao must be continuous and forceful. The right foot's landing and the dao's upward swing must utilize the yao power and be synchronous.

   ii. The dao blade and the right leg are aligned. Power must permeate to the front half of the dao. Incorporate pushing, grinding, and upswing energies.

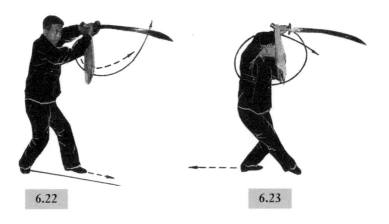

6.22                                        6.23

## 11. *Tui Bu Ti Xi Guo Nao Dao* (退步提膝裹脑刀;
## Backward-Stepping Knee-Lifting Wrapping-Overhead *Dao*)

1) The left foot takes one big step backward to form a right Bow Stance (a transitional stepping). With the forearm and wrist power, the right hand gua the dao downward, then leftward, one circle on the left side of the body. The left hand does not move. Eyes look to the front of the dao (picture 6.24).

2) Do not pause. The right foot takes one step backward to form a left Bow Stance (a transitional stepping). Simultaneously, with the forearm and wrist power, the right hand gua the dao downward, backward, then forward to draw another circle on the right side of the body, then pull the dao to the right side of the kua. As the right hand is pulling the dao backward, the left palm maintains contact with the right forearm to lv along to the dao and then become a standup palm and push forward. Eyes look forward (picture 6.25).

3) Do not pause. The body weight shifts to the right foot. The left knee lifts upward to form a single-foot stand. Simultaneously, the right hand turns the wrist outward to wrap around the head from behind, then leftward, then forward, then rightward, so the dao wraps around the body once, before pulling the dao to over the right side of the head. The dao is pointing forward; the blade is facing upward. Simultaneously, the left wrist turns downward and inward as it maintains contact with the body to pierce to the inside of the right forearm. Eyes look forward (picture 6.26).

| 6.24 | 6.25 | 6.26 |

PRINCIPLES

i. The three steps of the movement must be continuous, swift, and be completed in one breath.

ii. The two circles drawn with the dao on both sides of the body are vertical circles. When wrapping the dao around the head, extend the arm and keep the dao upright as it goes around the back. Do not raise the shoulders or lower the head.

## 12. *Jin Bu Zuan Dao* (进步钻刀; **Forward-Stepping Drilling** *Dao*)

Continue from the preceding movement. The upper body twists to the left so that the right arm turns downward, rightward, then inward, passing in front of the yao, to drill the dao forward and upward. The dao is at eye level, with the blade facing upward; the tip of the dao is slightly lower. Power is focused on the front part of the blade. Simultaneously, the left palm turns downward, forward, then upward to over the left side of the head; the palm is facing upward, with the fingers pointing forward. As the right hand is drilling the dao forward, the body weight shifts forward as left foot tang forward by one big step. The right foot follows immediately with a half-step to form a Cannon Fist Stance. The dao and the foot must arrive synchronously. Eyes look to the front of the dao (picture 6.27).

PRINCIPLES

i. Movements 11 and 12 are linked movements. The body and the weapon must move in continuum. Utilize yao power to maneuver the dao.

ii. When drilling the dao forward, twist the body as much to the left as possible, so that the left leg is aligned with the dao. The tip of the dao, the left toes, and the tip of the nose must also be aligned.

6.27

## 13. *Deng Jiao Zhan Pi Dao* (蹬脚斩劈刀; **Heel-Kicking Sweeping** *Dao*) / *Li Mao Shang Shu Dao* (狸猫上树刀; **Leopard Cat Climbing Up the Tree Dao**)

Part 1) *Deng Jiao Heng Zhan Dao* (蹬脚横斩刀; Heel-Kicking Cross-Slicing *Dao*): The body weight shifts forward as the left foot takes one small step forward; immediately afterward, the right foot kicks with the heel forcefully upward, with the knee bent and the toes pointing outward. Simultaneously, the right hand wraps the dao around the head and around the back on the right, before sweeping it horizontally in front of the chest toward right side of the body. The dao blade is facing rightward, the tip is pointing forward at shoulder height. Simultaneously, the left palm turns downward and inward as it maintains contact with the body to pierce upward to the front of the chest. As the right hand is sweeping the dao rightward, the left palm swings to the left at shoulder height; the fingers are pointing forward. Eyes look forward (picture 6.28).

6.28

PRINCIPLES

i. The right foot's heel-kick must utilize the left foot's forward-stepping momentum.

ii. The right foot's heel-kick, the dao's horizontal sweep, and the left palm's outward swing must be synchronous, holistic, and balanced on both sides.

Part 2) *Luo Bu Xie Pi Dao* (落步斜劈刀; Landing Diagonal Chopping Dao): Do not pause. The right foot lands forward with toes pointing outward. The left foot follows immediately with a half-step to form a Backward-Stepping Smashing Fist Stance. Simultaneously, the right hand turns the wrist outward to wrap the dao around the head, from the right to top of the head. The left palm also turns around to the left to press on the right wrist. As the yao twists to the right, both hands combine forces to chop the dao forward from over the left shoulder; the tip of the dao is at shoulder height. Eyes look to the front of the dao (picture 6.29).

PRINCIPLES

i. Part 2 of the movement continues seamlessly after Part 1. There must not be a pause between the two parts.

ii. The right foot's landing and the forward chopping must utilize power from the yao's right twist. The dao and the foot must arrive at the same time. The movement must be swift and firm.

**6.29**

### 14. *Jin Bu Beng Dao* (进步崩刀; **Forward-Stepping Smashing** *Dao*)

1) Continue from the preceding movement. The tip of the dao probes forward with left hand holding end of the handle. The right foot tang forward by one big step. The left foot follows immediately to press on the inside of the right leg to form a left lift step. Simultaneously, the left hand pushes forward on the handle while the right hand pulls backward; together, they pull the dao to an upright position in front of the right shoulder. Both hands are in contact with the body; both arms are in contact with the ribs. Eyes look forward (picture 6.30).

2) Do not pause. The left foot tang forward by one big step. The right foot follows with a forward step to form a Smashing Fist Stance. Simultaneously, the right hand pushes on the handle while the left hand pulls to smash the dao forward. Eyes look forward (picture 6.31).

PRINCIPLES

i. The two hands' pulling the dao upright and the left foot's landing must be synchronous and holistic.

ii. In smashing the dao forward, utilize momentum from back foot's deng and front foot's forward tang to issue yao power.

iii. Movements 12, 13, and 14 are continuous movements; they are like the "one horse, three arrows" of Linking Fist. They must reflect the power of pushing mountains and turning the ocean so as to highlight the swift and mighty characteristics of Xingyi dao.

6.30                    6.31

### 15. *Che Bu Ning Shen Fan Pi Dao* (撤步拧身反劈刀; Retreat-Stepping Twist-Body Reverse-Chopping *Dao*)

1) The body turns to the left as the left foot takes one backward step toward the left to form a left Bow Stance. Simultaneously, the left hand changes into an upward-facing palm, then drops and maintains contact with the body to swing diagonally outward to over the left shoulder; the right hand turns the wrist inward as it drops lower so the dao bei is facing downward. Eyes look to the right (picture 6.32).

2) Do not pause. The right foot steps past the inside of the left foot to take one forward step toward the left. The right hand gua the dao downward, leftward, then upward to draw one circle in front of the body before chopping the dao backward; the dao is at center chest height. At the same time, the left elbow bends to maintain contact with the body as the left wrist twists inward to pierce the palm downward along the inside of the right arm before swinging upward over left side of the head; the palm is facing upward. Eyes follow the chopping dao (picture 6.33).

PRINCIPLE

In this reverse chop with backward-stepping movement, utilize the momentum from elbow-bending and yao-twisting, and gua the dao in a circle before the chop to achieve a holistic foot-weapon synchronization.

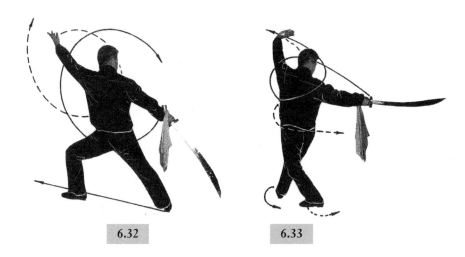

6.32                                    6.33

## 16. *Zhuan Sheng Shang Bu Pi Dao* (转身上步劈刀;
## Turn–Around Advance-Stepping Chopping *Dao*)

1) Do not pause. The toes of the right foot hook inward and the toes of the left foot hook outward to turn around [180°], turning to the left. As the body is turning around, the right hand sweeps the dao horizontally across toward the left; as the dao passes front of the body, the right wrist turns to wrap the dao over the head and left shoulder to the back of the right shoulder; the dao is pointing downward. Simultaneously, the left elbow bends to maintain contact with the body as the left palm pierces along inside of the right arm to swing outward to the left. Eyes look forward (picture 6.34).

2) Do not pause. The right foot tang forward by one big step. The left foot follows with a half-step forward to form a Zhuang Bu. Simultaneously, borrowing the momentum from twisting the yao to the left, the right hand chops the dao diagonally forward from behind the right shoulder; the tip of dao is at shoulder height. As the dao is chopping forward, the left palm holds on to the lower handle to aid the chop. Eyes look forward (picture 6.35).

PRINCIPLE

Following the preceding movement, utilize the momentum from the body's turning around to continue with the forward-stepping chop. The yao must be agile; the arms must swing; the movements must be swift. The chopping dao must be swift and forceful.

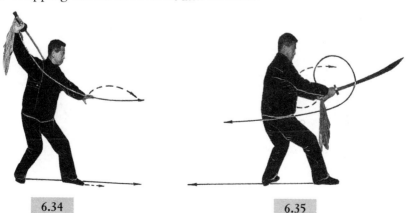

6.34                              6.35

## 17. *Tui Bu Shi Dao* (退步拖刀; **Backward-Stepping Dragging *Dao*)**

1) The left foot takes one step backward to form a left Bow Stance. Using forearm and wrist power, the right hand gua the dao in a clockwise circle to pull it back to the right side of the kua; the dao is pointing forward. Simultaneously, the left hand drops in front of the body, then maintains contact with the body as it turns the wrist and pierces upward to the chest, then *lv* along inside of the right forearm to the dao, then changes into a standup palm to push forward. Eyes look forward (picture 6.36).

2) Do not pause. The right toes swing outward; the body turns to the right; the left foot steps close to and past the inside of the right foot, and takes one forward step to the right to form a left Bow Stance. Because this movement is a retreat and includes looking backward and dragging the dao, it is an escape move that has a strategy to turn a defeat into victory; hence this turn-around Bow Stance should technically be named a "bai bu" (败步; defeat stance). The left palm changes into a hooked hand in the same position, with hooked fingers pointing upward. Simultaneously, the right hand gua the dao downward, then backward on the right, before turning the wrist to lift the dao upward so the dao bei is over the top of the left arm; dao blade lies diagonally upward. Twist the head to look backward (picture 6.37).

PRINCIPLE

The hand and feet movements must be coordinated and agile. The feet must move naturally with the body.

6.36

6.37

## 18. *Zhuan Sheng Jie Kang* (转身截砍; **Turn–Around Intercept and Chop)**

1) Do not pause. The toes of the left foot hook inward, while the right toes hook outward, to turn body around [180°], turning to the right, and shift body weight to the left leg to form a semi-horse-stand. With the body's turning, the right wrist twists outward and uses the dao bei to intercept in the diagonal upward direction behind the back. Simultaneously, the left hand changes into a palm and drops to press on top of the left knee; Hukou is facing inward. The dao bei is facing rightward. Eyes look to the dao blade (picture 6.38).

2) Do not pause. The right hand wraps the dao over top of the head, from right to left, one half circle before chopping it downward and diagonally forward; the dao bei is facing rightward; the tip of the dao is at knee height and pointing in the direction of the right foot. Eyes look to the tip of the dao (picture 6.39).

PRINCIPLE

Movements 17 and 18 are linked; there must not be any pause between them. The turning around to intercept and the chopping downward must utilize yao power; the movement must be swift and forceful.

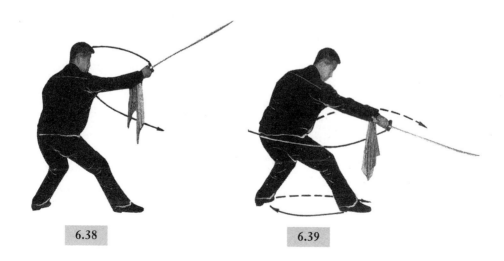

6.38

6.39

### 19. *Dao Bu Heng Pai Zhang* (倒步横拍掌; Exchange-Stepping Cross-Slapping Palm)

The left foot steps up to the inside of the right foot; the right foot immediately steps back to the left foot's original position to form a Zhuang Bu. With the right foot's backward stepping, the right hand simultaneously pulls the dao back behind the body on the right. Also simultaneously, the left palm slaps horizontally across from left to right; the palm is at center chest height. Eyes look to the front of the palm (picture 6.40).

PRINCIPLE

The exchange stepping must be swift and synchronous with the left slap; it must also utilize the yao power. The forward movements of the left hand and the left foot must be coordinated with right hand's backward pull.

**6.40**

## 20. *Jin Bu Ci Dao* (进步刺刀; **Forward-Stepping Stabbing Dao**)

1) The left foot takes one small step forward; the right foot follows immediately to press against inside of the left foot to form a right lift step. Simultaneously, the left palm swings downward, leftward, then upward to become a standup palm in front of the head; the Hukou is facing to the right. Eyes look forward (picture 6.41).

2) Do not pause. The right foot tang forward by one step to form a Zhuang Bu. The right hand stabs the dao forward by borrowing the momentum from the left foot's reverse deng to push body forward, as well as from the yao twisting to the left; the dao bei is diagonally facing rightward; the dao is at shoulder height. At the same time the dao is stabbing forward, the left palm drops to press on the inside of the right forearm. Eyes look to the front of the dao (picture 6.42).

PRINCIPLES

i. The swinging of the left palm upward with a forward step must be light, yet swift and coordinated. The forward stabbing and the right foot's stepping must also be coordinated.

ii. In stabbing the dao, shake the yao to issue power. Movement must be swift and forceful.

6.41          6.42

## 21. *Hui Shen Deng Jiao Zhang Pi Dao* (回身蹬脚斩劈刀; **Turn-Around with Heel-Kick Sweeping Dao)/ *Hui Shen Li Mao Dao Shang Shu Dao* (回身狸猫倒上树刀; Leopard Cat Turns Around to Climb Up the Tree Dao)**

1) The left toes hook inward; the body weight shifts to the right leg; the body turns around [180°], turning to the left; the left toes swing outward. Simultaneously, the right hand lifts the dao upward and wraps it over the head, then chops it downward from over the left shoulder. In conjunction, the left palm passes in front of the body to swing leftward, then upward, to press on the top of the right wrist. The tip of the dao is at shoulder height. Eyes look to the front of the dao tip (picture 6.43).

2) Do not pause. The body weight shifts to the left foot. The right leg bends at the knee and heel-kicks the foot upward, with toes swung outward. Simultaneously, the right hand sweeps the dao horizontally across to the right; the dao is at shoulder height; the tip of the dao is pointing forward. Also simultaneously, the left palm swings horizontally leftward at shoulder height; the palm is facing leftward; the fingers point forward. Eyes look forward (picture 6.44).

3) Do not pause. The right foot lands forward immediately with toes swung outward; the body weight is on the left foot. Simultaneously, the right hand twists the wrist to lift the dao upward and wrap it over the head to above the left shoulder, while the left palm also swings over the head to press on the right wrist. The two hands together chop the dao

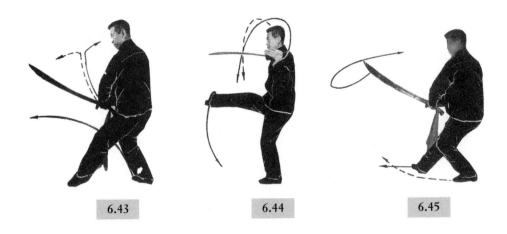

6.43                    6.44                    6.45

forward with a right twist of the yao; the dao is pointing in the direction of the right foot. Eyes look to the tip of the dao (picture 6.45).

PRINCIPLES

i. The two chopping dao in this movement are continuous movements; do not pause between them.

ii. The kick of the foot kick and the sweep of the dao, the foot's landing and dao's forward chopping must be coordinated. Utilize the yao-twist momentum to chop the dao; be swift yet firm. The two legs must press tight against each other. Even though this is an Au Bu stand, jing is forward.

## 22. *Jin Bu Beng Dao* (进步崩刀; Forward-Stepping Smashing *Dao*)

1) The right foot takes one big step forward; the left foot follows immediately to press on the inside of the right foot to form a left lift step. Simultaneously, the tip of the dao drops downward to probe forward; immediately afterward, with one hand pushing forward while the other hand pulls backward, the two hands pull the dao to an upright position in front of the right shoulder. Both hands and forearms press tight against the right side of the yao. Eyes look forward (picture 6.46).

2) Do not pause. The left foot tang forward by one big step. The right foot follows immediately with a forward step to form a Smashing Fist Stance. Simultaneously, the two hands together smash the dao

forward with yao power; the dao is horizontal at center chest height. Eyes look to the front of the dao (picture 6.47).

6.46 6.47

PRINCIPLE

Same as for movement 4 above.

In Xingyiquan and weapons, the movements in the first half and the second half of the forms are the same, except that they are executed in opposite directions.

In the traditional Linking Dao form, practice [from movement 1] up to movement 14, Forward-Stepping Smashing Dao, then follow with movement 21, Leopard Cat Turns Around to Climb Up the Tree Dao, to complete the first half. Start with movement 4, Forward-Stepping Smashing Dao to complete the second half.

In the long form, add movements 15 to 20 [after movement 14], follow with movement 21, "Leopard Cat Turns Around to Climb Up the Tree Dao, to complete one direction. For the second half, in the reverse direction, start with movement 4, Forward-Stepping Smashing Dao, then follow with movement 5, 6, and so on, up to movement 20. To close, proceed to movement 4 (picture 6.48), then movements 23 and 24.

**6.48**

### 23. *Bai Ko Bu Zuan Shen Sao Dao* (摆扣步转身扫刀; *Bai-*, *Kou-Bu* Turn-Around Sweeping *Dao*)

1) Shift the body weight slightly backward. With forearm and wrist power, the right hand turns the wrist to gua the dao downward, backward, and then forward to draw one vertical circle on the right side of the body. At the same time that the dao gua downward, the right foot takes one backward step. Immediately afterward, the left hand turns the wrist inward to pierce upward from the inside of the right arm, then becomes a *Tuo Zhang* (托掌; an upholding palm) over the left side of the head. Simultaneously, the body turns to the right and the left toes hook inward. With the body weight on the left leg, the right wrist turns inward to press dao bei under the left armpit. Eyes look to the right (picture 6.49).

2) Do not pause. The body turns to the right. The right toes swing outward to take one step forward to the right; the body weight remains

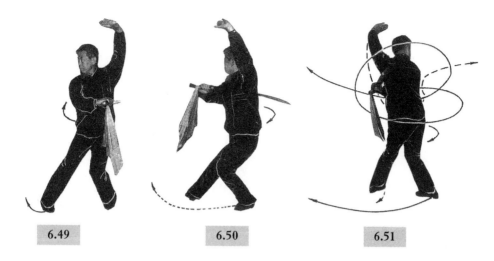

6.49    6.50    6.51

on the left foot (picture 6.50). The hands do not move. The body continues to turn to the right. The left foot steps around and toward the front of the right foot, with toes hooked inward; the two feet now point at each other. Eyes look to the right (picture 6.51).

3) Do not pause. The body turns to the right once more. The right foot steps behind the left foot, stepping backward by one big step. The left foot follows by pointing toes inward to form a right Bow Stance. The right toes point forward, parallel with the left toes. With the momentum from the body turning and the backward stepping, the right hand sweeps the dao horizontally rightward, then turns the wrist to lift the dao upward to wrap it over the head, around the back and left shoulder, to sweep it across to the right. The dao blade is facing backward at shoulder height. Simultaneously, the left palm drops downward to pierce from the inside of right arm upward to the chest. As the dao is sweeping across to the right, the left palm parts across to the left; the palm is facing outward at shoulder height. The eyes look to the dao on the right (picture 6.52).

6.52

PRINCIPLES

    i. There must not be any pause within this movement. Do not raise the body. The turning around must be agile, swift, and coordinated.

    ii. The turning around with the backward stepping and the separation of the palm and the dao must be coordinated with each other—the foot and the dao must arrive simultaneously, with holistic power.

## 24. *Shou Shi* (收势; Closing Stance)

1) The right wrist turns inward to wrap the dao past the front of the body, over the left shoulder and the head to behind the right shoulder. Simultaneously, the left arm bends at the elbow to pierce the palm downward, then leftward. Eyes look to the front-right direction (picture 6.53).

2) Do not pause. Shift the body weight to the left foot. The right hand continues to sweep the dao over the right shoulder and across to the front left of the body, then suddenly turns the wrist inward so that the dao bei is facing downward; the tip of the dao is pointing backward. Simultaneously, the left palm comes up to take hold of the dao at the front left of the body; the dao bei is against the left arm. Eyes look to the left (picture 6.54).

3) Do not pause. Shift the body weight to the right leg. The left hand holds the dao and drops by the left kua. The right hand changes into a palm and swings rightward to shoulder height; the palm is facing upward. Eyes look to the right palm (picture 6.55).

4) The left foot moves rightward to be together with the right foot. The right arm lifts upward and, with a quick upward wrist-swing, turns the palm upward. At the same time, the head turns to the left, with eyes looking to the left (picture 6.56).

5) The right foot takes one step backward. The left foot follows with another backward step to be together with the right foot. Simultaneously, the right palm turns leftward, then downward, to press on the inside of the left arm. Eyes look to the left (picture 6.57).

6) The left foot takes one step forward. The right foot follows with another step forward to be together with the left foot. The right palm drops to rest by the right kua. The head turns forward. Eyes look forward (picture 6.58).

6.53

6.54

6.55

6.56

6.57

6.58

# Xingyi Lian Huan Jian
## (形意连环剑; Xingyi Linking Sword)

NAMES OF THE MOVEMENTS IN *XINGYI LIAN HUAN JIAN*

1) *Yu Bei Shi* (预备式; Preparation Stance)

2) *San Ti Shi Jie Jian* (三体式接剑; *San Ti Shi* Switch-Hand *Jian*)

3) *Dian Bu Ba Chou* (点步拔抽; Toe-Pointing Sharp Slice and Pull-Back)/ *Ting Shen Bi Jian* (停身蔽剑; Pause with Hidden *Jian*)

4) *Jin Bu Beng Jian* (进步崩剑; Forward-Stepping Smashing *Jian*)

5) *Tui Bu Fan Beng Jian* (退步反崩剑; Backward-Stepping Reverse Smashing *Jian*)

6) *Xie Jin Bu Pi Jian* (斜进步劈剑; Diagonal Forward-Stepping Chopping *Jian*)

7) *Tui Bu Jiao Jian* (退步搅剑; Backward-Stepping Stirring *Jian*)

8) *Ti Xi Ci Jian* (提膝刺剑; Lift-Knee Stabbing *Jian*)

9) *Hui Shen Chou Jian* (回身抽剑; Turn-Around and Pull-Back *Jian*)

10) *Jin Bu Ci Jian* (进步刺剑; Forward-Stepping Stabbing *Jian*)

11) *Fan Shen Ti Xi Pi Jian* (翻身提膝劈剑; Twist and Turn Lift-Knee Chopping *Jian*)

12) *Jin Bu Pao Jian* (进步炮剑; Forward-Stepping Cannon *Jian*)

13) *Gua Jian Tui Bu Fan Beng Jian* (挂剑退步反崩剑; *Gua Jian* Backward-Stepping Reverse-Smashing *Jian*)

14) *Jin Bu Zuan Jian* (进步钻剑; Forward-Stepping Drilling *Jian*)

15) *Jin Bu Deng Jiao Fan Beng Jian* (进步蹬脚反崩剑; Forward-Stepping Heel-Kicking Reverse-Stabbing *Jian*)/ *Li Mao Shang Shu Jian* (狸猫上树剑; Leopard Cat Climbing Up the Tree *Jian*)

16) *Jin Bu Beng Jian* (进步崩剑; Forward-Stepping Smashing *Jian*)

17) *Che Bu Ning Shen Fan Pi Jian* (撤步拧身反劈剑; Retreat-Stepping Turn-Around Reverse-Chopping *Jian*)

18) *Zhuan Shen Yun Pi Jian* (转身云劈剑; Turn-Around Circling-Overhead Chopping *Jian*)

19) *Tui Bu Zhuan Shen Tui Jian* (退步转身推剑; Backward-Stepping Turn-Around Pushing *Jian*)

20) *Zhuan Shen Shang Yun Xia Zhan Jian* (转身上云下斩剑; Turn-Around *Yun* Above and Strike-Below *Jian*)

21) *Dao Bu Heng Pai Zhang* (倒步横拍掌; Exchange-Stepping Cross-Slapping Palm)

22) *Jin Bu Ci Jian* (进步刺剑; Forward-Stepping Stabbing *Jian*)

23) *Hui Shen Deng Jiao Zhan Pi Jian* (回身蹬脚斩劈剑; Turn-Around with Heel-Kicking Chopping *Jian*)/*Li Mao Dao Shang Shu Jian* (狸猫倒上树剑; Leopard Cat Turns Around to Climb Up the Tree *Jian*)

24) *Jin Bu Beng Jian* (进步崩剑; Forward-Stepping Smashing *Jian*)

25) *Bai Kou Bu Zhuan Shen Sao Jian* (摆扣步转身扫剑; *Bai- Kou-Bu* Turn-Around Sweeping *Jian*)

26) *Shou Shi* (收势; Closing Stance)

## EXPLANATIONS FOR THE MOVEMENTS IN XINGYI LIAN HUAN JIAN

### 1. *Yu Bei Shi* (预备式; Preparation Stance)

Stand up straight, with feet together. Shoulders and elbows are dropped; head is pulled upward; chin is slightly tucked back; jaw is closed; tip of the tongue touches the upper palate; qi is sunk to Dantian; relax the entire body. Eyes look forward. Arms drop naturally; elbows do not touch the body. The left hand holds the jian with the thumb, middle finger, and ring finger, with the small finger wrapping the jian guard; the index finger is extended to stabilize the handle. Jian is held close to the back of the left forearm. The right hand forms the jian finger with the palm facing backward (picture 6.59).

6.59

## 2. *San Ti Shi Jie Jian* (三体式接剑; *San Ti Shi* **Switch-Hand** *Jian*)

1) The right foot takes one step forward to form a right Bow Stance. Simultaneously, the right hand jian finger lifts upward on the right to shoulder height, with the palm facing forward; the left hand, holding the jian, lifts upward on the left, also to shoulder height, with the palm facing backward. Eyes look to the right (picture 6.60).

PRINCIPLE

The right foot's stepping forward and the two arms lifting to the sides must all be synchronized.

2) Do not pause. The left foot takes one step forward to the left side of the right foot; the right toes hook inward to form Zhuang Bu; the body weight is on the right leg. Simultaneously, both forearms fold to the front of the chest, with the left hand resting in front of the heart, palm facing outward, while the right hand's jian finger presses on the jian handle with the palm facing inward. Eyes look to the left (picture 6.61). The right hand immediately takes hold of the jian, and left hand turns into *jian* finger in preparation for the next movement.

PRINCIPLE

The folding of the forearms and the left foot's stepping forward must be synchronized. At the same time, the focus of the eyes must shift from the right to in front of the jian on the left. The turning of the head must be swift; the focus of the eyes must be sharp, with full intensity.

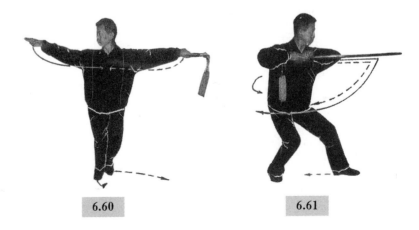

6.60          6.61

### 3. *Dian Bu Ba Chou* (点步拔抽; **Toe-Pointing Sharp Slice and Pull-Back**)/*Ting Shen Bi Jian* (停身蔽剑; **Pause with Hidden *Jian***)

Once the jian is passed to the right hand, the left hand's jian finger presses on the right hand Mai Men; the body weight shifts forward as the right hand stabs the jian forward, then immediately slices the jian rightward and downward and then pulls it back to the right side of kua. After the forward stab of the jian, the left arm also pulls back to rest the jian finger by the left kua. Simultaneously, the body weight shifts backward as the left foot takes one half-step backward, with the toes pointing at the ground. The right leg is straight. Eyes look forward (picture 6.62).

PRINCIPLES

i. When stabbing the jian forward, the height of the jian should be at the center of the chest. The stabbing, slicing across, and pulling back sequence must be continuous and smooth, with energy reaching the blade.

ii. The left-foot retreat and pulling back of the hands must be coordinated. At this point, the right palm and the jian blade are facing upward, with the jian hidden diagonally by the side of the body—hence this movement is named "hidden jian."

6.62

### 4. *Jin Bu Beng Jian* (进步崩剑; **Forward-Stepping Smashing** *Jian*)

1) Both hands reach outward to meet in front of the body; both hands hold the jian to stab it directly forward. Simultaneously, the left leg tang forward by one big step; the right leg follows immediately to form a right lift step (picture 6.63). Do not pause. Both arms pull back quickly, with both wrists lifted upward, and using opposing force (that is, the left hand pushes forward, the right hand pulls backward), the hands pull the jian back to the front of the right abdomen in an upright position; both the arms and the hands press against the body; the jian blade leans slightly in front of the right shoulder. Simultaneously, the right leg tang forward by one big step; the left leg follows immediately by lifting upward to form a left lift step (picture 6.64).

2) Do not pause. The left foot tang forward by one big step; the right foot follows immediately with a half-step forward to form a Smashing Fist Stance. At the same time, both hands apply opposing forces to push, drill, and smash the jian forward; the jian blade is vertical at center chest height. Eyes look to the front of the jian (picture 6.65).

PRINCIPLES

    i. When stabbing the jian forward with both hands, the hands and feet must arrive at the same time, with energy reaching the tip of the jian.

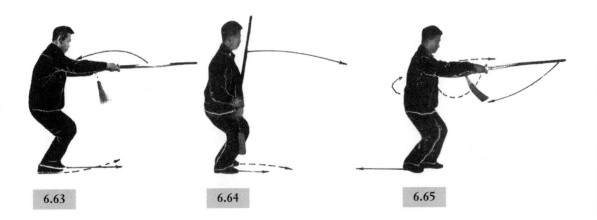

6.63                6.64                6.65

ii. The pulling back of the jian and the left lift step must also be coordinated; the hands and feet move as one.

iii. In smashing the jian forward, incorporate pushing, drilling, smashing, and stabbing energies; utilize momentum from the forward tang and backward deng to issue power from the *yao* to enable the stabbing to be swift and forceful.

### 5. *Tui Bu Fan Beng Jian* (退步反崩剑; **Backward-Stepping Reverse-Smashing** *Jian*)

1) The left hand changes into jian finger to pull downward and backward to touch the chest center, then point forward. Simultaneously, the right hand pulls the jian downward and backward to rest by the right kua. Also simultaneously, the right foot takes one big step backward to form a left Bow Stance (a transitional stance). Eyes look forward (picture 6.66).

2) Do not pause. Shift the body weight backward; the left foot then moves backward to rest by inside of the right foot to form a left lift step. The right hand lifts the jian backward and upward (with the tip of the jian still pointing forward) to above the head on the right. Left wrist sinks downward slightly. Eyes look forward (picture 6.67).

6.66                              6.67

3) Do not pause. The yao twists to the left; the jian in the right hand follows the twisting momentum to reverse-stab forward; the jian is level with the head; and the palm is facing outside. Simultaneously, the left jian finger retreats to rest under inside of the right elbow joint. Also simultaneously, the body weight shifts backward; and the right foot retreats to the inside of the left foot. Eyes look to the front of the jian (picture 6.68).

6.68a                                                    6.68b

PRINCIPLES

  i. The pullback of the jian, with backward stepping, and the jian finger's forward pointing should cross each other in front of the body before separating into two parallel lines.

 ii. In the left-foot retreat and right-hand reverse-stab, issue power from the yao; the body and the jian must be coordinated.

iii. The steps from the retreat and pullback to the reverse-stab are continuous movements; all details must be followed and should be executed with agility and power.

## 6. *Xie Jin Bu Pi Jian* (斜进步劈剑; **Diagonal Forward–Stepping Chopping Jian**)

1) The right hand gua the jian, keeping close to the left side of the body, downward, then backward, then upward to over the left side of the head; the left jian finger sinks downward and inward. At the same time,

the left foot moves past the inside of the right foot to take a diagonal forward step to the right; the right foot follows immediately to press against inside of the left foot to form a right lift step. Eyes look forward (picture 6.69).

2) Do not pause. The right foot tang forward by one big step in the right diagonal direction; the left foot follows immediately with a forward step to form a Zhuang Bu. At the same time, the right hand continues with the downward, backward, then upward gua jian to finally chop it forward. Simultaneously, the left jian finger also continues with the downward-backward sink, then swings upward to the left side of the head, and then throws the wrist, with some force, outward to have the jian finger facing upward and pointing forward. Eyes look to the tip of the jian (picture 6.70).

PRINCIPLES

i. Drawing circles with the jian on the left side of the body, with forward stepping, is to cover the body in advance. The lift step is to massage the channel and gather energy.

ii. The backward deng, forward tang, swinging the arm, and circling to chop forward must all issue power from the yao; the body and the jian must be coordinated, swift, and complete.

6.69                              6.70

### 7. *Tui Bu Jiao Jian* (退步搅剑; **Backward-Stepping Stirring** *Jian*)

The right forearm and wrist turn outward to stir the jian rightward, then upward, before pulling and pressing the jian back to the front of the abdomen; the forearm is against the right abdomen; the tip of the jian is at waist height. Simultaneously, the left jian finger drops down to the front of the body to press on the right Mai Men. While stirring the jian, the left foot takes one backward step; when pulling the jian backward, contract the body, then move the right foot back to rest by the inside of the left foot. Eyes look to the front of the jian (picture 6.71).

6.71

PRINCIPLES

    i. In stirring the jian and retreating the feet, the body and jian must be coordinated and move as one entity.

    ii. In stirring the jian, the tip of the jian is drawing a vertical circle; power is focused on the front end of the jian. When pulling back the jian, press it downward at the same time, with energy focused on the back end of the jian.

### 8. *Ti Xi Ci Jian* (提膝刺剑; **Lift-Knee Stabbing** *Jian*)

The right foot takes one big step forward, with toes pointing inward as it lands; the left foot follows immediately with a forward step, then lift the knee. Simultaneously, the left jian finger presses on the jian handle as the right hand stabs the jian diagonally upward with the body leaning forward; the jian blade lies flat, with tip of the jian no higher than top of the head. Eyes look to the tip of the jian (picture 6.72).

6.72

PRINCIPLES

i. The forward stepping, lifting of the knee, and the stabbing forward must all be coordinated; the body, hands, and feet move as one and arrive at the same time.

ii. Lean the body forward and twist the yao to enable power to reach the tip of the jian.

## 9. *Hui Shen Chou Jian* (回身抽剑; **Turn–Around and Pull-Back** *Jian*)

The body turns around to the left; the right hand turns the wrist to pull the jian, with jian handle leading, first forward, then downward, then backward, to rest by the right kua. Simultaneously, the left jian finger traces the body to point left-forward from below; the left foot follows the turning around to take one step toward the left front, while the right foot pivots outward on the ball to form a Zhuang Bu. Eyes look to the jian finger (picture 6.73).

PRINCIPLE

The pulling back of the jian, while turning around, the landing of the foot, and the pointing the jian finger outward must all be coordinated and fully executed.

6.73

### 10. *Jin Bu Ci Jian* (进步刺剑; **Forward-Stepping Stabbing** *Jian*)

1) The left foot takes one step forward; the right foot follows immediately by moving forward to press against the inside of the left foot to form a right lift step. Simultaneously, the left jian finger draws a curve from right, going downward, then left-forward, then upward, to stop in front of the head at no higher than eye level. Eyes look forward (picture 6.74).

2) The body weight shifts forward; the right hand turns the wrist outward to stab the jian forward; the palm is facing upward; the jian is aiming at the opponent's throat. Simultaneously, the left hand draws a small curve by turning rightward, then downward to rest at mid-section of the right forearm. Also simultaneously, the right foot steps forward and lands with the toes hooked inward. The body weight rests mostly on the left foot. Eyes look to the tip of the jian (picture 6.75).

PRINCIPLE

The pointing of the jian finger and the lift step should be coordinated. The stabbing and the forward step landing should utilize power from left-twisting the yao; the hand and foot should arrive at the same time, with power reaching the tip of the jian.

6.74                                            6.75

## 11. *Fan Shen Ti Xi Pi Jian* (翻身提膝劈剑; **Twist and Turn Lift–Knee Chopping** *Jian*)

The body turns around to the left while the jian chops forward from over the right side of the head to the front of the chest; the left jian finger traces downward along the chest, then leftward, then upward, to above the left side of the head, with the palm facing upward. Simultaneously, twist the body and shift the body weight to the right leg and lift the left leg with a bent knee to form a single-foot stand. Eyes look to the tip of the jian (picture 6.76).

PRINCIPLE

Chopping the jian, turning the jian finger upward, and lifting the knee must all be coordinated. The body should lean forward with the left knee held tight when chopping the jian forward, with pushing and drilling energy reaching the front of the jian.

6.76

### 12. *Jin Bu Pao Jian* (进步炮剑; **Forward-Stepping Cannon *Jian*)**

1) The upper body twists to the left; the right hand turns the wrist outward to gua the jian upward to the left front of the head. Simultaneously, the left-hand sword finger drops down to press on the Mai Men of the right hand as the left foot lands forward. Eyes look forward (picture 6.77).

2) Do not pause. The right foot tang one big step forward, passing the inside of the left foot; the right foot follows immediately with a half-step forward to form a Cannon Fist Stance. Simultaneously, the right hand draws a backward curve before lifting the jian upward and forward in a curve; in coordination, the left hand presses on the inside of the right forearm; the blade of the jian is vertical, with the tip of the jian slightly lower. Eyes look to the front of the jian (picture 6.78).

PRINCIPLES

  i. The two steps of the movement must be continuous. Issue power from the yao. The jian and foot must arrive at the same time.

  ii. The jian blade and the right foot must be aligned. Power should reach the front of the jian with pushing, drilling, and lifting energies.

| 6.77 | 6.78 |

### 13. *Gua Jian Tui Bu Fan Beng Jian* (挂剑退步反崩剑; Gua Jian Backward-Stepping Reverse-Smashing Jian)

1) The left foot takes one big step backward to form a right Bow Stance. At the same time, the right hand gua the jian downward, passing the left side of the body, then backward, then upward, then forward, to drop in front of the body. Eyes look to the front of the jian (picture 6.79).

2) Do not pause. The right foot also takes one step backward to form a left Bow Stance. Simultaneously, the right hand gua the jian downward on the right side of the body, then backward, then upward, then outward-forward to finally pull back to rest by the right kua. The left jian finger simultaneously points forward from the chest. Eyes look forward (picture 6.80).

6.79     6.80

3) The body weight shifts backward; the left foot lifts to retreat to the inside of the right foot to form a left lift step. At the same time, the right hand pulls the jian backward behind the right side of the body. Eyes look forward (picture 6.81).

6.81

4) The body weight shifts backward; the left foot retreats to the
back of the right foot to form a Backward-Stepping Beng Quan Bu.
Simultaneously, the right hand continues to lift the jian upward, then
reverse-smashes it forward from right side of the head; the palm is facing
outward, with the jian at brow height; the left jian finger turns downward, inward, then upward to press on the inside of the right elbow joint.
Eyes look to the front of the jian (picture 6.82).

**6.82**

PRINCIPLES

   i. In circling the jian on the left and the right with backward stepping,
use the forearm and wrist-twist to aid the power. The stepping and
the jian movements must be coordinated, natural, and agile.

   ii. Pulling the jian backward with the lift step is meant to gather
power. Utilize momentum from the backward stepping with the
backward deng and the twisting of the yao leftward to direct power
to the tip of the jian so the reverse smash is swift and forceful.

## 14. *Jin Bu Zuan Jian* (进步钻剑; **Forward–Stepping Drilling** *Jian*)

The right foot takes one small step forward; the left foot follows immediately by tang forward by one big step, staying close to the inside of
the right foot; the right foot then follows with one half-step forward to
form a Zhuang Bu. At the same time, the upper body twists slightly to
the right, so the jian in the right hand pulls backward, passing in front

of the body, and turns outward. Then utilize the momentum from twisting the yao leftward to drill the jian upward and forward, with the palm facing upward; the left jian finger swings downward, leftward, and upward to above the head; then twist the wrist, with a throwing energy, to have the palm facing upward; the fingers are pointing forward. Eyes look to the front of the jian (picture 6.83).

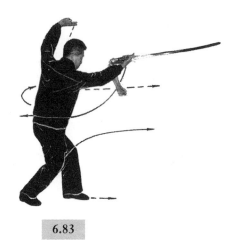

6.83

PRINCIPLES

  i. In pulling the jian backward, then drilling it forward, it is important to issue power by twisting the yao rightward, then leftward.

  ii. The drilling of the jian with the forward stepping and the landing of the left foot must be coordinated, with power reaching the tip of the jian.

### 15. *Jin Bu Deng Jiao Fan Beng Jian* (进步蹬脚反崩剑; **Forward-Stepping Heel-Kicking Reverse-Smashing** *Jian*) / *Li Mao Shang Shu Jian* (狸猫上树剑; **Leopard Cat Climbing Up the Tree** *Jian*)

1) The body weight shifts forward; the left foot takes one big step forward; the yao twists to the right; the right leg then immediately bends at the knee, and with the toes pointing outward, kicks forward with the heel, forcefully and with speed; the foot height does not exceed the kua. At the same time, the right hand turns the wrist inward as

it pulls the jian downward and backward, past right side of the body and behind; the palm is facing downward. Also simultaneously, the left jian finger points downward, passing left chest center, then forward; the palm is facing downward at center chest height. Eyes look forward (picture 6.84).

2) The body weight shifts forward as the right foot swings outward, then lands forward with the toes pointing forward; the left foot follows immediately with a half-step forward. Simultaneously, the yao twists to the left as the right arm bends at the elbow to lift the jian upward, then reverse-stabs it forward, passing the right side of the head; the palm is facing outward; the left jian finger presses on the bottom inside of the right elbow joint. Eyes look to the front of the jian (picture 6.85).

## PRINCIPLES

    i. Pulling back the jian, pointing the jian finger forward, and kicking the foot should all be coordinated; also gather energy by twisting the yao rightward.

    ii. In the reverse stabbing and the right foot landing, utilize the momentum from the left foot's backward deng to push the body forward; the jian and the foot must arrive at the same time. Issue power by twisting the yao leftward; direct energy to the tip of the jian.

    iii. When the left foot follows the right foot with a half-step forward, the left knee must press tight against inside of the right knee to make the pose firm and well-rooted.

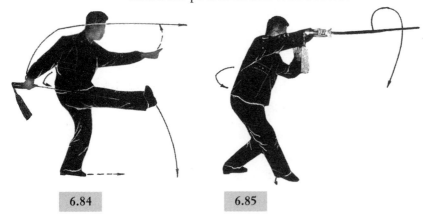

6.84             6.85

### 16. *Jin Bu Beng Jian* (进步崩剑; Forward-Stepping Smashing *Jian*)

1) The upper body twists to the left. The right hand turns the wrist outward as it presses the jian downward to the front of the abdomen. The right foot adjusts to point forward as the body weight begins to shift forward. Eyes look to the tip of the jian (picture 6.86).

2) The left foot deng backward to enable the right foot to take one big step forward; the left foot follows immediately and moves forward to press on the inside of the right foot and form a left lift step. At the same time, the right hand pulls on the jian handle, while the left pushes on it, to pull the jian back to the front of the right shoulder in an upright position; both hands press on the right abdomen, while both elbows press against the ribs. Eyes look forward (picture 6.87).

3) The right foot deng backward to push the body forward, thereby enabling the left foot to tang forward by one big step; the right foot follows immediately with a half-step forward to form a Smashing Fist Stance. Simultaneously, both hands hold the jian handle, and with opposing force, smash the jian forward with pushing, drilling, and smashing stab energies. Eyes look to the front of the jian (picture 6.88).

PRINCIPLES

i. The pulling back of the jian and the right lift step must be coordinated and completed as a single movement.

ii. In smashing the jian forward, utilize the momentum from the backward deng and the forward tang to issue power from the yao, thereby enabling the smash to be swift and forceful.

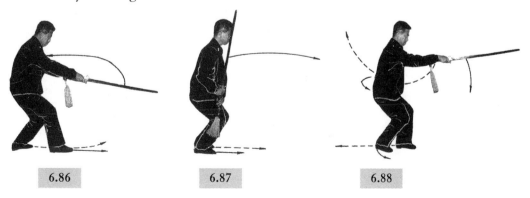

| 6.86 | 6.87 | 6.88 |

iii. Movements 14 (Forward-Stepping Drilling Jian) to 16 (Forward-Stepping Smashing Jian) are like the One Horse with Three Arrows of the Linking Fist; they must be executed with speed, power, and continuity.

### 17. *Che Bu Ning Shen Fan Pi Jian* (撤步拧身反劈剑; Retreat-Stepping Turn-Around Reverse-Chopping *Jian*)

1) The body turns to the left as the left foot steps past inside of the right foot to take a backward step; body then turns around while right foot pivots on the ball to form a left Bow Stance. Simultaneously, left hand forms jian finger and turns downward in front of the body, then leftward, then upward. Also simultaneously, right hand twists the wrist inward as it presses the jian downward with the palm facing backward. Eyes look to the right (picture 6.89).

2) Do not pause. The right foot steps past inside of the left foot to take a forward step toward the left. The right hand gua the jian downward, then left-upward, passing in front of the body, then upward to finally reverse-chop rightward with the jian at center-chest height. At the same time, left-hand jian finger turns downward, passing in front of the chest, then turns rightward, to finally throw the wrist upward to rest over the head on the left; palm is facing forward. Eyes follow the chopping jian (picture 6.90).

PRINCIPLE

In circling the jian, then reverse-chopping, utilize the momentum from the backward stepping and twisting the yao; the foot and the jian must arrive at the same time. The jian and the jian finger must also be coordinated.

**6.89**        **6.90**

## 18. *Zhuan Shen Yun Pi Jian* (转身云劈剑; **Turn-Around Circling-Overhead Chopping** *Jian*)

1) The body turns to the left as the right foot hooks inward. As the body is turning, the right hand pulls the jian back so that the hand rests in front of the left ribs; the jian now lies horizontally across the front of the chest with the tip pointing to the right. At the same time, the left jian finger drops to press on the jian handle. Eyes look to the tip of the jian (picture 6.91).

   2) The body turns to the left as the left foot swings outward; the right foot stays very close to the inside of the left foot to take one step forward to form a Zhuang Bu. At the same time, the right hand circles the jian overhead once by swinging upward to the left, then chops diagonally forward toward the right; the tip of the jian is no higher than the shoulder. As the jian chops forward, the left hand holds onto the back of the handle to support the right hand (picture 6.92).

PRINCIPLES

    i. The circling overhead and chopping of the jian must utilize yao power from the turning of the body and from the forward-stepping momentum, and it must be completed in one breath. The jian and foot must arrive at the same time.

    ii. When turning around and circling the jian overhead, the eyes look to the front part of the jian. When drawing the jian upward, the power should reach the upper blade, as to intercept an attack; whereas when chopping the jian forward, the power should reach the lower blade. The body and weapon must be coordinated and move as one unit.

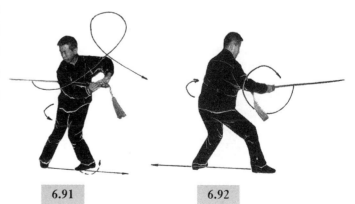

6.91                    6.92

## 19. *Tui Bu Zhuan Shen Tui Jian* (退步转身推剑; Backward-Stepping Turn-Around Pushing *Jian*)

1) The body turns to the right; the left jian finger presses on the Mai Men; the right hand, holding the jian, twists the wrist outward to gua the jian downward, backward, then upward and outward so the jian draws a circle by the right side of the body. The right foot steps past the inside of the left foot to take one step backward to form a left Bow Stance. Eyes look forward (picture 6.93).

2) Do not pause. The body turns around to the right by pivoting on the heels; the left foot follows immediately to rest by the inside of the right foot and form a left lift step. At the same time that the body turns around, the right hand pulls the jian to the front of the center of the chest; the jian is level, about a distance of two fists from the chest, with the palm facing downward. The left jian finger presses on the inside of the right wrist. Eyes look forward (picture 6.94).

3) The left foot tang forward by one big step; the right foot follows immediately with a half-step forward to form a Zhuang Bu. At the same time, the right hand pushes the jian forward with the front blade; the jian is level and no higher than the shoulders. Eyes look forward (picture 6.95).

PRINCIPLE

When pulling the jian to the front of the chest, utilize the pulling momentum to step forward. When pushing the jian forward, the focus is on the back half of the blade; issue power from the yao.

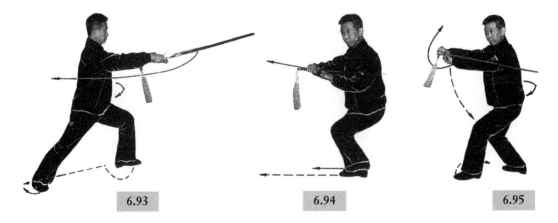

6.93          6.94          6.95

## 20. *Zhuan Shen Shang Yun Xia Zhan Jian* (转身上云下斩剑; Turn-Around *Yun* and Strike-Below *Jian*)

1) The body turns to the right; the left toes hook inward; the left hand opens to a palm and twists the wrist inward to press on the left knee, with the Hukou facing inward; the right hand twists the wrist outward to pull back the jian to rest diagonally across the chest with the tip of the jian pointing to the left and at shoulder height. Eyes look to the tip of the jian (picture 6.96).

    2) Do not pause. The body twists to the right while the right toes turn slightly to the right. At the same time, the right hand yun the jian outward and upward to the right. Eyes look to the tip of the jian (picture 6.97).

    3) Do not pause. The right hand continues to yun the jian leftward, then strikes it diagonally downward and forward. The right foot adjusts forward to form a Zhuang Bu. Eyes look to the tip of the jian (picture 6.98).

PRINCIPLES

  i. The hooking in of the foot and the twisting of the wrist to pull back the jian are used to gather power and wait to issue.

  ii. Turn the yao to yun the jian and allow energy to reach the front half of the jian; the upward yun and downward strike must utilize power from the yao and be completed in one breath.

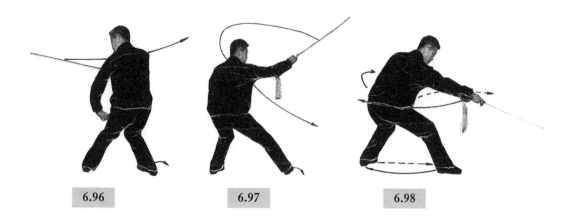

| 6.96 | 6.97 | 6.98 |

### 21. *Dao Bu Heng Pai Zhang* (倒步横拍掌; **Exchange-Stepping Cross-Slapping Palm**)

The left foot steps up to the inside of the right foot; the right foot then immediately steps backward to the original position of the left foot to form a Zhuang Bu. At the same time that the right foot steps backward, the right hand follows the body's twist to pull the jian backward behind the right side of the body, with the the palm facing inside. The left palm also follows the body's twist to slap across to the right; the palm is facing rightward at heart height. Eyes look to the front of the palm (picture 6.99).

PRINCIPLES

i. The backward stepping must be swift and arrive at the same time that the left palm slaps across; utilize the yao power. The left palm's slapping across and left foot's forward stepping must be coordinated. The right hand's pulling back and the right foot's backward stepping must also be coordinated.

ii. This movement is a special defense movement in a situation when the preceding movement fails to strike the target (i.e., when the opponent's qian or dao is striking toward your chest, and you're not able to strike back).

6.99

### 22. *Jin Bu Ci Jian* (进步刺剑; **Forward-Stepping Stabbing** *Jian*)

1) The left foot takes one step forward; the right foot follows immediately forward to form a right lift step. At the same time, the left palm turns into jian finger and twists the wrist inward to turn leftward, then throws the wrist upward to be horizontally in front of the face. The jian in the right hand does not move; only the palm turns downward. Eyes look forward (picture 6.100).

2) Do not pause. The right foot tang forward by one big step; the left foot follows immediately with a half-step forward to form a Zhuang Bu. Simultaneously, with the jian in the right hand pressed against the right side of the body, utilize the power from twisting the yao leftward to stab the jian forward; the blade of the jian is vertical and at center chest height. The left jian finger drops to press on the right hand's Mai Men. Eyes look to the front of the jian (picture 6.101).

PRINCIPLES

i.  The swinging of the jian finger upward and the forward stepping should be swift, light, and coordinated; gather power to issue.

ii. The right foot's forward tang and the forward stabbing of the jian must also be coordinated.

iii. Stab the jian by issuing power from the yao; be swift and forceful.

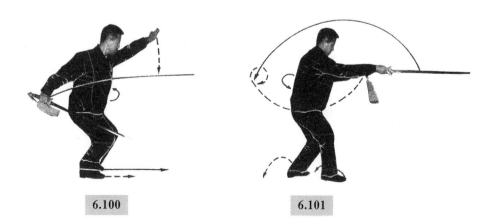

6.100          6.101

### 23. *Hui Shen Deng Jiao Zhan Pi Jian* (回身蹬脚斩劈剑; Turn-Around with Heel-Kicking Chopping *Jian*) / *Li Mao Dao Shang Shu Jian* (狸猫倒上树剑; Leopard Cat Turns Around to Climb Up the Tree *Jian*)

1) The right toes hook inward; the body weight shifts to the right leg; the body then turns around to the left; and the left foot lifts up and swings the toes outward, then lands on the toes. Simultaneously, the right hand turns the jian outward so the jian handle is swung by the right side of the head to chop the jian forward to the front of the body; the tip of the jian is pointing diagonally upward and does not exceed the shoulder height. The left jian finger draws a curve by pointing downward first, then leftward, then upward, then inward to rest on the right hand's Mai Men. Eyes look forward (picture 6.102).

2) Do not pause. The body weight shifts forward to the left foot; the right foot steps up to the inside of the left foot, then kicks upward from the heel, with the toes pointing outward, to no higher than the kua; both legs are slightly bent. Simultaneously, the right hand chops the jian across to the right at shoulder height, while the left jian finger swings across to the left with the palm facing left, also at shoulder height. Eyes look forward (picture 6.103).

3) Do not pause. The body weight shifts forward; the right leg bends slightly to land on the ground, with the toes still pointing outward; the left foot follows immediately with a half-step forward to form a Backward-Stepping Smashing Fist Stance. Simultaneously, the body twists to the right as the right hand chops the jian upward, then forward, passing the right side of the head, with the tip of the jian pointing diagonally left-forward; the blade of the jian is diagonally covering the upper body, with the tip of the jian no higher than the shoulder.

6.102

6.103

Also simultaneously, the left jian finger turns upward, then forward, to press on top of the Mai Men. Eyes look forward (picture 6.104).

PRINCIPLES

i. In turning around and chopping forward with a hooked-in step, the body and the weapon must be coordinated, agile, and natural.

ii. In parting the jian and jian finger to the two sides, the hands and the kicking of the foot must all be coordinated.

iii. In the landing of the right foot and chopping the jian forward, utilize the momentum from backward deng and from twisting the yao. The jian and the foot must arrive at the same time.

Up to this point, the first half of the form is completed. To continue with the second half of the form after turning around, the front foot steps forward to form a left lift step. Simultaneously, both hands hold onto the jian to pull it back into an upright position; immediately afterward, the left foot tang one step forward; the right foot follows with another forward step, and then continues with Forward-Stepping Smashing Jian [movement 4] (picture 6.105). Follow with Backward-Stepping Reverse Smashing Jian [movement 5] and the remaining movements as described above, only with the direction reversed.

Practice in the original direction, then continue with Leopard Cat Turns Around to Climb Up the Tree Jian [movement 23] to turn around. In order to close, practice the movements described below.

6.104                6.105

## 24. *Jin Bu Beng Jian* (进步崩剑; **Forward-Stepping Smashing** *Jian*)

This movement is identical to movement 4 above in description and principles (picture 6.106). After completing this movement, you may proceed to the following transitional movement before the closing movement.

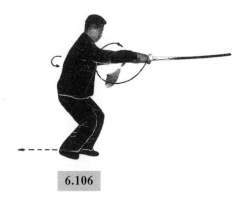

6.106

## 25. *Bai Kou Bu Zhuan Shen Sao Jian* (摆扣步转身扫剑; *Bai-Kou-Bu* **Turn-Around Sweeping** *Jian*)

1) The left foot stays close to the inside of the right foot, then takes one backward step to form a right Bow Stance. Simultaneously, the left jian finger drops to press on the right Mai Men; the right hand gua the jian downward and backward, then upward and forward to trace one circle on the left side of the body. Eyes look to the front part of the jian (picture 6.107).

2) Do not pause. The right foot stays close to the inside of the left foot and takes one backward step to form a left Bow Stance. At the same time, the right hand gua the jian downward and backward, then upward and forward to trace one circle on the right side of the body. Eyes look to the front part of the jian (picture 6.108).

3) The body turns to the right as the left toes hook inward and the right toes swing outward to take one step forward to the right. As the body is turning to the right, the right hand twists the wrist inward to have the palm facing outward and the jian blade vertical, and it then pulls the jian backward toward the chest front so that the blade presses on the outside of the left forearm. Simultaneously, the left jian finger

turns outward to press on the back of the right wrist. Eyes look toward the left (picture 6.109).

**6.107**                          **6.108**                          **6.109**

4) Do not pause. The body continues to turn toward the right so that the left foot can stay close to the inside of the right foot to take one Kou Bu forward; the toes of the two feet are thus pointing at each other. The jian finger does not move. Eyes look to the left (picture 6.110).

5) Do not pause. The body continues to turn to the right, while right foot takes one Bai Bu forward, behind the left foot; then the toes adjust to point forward. Simultaneously, the left foot pivots on the heel and hooks the toes inward to form a right Bow Stance. With the body's turning around, the right arm extends and the right wrist turns outward and, with the palm facing upward, sweeps the jian horizontally rightward; the tip of the jian is slightly higher than the shoulder. Simultaneous with the rightward sweep of the jian, the left jian finger sweeps leftward with the palm facing outward and the jian finger pointing forward at shoulder height. Eyes look to the tip of the jian (picture 6.111).

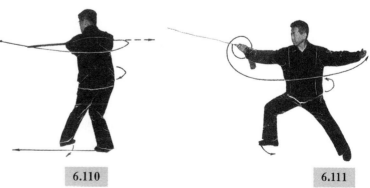

**6.110**                                            **6.111**

PRINCIPLES

   i. The wrist must be agile when swinging the jian on the left and on the right with backward stepping; the body and the jian must be coordinated.

  ii. Carrying the jian to turn around with Bai Bu and Kou Bu must be light, natural, and smooth.

 iii. In the horizontal-sweep of the jian with the stepping of the right foot, utilize power from the yao; the foot and the jian must arrive at the same time. Power in this sweeping jian is similar to other horizontal smashing jian techniques—shake the arm and wrist to issue explosive power; emphasis is on crispness, speed, and forcefulness.

## 26. *Shou Shi* (收势; Closing Stance)

1) The right hand gua the jian, in front of the body, leftward and downward, then rightward and upward to draw one [vertical] circle; with the palm facing upward, it then sweeps the jian across the front of the chest to the left. At the same time, the left forearm is extended on the left side of the body at shoulder height, with the palm facing leftward. As the jian is sweeping near the left hand, right wrist turns inward to have palm facing outward, pressing the handle (guard) on the left hand; the jian blade is vertical and pressed against outside of the left forearm. When the jian is sweeping leftward, the yao must also turn leftward; the body weight shifts to the left, and the right toes hook leftward to form a sideways left Bow Stance. Eyes look to the left (picture 6.112).

2) Shift the body weight to the right, and the left foot comes together with the right foot. At the same time, the left hand takes hold of the jian and drops to rest by the left kua. The right hand changes into a jian finger as the right arm swings rightward and upward by the front of the body, with the right wrist turning upward with a throwing energy over the head on the right with the finger pointing to the left. The head turns to the left (picture 6.113). Immediately, the left foot takes one backward step; the right foot follows immediately, also with a backward step; and

then two feet are together. The right jian finger drops to rest by the right kua. Eyes look forward (picture 6.114).

PRINCIPLE

The body, hands, and feet must all be coordinated; the focus of the eyes must be coordinated with the movements. Be restful and natural.

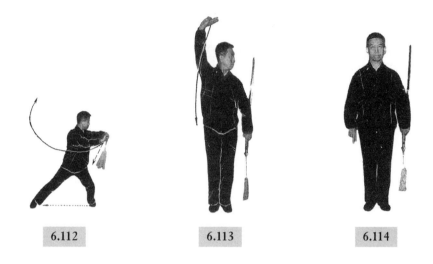

6.112          6.113          6.114

# Xingyi Lian Huan Gun (形意连环棍; *Xingyi Linking Staff*)

NAMES OF THE MOVEMENTS IN *XINGYI LIAN HUAN GUN*

1) *Yu Bei Shi* (预备式; Preparation Stance)

2) *Qi Shi* (起式; Beginning Stance)

3) *Jin Bu Beng Gun* (进步崩棍; Forward-Stepping Smashing *Gun*)

4) *Tui Bu Beng Gun* (退步崩棍; Backward-Stepping Smashing *Gun*)

5) *Xie Jin Bu Pi Gun* (斜进步劈棍; Diagonal Forward-Stepping Chopping *Gun*)

6) *Che Bu Jiao Qun* (撤步绞棍; Retreat-Stepping Stirring *Gun*)

7) *Ti Xi Chuo Gun* (提膝戳棍; Lift-Knee Stabbing *Gun*)

8) *Fan Shen Ti Xi Pi Gun* (翻身提膝劈棍; Twist and Turn-Around Lift-Knee Chopping *Gun*)

9) *Jin Bu Pao Gun* (进步炮棍; Forward-Stepping Cannon *Gun*)

10) *Tui Bu Ti Xi Lun Gua Gun* (退步提膝抡挂棍; Backward-Stepping Lift-Knee *Lun Gua Gun*)

11) *Shang Bu Zuan Qun* (上步钻棍; Advance-Stepping Drilling *Gun*)

12) *Jin Bu Deng Jiao Gua Pi Gun* (进步蹬脚挂劈棍; Forward-Stepping Kick-Heel *Gua Pi Gun*)/*Li Mao Shang Shu Gun* (狸猫上树棍; Leopard Cat Climbing Up the Tree *Gun*)

13) *Jin Bu Beng Gun* (进步崩棍; Forward-Stepping Smashing *Gun*)

14) *Hui Shen Deng Jiao Gua Pi Gun* (回身蹬脚挂劈棍; Turn Around with Heel-Kick *Gua Pi Gun*)/*Li Mao Dao Shang Shu* (狸猫倒上树; Leopard Cat Turns Around to Climb Up the Tree *Gun*)

15) *Zhuan Shen Yun Pi Gun* (转身云劈棍; Turn-Around *Yun Pi Gun*)/*Yao Zhuan Pi Gun* (摇转劈棍; Swing-Around Chopping *Gun*)

16) *Jin Bu Ti Xi Ba Ti Gun* (进步提膝拔提棍; Forward-Stepping Lift-Knee Pull-Up *Gun*)/*Wu Long Jiao Shui* (乌龙搅水; Black Dragon Stirring the Water)

17) *Luo Bu Ao Ba Qian Pi Gun* (落步拗把前劈棍; Landing *Ao Ba* Forward-Chopping *Gun*)

18) *Jin Bu Beng Gun* (进步崩棍; Forward-Stepping Smashing *Gun*)

19) *Hui Shen Deng Jiao Gua Pi Gun* (回身蹬脚挂劈棍; Turn-Around with Heel-Kick *Gua Pi Gun*)/*Li Mao Dao Shang Shu* (狸猫倒上树; Leopard Cat Turns Around to Climb Up the Tree)

20) *Jin Bu Beng Gun* (进步崩棍; Forward-Stepping Smashing *Gun*)

21) *Shou Shi Zhi Yi* (收势之一; Closing Stance Part 1)/*Che Bu Wu Hua Shang Gia* (撤步舞花上架; Retreat-Stepping Spinning Parry Upward)

22) *Shou Shi Zhi Er* (收势之二; Closing Stance Part 2)

## EXPLANATIONS FOR THE MOVEMENTS IN *XINGYI LIAN HUAN GUN*

### 1. *Yu Bei Shi* (预备式; Preparation Stance)

Stand up straight with the feet together. Head is erect; chin is slightly tucked back; jaws are tightly closed; tip of the tongue is placed against the upper palate. Shoulders and elbows are dropped. Qi is sunk to Dantian. Relax the entire body. Eyes look straight forward. The left hand holds the *gun,* which stands in front and to the left of the left foot. The right hand rests naturally by the right kua, with all fingers closed together (picture 6.115).

**6.115**

### 2. *Qi Shi* (起式; Beginning Stance)

Keeping the elbow straight, the right palm turns outward, then lifts upward, then turns leftward to pass over the head, then continues to drop downward, to rest by the left chest as a standup palm; the palm is facing the left. Eyes follow the palm to finally look to the left front (picture 6.116).

### 3. *Jin Bu Beng Gun* (进步崩棍; Forward-Stepping Smashing *Gun*)

**6.116**

1) The body turns to the left; the left toes swing outward to the left front. Simultaneously, the right hand takes hold of the *gun* above the left hand, with the palm facing inside; without pausing, the right foot kicks the *gun* forward with inside of the ball of the foot. The right hand holds the *gun* and bends at the elbow to pull the *gun* backward to the front of the right shoulder, while left elbow relaxes to allow the left hand to slide downward to hold the lower section of the *gun*. Eyes look to the front (picture 6.117).

2) Do not pause. The right foot lands toward the front of the left foot, the left foot tang forward by one big step; the right foot follows immediately with a forward step to form a left Smashing Fist Stance. At the same time, the left hand pulls the *gun* backward so that both the forearm and the front part of the *gun* press tight against the left yao.

Simultaneously, the right hand slides forward along the *gun* and smashes the *gun* forward, issuing power when the *gun* is parallel to the ground. The *gun* is pointing in the direction in which the left foot steps forward. Eyes look forward (picture 6.118).

6.117                                6.118

PRINCIPLES

    i. In smashing the *gun,* borrow power from the back foot's deng and the front foot's forward tang. The smash must be coordinated with the left foot's landing. Issue power by aligning the yao forward, as in Beng Quan (Smashing Fist).

    ii. The left hand holds the *gun* tight; the right hand slides along the *gun,* then also tightens the hold when it reaches the proper spot; the two hands support each other by smashing in opposite directions to issue a coordinated power, which must encompass pushing, grinding, and jabbing energies.

## 4. *Tui Bu Beng Gun* (退步崩棍; Backward-Stepping Smashing *Gun*)

1) The body turns to the right; the right foot takes one big step backward to form a left Bow Stance. Simultaneously, the left hand pushes the *gun* upward then forward, while the right hand slides downward along the *gun* then pulls the *gun* backward so the right hand is touching

the right rib cage. [A *lun gua* is completed on the right side of the body.] Eyes look forward (picture 6.119).

  2) Do not pause. The upper body twists to the left; the left foot stays close to the inside of the right foot as it takes one quick step backward to form a backward-stepping Smashing Fist Stance. The left hand pulls the *gun* under the right armpit, from below; the hand, forearm, and *gun* are all snugly pressed under the right armpit. The right hand slides along the *gun* to smash the *gun* forward from above. The *gun* is parallel to the ground and pointing in the direction in which the right foot points to. Eyes look forward (picture 6.120).

PRINCIPLES

  i. Borrow power from the left foot's quick landing and reverse deng to enhance the power of the smashing *gun*. The power is like that in the Retreat-Stepping Smashing Fist, fully exploiting the principle of "attack when advancing, also attack when retreating."

  ii. Pressing the *gun* under the right armpit increases the force of the forward-smashing *gun*. Borrow power from yao-twist and the mutual support of the two hands to direct power to the tip of the *gun*, thereby achieving power without momentum.

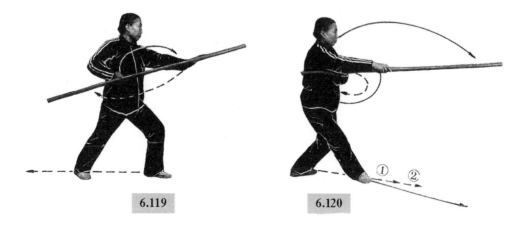

6.119                    6.120

### 5. *Xie Jin Bu Pi Gun* (斜进步劈棍; **Diagonal Forward–Stepping Chopping** *Gun*)

The left foot steps diagonally forward, past the front of the right foot, toward the right. The right hand spins the *gun* over the advancing left leg by pointing the *gun* downward first, then backward, then upward, and then smashing it forward. In conjunction, the left hand pulls the *gun* from under the right forearm upward and forward to rest by the left side of the yao, holding the *gun* tight under the left forearm. At the same time the *gun* is smashed forward, the right foot tang forward by one big step along the inside of the left foot; the left foot follows immediately with a half-step forward to form a Zhuang Bu. The tip of the gun is at shoulder height and pointing in the direction in which the right foot advanced. Eyes look to the front of the gun (picture 6.121).

PRINCIPLES

   i. Spinning the *gun* to cover the left leg with diagonal stepping is a strike-in-defense technique; its transition to chopping the *gun* must be smooth.

   ii. The chopping of the *gun* must be coordinated with the right foot's landing; totality and completeness of the power must be the same as that in a Pi Quan, with energy reaching front part of the *gun*.

6.121

## 6. *Che Bu Jiao Gun* (撤步绞棍; **Retreat-Stepping Stirring** *Gun*)

The left foot takes one half-step backward; the right foot then immediately retreats to the inside of the left foot, with the toes pointing forward. Simultaneously, the left hand rotates the wrist from outward to upward to pull the *gun* behind the body, while the right hand rotates the wrist from the left to upward, then rightward, to draw one clockwise circle with the *gun,* then it pulls the *gun* back to the front of the right chest. The two hands thus combine forces to move the *gun* in a circle and pull it back so the tip of the *gun* is at brow height. Eyes look to the front of the *gun* (picture 6.122).

PRINCIPLES

i. The retreat of the feet must be coordinated with the moving the *gun* in a circle and pulling it back. Not only do you move it in a circle and pull it back at the same time, there should also be a smashing energy within the circle.

ii. The turning of the left wrist and its pulling back is to enforce the right hand's moving the *gun* in a circle and smashing it; the two hands must be coordinated and utilize the yao power.

**6.122**

### 7. *Ti Xi Chuo Gun* (提膝戳棍; **Lift–Knee Stabbing *Gun***)

The right foot takes one step forward to the right; the left foot follows immediately with a knee lift to form a single-foot stand. Simultaneously, the right hand twists the *gun* inward and stabs it forward with the aid of a yao-shake, while the left hand twists the *gun* outward and pushes the *gun* forward; the two hands thus combine forces to twist and stab the *gun* forward at shoulder height. Eyes look to the front of the *gun* (picture 6.123).

PRINCIPLES

i. Issue power by shaking the yao, and focus on utilizing spiraling energy in the twisting stab.

ii. The knee lift and the *gun* stab must be coordinated.

6.123

## 8. *Fan Shen Ti Xi Pi Gun* (翻身提膝劈棍; **Twist and Turn–Around Lift-Knee Chopping *Gun*)**

1) The body turns to the left; the left foot takes one big step directly backward to form a left Bow Stance; the left hand pulls the *gun* toward the upper left, while right hand slides downward along the *gun* and turns the wrist to press the *gun* downward. Eyes look downward to the right (picture 6.124).

2) Do not pause. The right foot takes one Kou Bu toward the front of the left foot; the body turns around to the left; the left foot follows immediately with a knee lift. At the same time, the left arm straightens to pull the *gun* upward and backward to the left side of the yao as the body twists and turns around. The right hand slides downward along the *gun* then spins the *gun* once over right side of the head before chopping the *gun* forward and downward with lower end of the *gun* at the shoulder level. Eyes look to the tip of the *gun* (picture 6.125).

PRINCIPLES

i. The body's turning and the retreat stepping should be swift. Chopping with a knee lift must be forceful.

ii. In chopping the *gun,* utilize power from the yao-twist during the turning. The stability of the knee lift in the single-foot stand relies on pressing the knees inward toward each other.

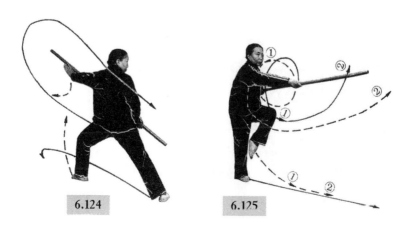

6.124                     6.125

### 9. *Jin Bu Pao Gun* (进步炮棍; **Forward–Stepping Cannon *Gun***)

The left foot lands forward. The right hand slides upward along the *gun* to *gua* the *gun* backward by the left side of the body. Simultaneous with the *gun's* rotation, the right hand slides downward along the *gun* and the left hand slides upward along the *gun;* the two hands have now switched positions. Without pausing, the right foot tang forward by one big step; the left foot follows immediately with a half-step forward to form a Cannon Fist Stance. Simultaneously, the right hand slides upward along the *gun* to twist the gun and lift it over the head, as the left hand stabs the *gun* forward and upward with tip of the *gun* at shoulder height. Eyes look to the front of the *gun* (picture 6.126).

PRINCIPLES

i. It is important to practice, in particular, the switch-hand *gun* rotation. In the form, the switch-hand *gun* rotation must be smooth and fast.

ii. In the Cannon *Gun,* the twisting and lifting upward of the right hand and the forward stabbing of the left hand have the same energy as in the *Pao Quan* (Cannon Fist); the two hands must be coordinated; the power must be forceful; the *gun* and foot must arrive simultaneously.

6.126

## 10. *Tui Bu Ti Xi Lun Gua Gun* (退步提膝抡挂棍; Backward-Stepping Lift-Knee *Lun Gua Gun*)

1) The body turns to the left; the left foot takes one big step backward to form a right Bow Stance. Simultaneously, the left hand slides upward along the *gun,* so that the upper part of the *gun* is close to the left side of the body, and lun gua with the *gun* once. In conjunction, the right hand drops down to the front of the chest to hold the *gun* at the opposite end. The left hand then pulls the *gun* backward to the front of the left kua. The *gun* is now higher in the front and lower in the back. Eyes look forward (picture 6.127).

2) Do not pause. The body turns to the right; the right foot steps backward to form a left Bow Stance. Simultaneously, the right hand pulls the *gun* to cover the retreating right leg, then lun gua with the *gun* once by the right side of the body; in conjunction, the left hand lifts the *gun* upward from the left side of the body to reinforce the power. Eyes look forward (picture 6.128).

3) Do not pause. The body weight shifts to the right leg; the left knee lifts upward to form a single-foot stand. Simultaneously, the right hand continues to gua the *gun* backward, then upward, crossing to the left side of the body to gua the *gun* backward; in conjunction, the left hand slides along the *gun* to draw it downward, backward, then upward and to the front of the right armpit. Eyes look downward to the left (picture 6.129).

| 6.127 | 6.128 | 6.129 |

4) Do not pause. The right hand draws the *gun* upward, passing in front of the body, to drop in front of the right leg. In conjunction, the left hand draws the *gun* downward, backward, then upward to the upper left-front of the body. Eyes look downward to the right (picture 6.130).

PRINCIPLES

   i. Lun gua with the *gun* with left and right backward steps are defense techniques; you must protect the leg by covering it with the *gun* as you step backward; the body and weapon must move with coordination.

   ii. The lifting of the knee and the gua of *gun* on the left should utilize power from twisting the yao and extending the arms. It must be executed with speed and agility.

**6.130**

## 11. *Shang Bu Zuan Gun* (上步钻棍; **Advance-Stepping Drilling *Gun*)**

Do not stop from the preceding movement. The left foot tang forward by one big step; the right foot follows immediately with a half-step forward to form a Cannon Fist Stance. The right hand twists the wrist outward to stab the *gun* upward and forward; the tip of the *gun* should not be higher than the shoulder. In conjunction, the left hand, holding the back of the *gun,* twists the wrist inward to tighten the hold and lifts the *gun* upward and forward, aiding the forward-stabbing and drilling force of the *gun*. The back of the *gun* is at about the height of the head. Eyes look to the front of the *gun* (picture 6.131).

PRINCIPLES

i. The drilling and stabbing of the *gun* and the forward stepping of the left foot must be coordinated; the foot and *gun* must arrive simultaneously. There should be a combination of pushing, grinding, drilling, and jabbing energies in the *gun*. The tip of the *gun* should be aligned with the direction of the left foot.

ii. This and the preceding movement (movement 10, Backward-Stepping Lift-Knee Lun Gua Gun) must be executed with continuity, without any pause between them.

**6.131**

## 12. *Jin Bu Deng Jiao Gua Pi Gun* (进步蹬脚挂劈棍; Forward-Stepping Kick-Heel *Gua Pi Gun*) / *Li Mao Shang Shu Gun* (狸猫上树棍; Leopard Cat Climbing Up the Tree *Gun*)

1) The body weight shifts forward, the left foot moves forward by one step, while the right leg bends at the knee and kicks forward with the heel. At the same time, the right hand slides downward along the *gun* and gua the *gun* downward, then backward, to the right side of the body, resting the hand by the right side of the yao. Following the same momentum, the left hand gai the *gun* forward from above, with the power reaching the rear end of the *gun*. Eyes look to the front of the *gun* (picture 6.132).

2) Do not pause. The right foot lands forward, with the toes swung outward; the left foot follows with a half-step forward. Simultaneously, the left hand pulls the *gun* downward and backward to under the right armpit. In conjunction, the right hand lifts the *gun* upward then chops it forward. The *gun* is at center chest height and pointing in the direction of the right foot. Eyes look to the front of the *gun* (picture 6.133).

PRINCIPLES

i. The heel-kick and the gai of the *gun* should be coordinated. The right-hand gua and left-hand gai of the *gun* are two opposing forces that reinforce each other; they must also utilize power from the yao twisting to the right.

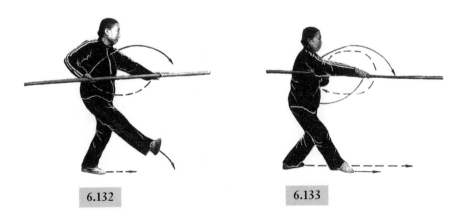

6.132                         6.133

ii. The landing of the right foot and the forward chopping of the *gun* must be swift and solid. The pulling back of the *gun* by the left hand and the chopping forward by the right hand are, again, two opposing forces that complement each other to create one holistic power.

### 13. *Jin Bu Beng Gun* (进步崩棍; **Forward-Stepping Smashing *Gun*)**

Do not pause from the preceding movement. The left foot tang forward by one big step; the right foot follows immediately with a forward step to form a left Smashing Fist Stance. Simultaneously, the yao twists to the left as the right hand pulls the *gun* backward to the left side of the body, and then it pushes it upward and forward with combined pushing, grinding, and smashing energies. In conjunction, the left hand slides downward along the *gun* and pulls it backward to press the hand and the *gun* tightly between the arm and the yao. The tip of the *gun* must be aligned with the left foot. Eyes look to the front of the *gun* (picture 6.134).

PRINCIPLES

i. Movement 12 (Forward-Stepping Kick-Heel *Gua* Pi Gun / Leopard Cat Climbing Up the Tree *Gun*) and this movement are like the *Yi Ma San Jian* (一马三箭; One Horse with Three Arrows) of Linking Fist—they must be executed with continuity and speed, which are the characteristics of Xingyi weapons.

ii. To facilitate the turning around in the next movement, keep a bigger distance between the two feet when the right foot follows the left foot's forward stepping.

**6.134**

## 14. *Hui Shen Deng Jiao Gua Pi Gun* (回身蹬脚挂劈棍; **Turn-Around with Heel-Kick *Gua Pi Gun*)** / *Li Mao Dao Shang Shu* (狸猫倒上树; **Leopard Cat Turns Around to Climb Up the Tree)**

1) The left foot hooks inward; the body turns around to the right side; the body weight shifts to the left leg to enable the right knee to lift up, then swing the toes outward to kick forward with the heel. As the body is turning, the right hand slides upward along the *gun* and *gua* the *gun* forward, then downward, then backward so that the end of the *gun* is on the right side of the body. In conjunction, the left hand gai the *gun* forward from above, with the palm facing downward. The front of the *gun* is at waist level. Eyes look to the front of the *gun* (picture 6.135).

2) Do not pause. The right foot lands forward, with the toes swung outward; the left foot follows immediately with a half-step forward. Simultaneously, the upper body twists to the left as right hand slides along the *gun* to chop it forward from above, while the left hand pulls the *gun* backward to under the right armpit and presses the hand and *gun* tightly against the armpit. The *gun* is level, pointing in the direction of the right foot. Eyes look to the front of the *gun* (picture 6.136).

PRINCIPLES

   i. The turning around to gai and gua the *gun* should be coordinated with the right foot's heel-kick; both must borrow power from twisting the yao.

6.135      6.136

ii. The landing of the right foot and the gua pi of the *gun* should bor-row power from the right heel-kick and the shaking of the yao to achieve a holistic power.

### 15. *Zhuan Shen Yun Pi Gun* (转身云劈棍; **Turn–Around** *Yun Pi Gun*) / *Yao Zhuan Pi Gun* (摇转劈棍; **Swing–Around Chopping** *Gun*)

1) The left foot steps past the inside of the right foot and hooks inward to land toward the left-front as the body turns to the left. The right hand, holding the *gun* with palm facing downward, parries the *gun* upward to the left. Eyes look upward to the left (picture 6.137).

2) Do not pause. The body continues to turn to the left; the right foot takes a Kou Bu toward the front of the left foot, so that toes of the two feet are pointing at each other. The left foot then takes a big step backward; simultaneously, the right foot also takes a half-step back-ward to form a Zhuang Bu. The body turns around with the Kou Bu as the right hand circles the *gun* past the left side of the head toward the back, then chops it forward. In conjunction, the left hand holds the *gun* and swings it from the right side of the body toward the left and to bring it to rest by the left abdomen. The tip of the *gun* should be at shoulder height, pointing in the direction of the right foot. Eyes look to the front of the *gun* (picture 6.138).

PRINCIPLES

i. The hands, body, and the weapon must all be coordinated in the yun pi.

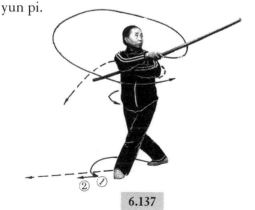

**6.137**

**6.138**

ii. Turning around with Kou Bu and Bai Bu must be swift and agile, allowing no hesitation between them.

iii. The *yun* of the *gun* should utilize energy generated from the turning of the body; issue power by the forward chopping of the *gun*.

## 16. *Jin Bu Ti Xi Ba Ti Gun* (进步提膝拔提棍; **Forward-Stepping Lift-Knee Pull-Up Gun**)/*Wu Long Jiao Shui* (乌龙搅水; **Black Dragon Stirring the Water**)

1) The right foot takes one step forward to form a right Bow Stance. Simultaneously, the upper body twists to the right, as the left hand holds the *gun* and pushes it upward, with the palm facing rightward and the tip of the *gun* level with the top of the head; in conjunction, the right hand slides along the *gun* and turns the wrist outward to pull the *gun* from above toward the right, then backward to rest by the right kua; the arm must squeeze tight; the hand grip must be firm. Eyes look to the tip of the *gun* (picture 6.139).

2) Do not pause. The left foot steps past the inside of the right foot to take one big step forward; the right knee then immediately lifts up to form a single-foot stand. At the same time, the right hand slides along the *gun* to lift it forward, then upward, so that the tip of the *gun* is at chest level. The left hand simultaneously pulls the *gun* upward toward the left side of the head to aid the lifting by the right hand. Eyes look to the tip of the *gun* (picture 6.140).

6.139                    6.140

PRINCIPLES

i. In stepping forward to lift the *gun* upward, it is important to twist the yao and swing the arm; the body and the *gun* must be coordinated.

ii. In the single-foot stand and the lifting of the *gun,* the movement must be stable; the body and feet must be coordinated.

iii. The two steps in this movement must be executed in smooth succession, without hesitation between them.

### 17. *Luo Bu Ao Ba Qian Pi Gun* (落步拗把前劈棍; Landing *Ao Ba* Forward-Chopping *Gun*)

This movement is a continuation of the preceding movement. The right foot lands forward, while the upper body twists to the right as the right hand slides downward along the *gun* to pull it past the right side of the body; then the right hand gua the *gun* backward and upward and chops it forward. In conjunction, the left hand holds the *gun* and swings it forward, downward, then rightward, and to press it tightly under the right armpit. The *gun* is now at center chest height. Eyes look to the tip of the *gun* (picture 6.141).

PRINCIPLE

This movement is an attack in defense, because the knee is lifted, leaving the lower body unprotected. Block an attack with a gua on the right, then attack with a forward chop. Hence, the landing of the foot and the forward chopping must be coordinated.

**6.141**

**18.** *Jin Bu Beng Gun* (进步崩棍; **Forward–Stepping Smashing** *Gun*)

This movement is identical to movement 13 above. In principle, this movement stays on the same spot to issue power. It is, again, important to keep a distance between the two feet when the right foot follows the left foot's forward stepping. This will facilitate the turning around in the following movement (picture 6.142).

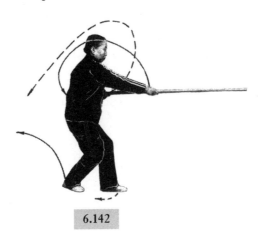

6.142

**19.** *Hui Shen Deng Jiao Gua Pi Gun* (回身蹬脚挂劈棍; **Turn-Around with Heel-Kick** *Gua Pi Gun*)/ *Li Mao Dao Shang Shu* (狸猫倒上树; **Leopard Cat Turns Around to Climb Up the Tree**)

This movement is identical to movement 14 above (pictures 6.143 and 6.144).

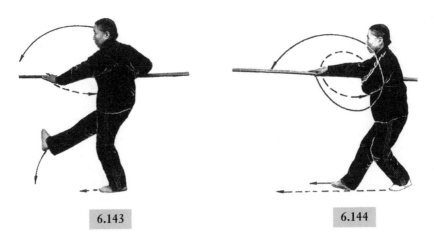

6.143                           6.144

## 20. *Jin Bu Beng Gun* (进步崩棍; **Forward–Stepping Smashing *Gun***)

This movement and its principles are identical to those of movement 18, except that one faces the opposite direction (picture 6.145).

Up until this point, the first half of the Linking Staff form is complete, and you may wrap up here. To complete the second half, continue with Backward-Stepping Smashing *Gun* and Diagonal Forward-Stepping Chopping *Gun,* which are identical to the movements in the first half, except facing the opposite direction. Then continue with movements up to movement 19 to turn around, follow with movement 20 (picture 6.146), and then proceed to the closing movements.

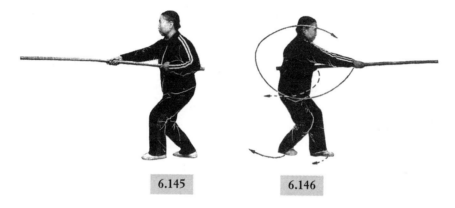

6.145                         6.146

### 21. *Shou Shi Zhi Yi* (收势之一; **Closing Stance Part 1**)/*Che Bu Wu Hua Shang Gia* (撤步舞花上架; **Retreat-Stepping Spinning Parry Upward**)

1) This movement is to follow movement 20 above. The body turns to the right as the left foot hooks the toes inward; the right foot takes one step backward with the toes swung outward to form a Bai Bu. Simultaneously, as the body turns, the right hand slides forward along the *gun* and spins it counter-clockwise in front of body to reach the left shoulder. In conjunction, the left hand gua the *gun* clockwise to the front of the right kua. The two hands thus gua the *gun* one vertical circle in front of the body. Eyes look past the *gun* on the left (picture 6.147).

2) Do not pause. The body continues to turn around to the right; the left foot takes one Kao Bu in front of the right foot so that toes of the two feet point at each other. Simultaneously, the right hand gua the *gun* clockwise once on the right side of body to reach outside of the right leg, while the left hand slides upward along the *gun* to raise the *gun* above the left shoulder. Eyes look to the lower end of the *gun* on the right (picture 6.148).

3) Do not pause. The body turns to the right as the right foot takes one backward step behind the left foot to form a Zhuang Bu. Following the body's turning around, the right hand lifts the *gun* upward to the front of the right shoulder, while the left hand presses the *gun* downward to the front of the left knee. Eyes look to the left front (picture 6.149).

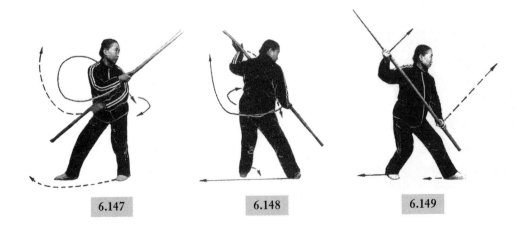

6.147      6.148      6.149

4) Do not pause. Borrowing the momentum from the left foot's backward *deng* and the body shifting backward, both feet retreat and land synchronously to form a *San Ti Shi*. Simultaneously, both hands hold the *gun* and push it forward and upward to above the head. Eyes look forward (picture 6.150).

6.150

PRINCIPLES

i. In turning the body around with backward stepping, both the stepping and the body movement must be agile and natural; the body and weapon must move together.

ii. When both feet retreat at the same time to form the San Ti Shi and push the *gun* upward, there should be a rubbing energy in the retreat stepping. The whole body must move as one; the feet and the *gun* must arrive at the same time.

iii. The entire movement must be executed with continuity; the requirements for each step must be fulfilled, yet without hesitation between them.

## 22. *Shou Shi Zhi Er* (收势之二; Closing Stance Part 2)

1) The left foot hooks the ball of the foot inward; the body weight shifts to the left leg to form a sideways Bow Stance; both hands hold the *gun* and allow it to drop upright by the left side of the body; the right foot comes together with the left foot. At the same time, the body turns to the right as the right hand releases the *gun* and changes into a palm to draw a circle by first dropping in front of the body, then drawing rightward, then upward, then leftward to come down as a standup palm and rest by the inside of the left arm. Eyes look to the left (picture 6.151).

2) Do not pause. The head turns to look forward as the right palm drops to rest by the outside of the right thigh (picture 6.152).

6.151     6.152

# Xingyi Lian Huan Qiang
## (形意连环枪; Xingyi Linking Spear)
N<small>AMES OF THE</small> M<small>OVEMENTS</small>
<small>IN</small> X<small>INGYI</small> L<small>IAN</small> H<small>UAN</small> Q<small>IANG</small>

1) *Yu Bei Shi* (预备式; Preparation Stance)

2) *Zhuang Bu Quan Qiang Shi* (桩步圈枪势; Zhuang Bu Circling *Qiang* Stance)

3) *Jin Bu Beng, Kou, Zha Qiang* (进步崩,扣,扎枪; Forward-Stepping Smashing, Hooking, Stabbing *Qiang*)

4) *Tui Bu Shang Beng Qiang* (退步上崩枪; Backward-Stepping Upward-Smashing *Qiang*)

5) *Qian Jin Cha Bu Fan Zha Qiang* (前进插步反扎枪; Forward-Stepping Cross-Feet Reverse-Stabbing *Qiang*)

6) *Jin Bu Zha Qiang* (进步扎枪; Forward-Stepping Stabbing *Qiang*) / *Jin Bu You Beng Qiang* (进步右崩枪; Forward-Stepping Right-Smashing *Qiang*)

7) *Tui Bu Shang Tiao Qiang* (退步上挑枪; Backward-Stepping Upward-Lifting *Qiang*) / *Tai Gong Diao Yu* (太公釣鱼; *Tai Gong Fishing*)

8) *Zhi Li Dian Qiang* (直立点枪; Stand Upright Pointing *Qiang*)

9) *Xie Jin Bu You Pao Qiang* (斜进步右炮枪; Diagonal Forward-Stepping Right Cannon *Qiang*)

10) *Heng Kua Bu Zuo Heng Qiang* (横跨步左横枪; Sideways-Stepping Left-Crossing *Qiang*)

11) *Li Mao Shang Shu Qiang* (狸猫上树枪; Leopard Cat Climbing Up the Tree Qiang)

12) *Quan Qiang Jin Bu Zha Qiang* (圈枪进步扎枪; Circling Qiang Forward-Stepping Stabbing *Qiang*) / *Jin Bu You Beng Qiang* (进步右崩枪; Forward-Stepping Right-Smashing *Qiang*)

13) *Zuo Che Bu Quan Ti Qiang* (左撤步圈提枪; Left Retreat-Stepping Circling and Up-Lifting *Qiang*)

14) *Zuo Hu Xing Bu Dao Ba* (左弧行步倒把; Left Curved-Stepping Handle-Swap)

15) *Jin Bu Zha Qiang* (进步扎枪; Forward-Stepping Stabbing *Qiang*) / *Jin Bu You Beng Qiang* (进步右崩枪; Forward-Stepping Right-Smashing *Qiang*)

16) *You Che Bu Quan Ti Qiang* (右撤步圈提枪; Right Retreat-Stepping Circling and Up-Lifting *Qiang*)

17) *You Hu Xing Bu Dao Ba* (右弧行步倒把; Right Curved-Stepping Handle-Swap)

18) *Jin Bu Zha Qiang* (进步扎枪; Forward-Stepping Stabbing *Qiang*) / *Jin Bu You Beng Qiang* (进步右崩枪; Forward-Stepping Right-Smashing *Qiang*)

19) *Hui Shen Shang Bu Pi Qiang* (回身上步劈枪; Turn-Around Advance-Stepping Chopping *Qiang*)

20) *Jin Bu Beng, Kou, Zha Qiang* (进步崩,扣,扎枪; Forward-Stepping Smashing, Hooking, Stabbing *Qiang*)

21) *Che Bu Hui Shen Wu Hua Jia Qiang* (撤步回身舞花架枪; Retreat-Stepping Turn-Around Spinning Parry *Qiang*)

22) *Shou Shi* (收势; Closing Stance)

## EXPLANATIONS FOR THE MOVEMENTS IN XINGYI LIAN HUAN QIANG

### 1. *Yu Bei Shi* (预备式; Preparation Stance)

1) Stand up straight with feet together. Head is erect; chin is slightly tucked back; jaws are closed tight; tip of the tongue is placed against the upper palate. Shoulders and elbows are dropped; qi is sunk to Dantian. Relax the entire body. The right hand is dropped by the right side of the body with the fingers naturally together. The left hand holds the qiang, which stands upright by the left side of the body. Eyes look forward (picture 6.153).

**6.153**

6.154

2) The right hand lifts upward, with the palm facing upward, then turns leftward, passing in front of the face and the left shoulder to press on the front of the left armpit; the palm is diagonally facing downward. Eyes follow the right hand to finally look leftward (picture 6.154).

3) The left arm bends and lifts the qiang upward. The right hand slides along the qiang to hold the qiang by the end. The left hand then slides downward along the qiang toward the front. The right hand pushes the qiang forward from the end so that the qiang and the arms form a straight line with the tip of the qiang pointing at the ground. Simultaneously, both feet turn 90° to the left, with the feet together. Eyes look to the tip of the qiang (picture 6.155).

4) The body weight shifts backward, and the body turns to the right. The right foot takes one step backward to form a Zhuang Bu. Simultaneously, the right palm drops in front of the body, then swings rightward, then upward, to over the right side of the head. Shake the wrist to turn the palm upward, with the fingers pointing forward. The left hand holds the qiang and does not move; the elbow is slightly sunk. Eyes look forward (picture 6.156).

PRINCIPLE
Swinging the arm, turning the body, holding the qiang with two hands, and swinging the palm upward, with backward stepping, must all be relaxed and natural, yet with focus and shen in the eyes.

6.155                              6.156

## 2. *Zhuang Bu Quan Qiang Shi* (桩步圈枪势; *Zhuang Bu* Circling *Qiang* Stance)

The right palm drops to take hold of the qiang. The left hand slides along the qiang with a loose hold. Subsequently, the right wrist maintains contact with the yao as it twists outward to pull the qiang backward; both the hand and the qiang must press close to the body. Simultaneous with the pull-back, the right hand combines force with the left wrist, turning inward to draw a clockwise vertical circle with tip of the qiang, ending with the qiang lying horizontally flat with Zhuang Bu. Eyes look forward (picture 6.157).

PRINCIPLES

i. The right hand's pulling back and left hand's sliding along the qiang must both utilize the yao power to twist the qiang. In circling the qiang, both hands must combine forces. The movement must be swift yet natural.

ii. The circle drawn by twisting the qiang must be a vertical circle of over a third of a meter in diameter. Power must permeate to the front tip of the qiang.

6.157

### 3. *Jin Bu Beng, Kou, Zha Qiang* (进步崩,扣,扎枪; Forward-Stepping Smashing, Hooking, Stabbing *Qiang*)

1) The right foot steps past the inside of the left foot to take one forward step. Simultaneously, the left wrist turns outward to point the tip of the qiang downward, rightward, upward, then leftward to draw a counterclockwise circle with smashing energy; at the same time, keep the qiang in contact with the body and pull it backward until the arm is bent, with the upper arm pressing on the body; the palm is facing upward and to the left. The right hand turns the wrist upward as it pulls the qiang backward; the palm is facing down, but slightly outward. Eyes look to the tip of the qiang (picture 6.158).

2) Do not pause. The left foot steps past the inside of the right foot to take one forward step, forming a Zhuang Bu. At the same time, the right hand rotates the wrist inward to push the qiang forward. The left hand kou the wrist inward to press the qiang forward and downward. With the combined force of two hands twisting the qiang, draw a vertical circle, by pointing the qiang tip downward, then leftward, then upward, then rightward, to form the Zhuang Bu Hooking Qiang Stance. Eyes look to the tip of the qiang (picture 6.159).

6.158     6.159

3) Do not pause. The right foot steps forward to form a Smashing Fist Stance. Simultaneously, the body turns to the left. The right hand pushes the qiang forward by shaking the yao so the qiang stabs outward with power. Both arms must be extended; the qiang must be level at center chest height (this is referred to as the Forward-Stepping Smashing Qiang). Eyes look forward (picture 6.160).

## PRINCIPLES

  i. Each of the smashing, hooking, and stabbing components of the movement must be continuous; utilize the yao power to complete in one breath.

  ii. The forward stepping must be swift; the landing must be firm. When executing the smashing, hooking, and stabbing movements, the body and the qiang must be coordinated; hands and feet must also be coordinated.

  iii. When executing the smashing, hooking, and stabbing components, it's important not only to utilize the yao power but also to incorporate the explosive power of pulling, pushing, and wrist-twisting.

**6.160**

### 4. *Tui Bu Shang Beng Qiang* (退步上崩枪; **Backward-Stepping Upward-Smashing Qiang**)

Continue from the preceding movement. The body weight shifts backward. Both hands holding the qiang drop slightly. The right foot retreats by one big step; the left foot follows immediately by dragging backward past the inside of the left foot, then it lands abruptly, with jamming energy, thus forming the Retreat-Stepping Smashing Fist Stance. As the left foot is retreating, the right hand borrows the retreating momentum to pull and push the qiang to the right side of the kua. With the left foot's landing momentum and the right hand's pull-and-push momentum, the left hand slides upward along the qiang to take hold and smash the qiang upward; power should permeate to the front of the qiang. This is the Retreat-Stepping Upward-Smashing Qiang Stance. Eyes look to the tip of the qiang (picture 6.161).

PRINCIPLES

i. The left foot's retreat, the right hand's pull and push, and the left hand's smashing the qiang upward must all utilize the yao power; practice until you're able to achieve a coordinated and holistic power.

ii. As in Retreat-Stepping Smashing Fist, it is essential to be able to issue power in retreat-stepping qiang so as to exemplify the "attack when advancing; also attack when retreating" characteristic. The more explosive the power, the better.

6.161

## 5. *Qian Jin Cha Bu Fan Zha Qiang* (前进插步反扎枪; Forward-Stepping Cross-Feet Reverse-Stabbing Qiang)

1) The right foot steps forward by half a step; the left foot takes one forward step, passing inside of the right foot, and lands directly in front of the right foot with the toes hooked inward. Simultaneously, the right hand maintains the qiang's contact with the body as it pulls the qiang upward, leftward, downward, then backward, then continues to twist the wrist outward to lift the qiang up over the right shoulder. Also simultaneously, the left hand rotates the wrist downward, rightward, and outward to stir the qiang toward the lower-right direction; tip of qiang is no lower than the knee. Eyes look forward (picture 6.162).

2) Do not pause. The right foot takes one cross step behind the right foot. Simultaneously, the left hand slides along the qiang to hold it upward. The body twists to the left; the right hand rotates the wrist inward to reverse-stab the qiang forward from right-front side of the head; the curve of the small finger is facing upward. The qiang is level and no higher than brow height. Eyes look to the tip of the qiang (picture 6.163).

PRINCIPLES

i. Stirring the qiang must be coordinated with the left foot's forward hooked-in stepping. Stabbing the qiang forward should be coordinated with the right foot's cross stepping. The body and the qiang must move as one.

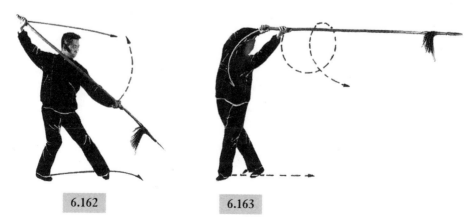

| 6.162 | 6.163 |

ii. The two steps in this movement are continuous; do not pause between them. The stepping must be agile, with power; the stabbing must be forceful.

## 6. *Jin Bu Zha Qiang* (进步扎枪; **Forward-Stepping Stabbing Qiang**) / *Jin Bu You Beng Qiang* (进步右崩枪; **Forward-Stepping Right-Smashing Qiang**)

1) Do not pause from the preceding movement. The left foot takes one forward step to form a Zhuang Bu. Simultaneously, the right wrist twists inward to pull the qiang downward and press it tightly against the yao; the left hand guides the qiang tip downward, then leftward, then upward, to finally kou the qiang downward. Thus, both hands together circle and kou the qiang by combining the force of backward pull and downward press, and form the Zhuang Bu Kou Qiang Stance. Eyes look to the tip of the qiang (picture 6.164).

  2) Do not pause. The right foot follows with a forward step to form the Smashing Fist Stance. Simultaneously, with a left-twist of the waist, the right hand forcefully stabs the qiang forward; the qiang is level at center chest height. Eyes look forward (picture 6.165).

PRINCIPLES

  i. In step 1, the left foot's forward stepping, the right hand's backward pull, and the left hand's downward kou must fully exploit the holistic power of circling qiang and yao-twist.

  ii. In step 2, the foot and the qiang must arrive simultaneously. Be forceful, so that power reaches the tip of the qiang.

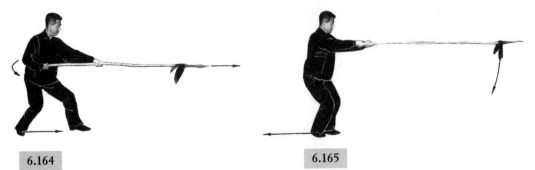

6.164                                    6.165

## 7. *Tui Bu Shang Tiao Qiang* (退步上挑枪; **Backward–Stepping Upward–Lifting Qiang**) / *Tai Gong Diao Yu* (太公釣鱼; *Tai Gong* **Fishing**)

1) The right foot takes one big step backward to form a left Gong Bu. Both hands hold the qiang to let the tip drop slightly. Eyes look to the tip of the qiang (picture 6.166).

2) Do not pause. The left foot immediately takes one retreating step; the body squats slightly; the heel touches the inside of the right ankle; the toes point forward. Simultaneously, the right hand pulls and presses the qiang downward to the outside of the right upper leg. The left hand slides along the qiang to tiao it upward; the tip of qiang is slightly over the head. The Fishing Stance is formed. Eyes look forward (picture 6.167).

PRINCIPLES

i. When stepping back with the right foot, open the stepping to form a left Bow Stance; but do not pause, so as to reinforce the power in the tiao of the qiang. The two hands holding the qiang and pressing downward is to gather power and wait to issue; power must be contained.

ii. The tiao qiang in the Fishing Stance should utilize the momentum from squatting the body, twisting the yao, and the combined force from both hands to issue power. Hence, the tiao qiang and the left foot's retreat stepping must be synchronized.

6.166

6.167

**8. *Zhi Li Dian Qiang* (直立点枪; Stand Upright Pointing *Qiang*)**

Continue from the preceding movement. The stance does not change; both legs deng and straighten to stand up. Simultaneously, the right hand turns the wrist inward to push forward while quickly lifting the qiang upward to the front of the head. Use the left hand to hold up the qiang, and use it as a leverage to point the qiang tip forward and downward swiftly. Eyes look to the tip of the qiang (picture 6.168).

6.168

PRINCIPLE

The two legs stand up by bouncing on the heels; the movement must be swift in order to aid the forward-pushing, upward-lifting, and downward-pointing power. The movement must be coordinated; the power must be holistic. Be swift. Power should reach tip of the qiang.

**9. *Xie Jin Bu You Pao Qiang* (斜进步右炮枪; Diagonal Forward-Stepping Right Cannon *Qiang*)**

1) The body weight shifts downward; the left foot takes one step forward toward the front of the right foot. Simultaneously, the right hand pulls the qiang downward along the inside of the left arm to under the left elbow. At the same time, the left hand, holding the qiang, draws a curve toward the lower right before lifting it upward. Thus, both hands combine forces to stir the qiang in a left-to-right downward curve before

lifting it upward, with the tip of the qiang slightly over the head. Eyes look forward (picture 6.169).

2) Do not pause. The right foot tang forward by one big step in the diagonal right direction. The left foot follows immediately with a forward half-step to form a Cannon Fist Stance. Simultaneously, the body twists to the right; both hands hold the qiang to go downward, then upward toward the upper right to issue Pao Quan power; the qiang is level and no higher than the brows. Eyes look to the tip of the qiang (picture 6.170).

PRINCIPLES

i. Step 1 is done to gather power and wait to issue. The movement must be coordinated. The power must be contained.

ii. In extending the qiang upward to the right, borrow momentum from turning the qiang and twisting the yao. The foot and the qiang must arrive at the same time. Power must be swift and forceful, with explosive energy permeating to the tip of the qiang.

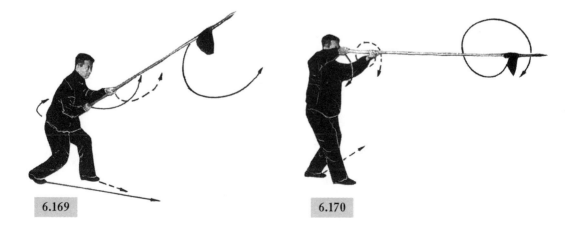

6.169                                           6.170

## 10. *Heng Kua Bu Zuo Heng Qiang* (横跨步左横枪; Sideways-Stepping Left-Crossing Qiang)

1) The left foot takes one step to the left. Simultaneously, the left hand holds the qiang and hooks in the wrist, while right hand holds the qiang and twists the wrist inward; both hands hold the qiang to make a lower-left-to-right [clockwise] circle, ending with the left hand at chest height while the right hand is under the inside of the left elbow, so that the tip of qiang draws a downward-then-leftward-then-upward-then-rightward [clockwise] circle to finally kou the qiang; the tip of the qiang is level with the head. Eyes look to the tip of the qiang (picture 6.171).

2) Do not pause. The right foot takes one step to the left, behind the left foot, to form the Zhuang Bu. Simultaneously, the body turns to the left; both hands combine forces to strike the qiang across to the left; qiang is at shoulder height. Eyes look to the tip of the qiang (picture 6.172).

PRINCIPLES

  i. In step 1, the hands and foot movement must be coordinated. After drawing the circle with the qiang, gather power within and wait to issue.

 ii. In step 2, the hand and foot movement must be coordinated and completed at the same time. The cross striking must be swift and explosive, with power reaching tip of the qiang.

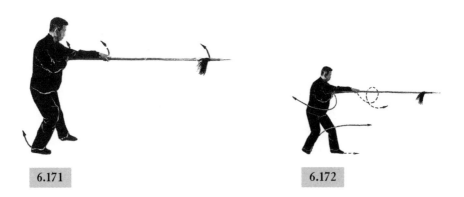

6.171                 6.172

## 11. *Li Mao Shang Shu Qiang* (狸猫上树枪; **Leopard Cat Climbing Up the Tree** *Qiang*)

1) The left foot takes one half-step forward; the body twists to the right; the right foot lifts up immediately, with the toes swinging outward, and kicks forward with the heel. Simultaneously, the right hand turns the wrist inward and pulls the qiang backward from the yao; in conjunction, the left hand turns the wrist outward and also pulls the qiang backward so that tip of the qiang circles counter-clockwise once, from the lower left toward the right. The qiang is level, at center chest height. Eyes look forward (picture 6.173).

2) Do not pause. The right foot lands forward swiftly; the left foot follows immediately, with one half-step forward; the two legs press tightly together, with the left knee pressing against the back of the right knee. Simultaneously, the left hand slides along the shaft to lift the qiang upward as body twists slightly toward the left. The right hand reverse-stabs the qiang forward with force from above the right shoulder; the qiang is at eye level. Eyes look to the tip of the qiang (picture 6.174).

PRINCIPLES

   i. The kick of the left foot must be swift and forceful and must be coordinated with the pullback of the qiang.

   ii. The right foot's landing and the qiang's forward stabbing must also be coordinated. The stabbing must be swift and with explosive power.

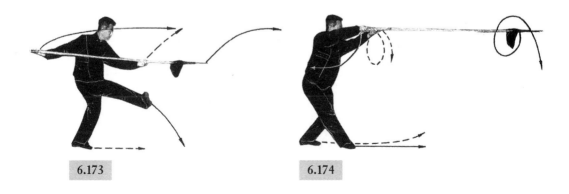

6.173          6.174

### 12. *Quan Qiang Jin Bu Zha Qiang* (圈枪进步扎枪; Circling *Qiang* Forward-Stepping Stabbing *Qiang*)/*Jin Bu You Beng Qiang* (进步右崩枪; Forward-Stepping Right-Smashing *Qiang*)

1) Do not pause from the preceding movement. The right foot steps forward by half-step; the left foot follows immediately to form a left lift step. Simultaneously, the right hand twists the wrist outward and pulls the qiang back to the right side of the yao; the left hand hooks in the wrist so that the qiang circles [clockwise] once from the lower left to the upper right before pressing it downward to form the *Ti Bu Kou Qiang Shi* (提步扣抢势; Lift Step *Kou Qiang* Stance). Eyes look forward (picture 6.175).

2) Do not pause. The left foot tang forward by one big step; the right foot follows immediately with a forward step to form a left Smashing Fist Stance. Simultaneously, the right hand turns the wrist inward and, with a left-twist of the yao, forcefully stabs the qiang forward; the qiang is level at center chest height. Eyes look forward (picture 6.176).

PRINCIPLES

  i. In both steps, the body and the qiang must be coordinated; the power must be holistic. The forward stabbing must be swift and forceful, fully exploiting the power of twisting and shaking the yao.

  ii. Movements 11 and 12 must be continuous and executed with power that's beyond counter.

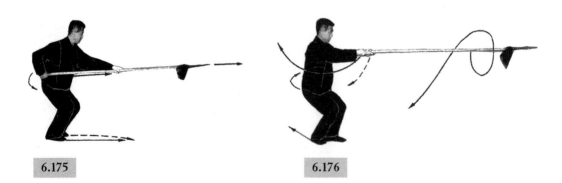

6.175                              6.176

### 13. *Zuo Che Bu Quan Ti Qiang* (左撤步圈提枪; Left Retreat-Stepping Circling and Lifting *Qiang*)

1) The body turns to the right; the right foot retreats by one big step behind the body, toward the left, to form a left Bow Stance. Simultaneously, the right hand twists the wrist outward to pull the qiang, by the end of the qiang and in contact with the body, past the yao, then upward to behind the body over the right shoulder, with the right arm fully extended. Also simultaneously, the left hand slides along the qiang toward the front and makes the qiang circle [counter-clockwise] once from the lower right toward the upper left before going downward toward the lower right. Eyes look to the tip of the qiang (picture 6.177).

2) Do not pause. The body weight shifts backward and the body turns to the right; the left knee lifts upward to form a single-foot stand. Simultaneously, the left arm lifts the qiang upward so that the left arm is pressed tightly against the left upper chest; the tip of the qiang is on the outside of the left knee. At the same time, right hand slides along to the middle of the qiang to lift it over the right side of the head with the arm fully extended. Eyes look downward to the left (picture 6.178).

PRINCIPLE

The two steps in this movement are linked movements; there should not be any pause between the two steps. The yao must be facing forward; the kua must be agile, so that circling of the qiang is soft and flexible. Utilize body movement fully to achieve body-qiang coordination, and be relaxed and natural at the same time.

6.177

6.178

### 14. *Zuo Hu Xing Bu Dao Ba* (左弧行步倒把; Left Curved-Stepping Handle-Swap)

1) Continue from the preceding movement. The body twists to the left, the left foot swings outward and steps toward the left front to form a Bai Bu. The hands, holding the qiang, do not change. Eyes look downward to the left (picture 6.179).

2) Do not pause. The body turns to the left; the right foot takes one curved forward step toward front of the left foot, with the toes hooked inward so that the two feet now point diagonally at each other. The hands, holding the qiang, do not change. Eyes look to the lower left (picture 6.180).

3) Do not pause. The body continues to turn to the left; the left foot swings outward and takes one curved step toward the left front to form a Bai Bu. The hands, holding the qiang, do not change. Eyes look to the lower left (picture 6.181).

4) Do not pause. The body continues to turn to the left; the right foot takes one curved step toward front of the left foot; the toes are hooked inward so that the two feet are pointing diagonally at each other. The hands, holding the qiang, do not change. Eyes look to the lower left (picture 6.182).

6.179                    6.180                    6.181

5) Do not pause. The body continues to turn to the left; the left foot takes a half-step forward toward the left, with toes pointing forward to form a Zhuang Bu. At this point, a curved-stepping turning around is completed; the stepping should be in the direction of the original form. Simultaneously, both hands pierce and lift the qiang so that the tip of the qiang draws upward, passing in front of the body, then backward; when tip of the qiang passes in front of the body, the left hand slides downward along the qiang, while the right hand moves upward over the qiang to complete a Forward-Stepping Handle-Swap. Eyes look to the tip of the qiang behind the body (picture 6.183).

PRINCIPLES

i. The stepping in this movement are the curved Bai Bu and Kou Bu to complete one turn around; the stepping must be swift and natural; the body must not rise. The feet must step to the right position so that the turn around takes you back to the starting position.

ii. There must not be any pause between the steps. Maintain the same center of gravity in the stepping.

iii. In changing the qiang's direction by switching the positions of the hands on the qiang, the movement must be natural, swift, and coordinated with the left foot's stepping.

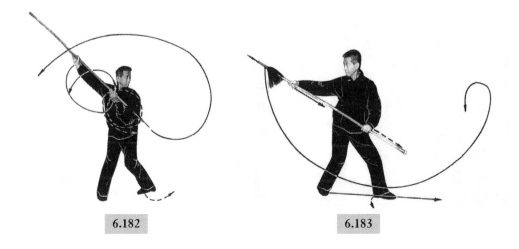

6.182                                    6.183

### 15. *Jin Bu Zha Qiang* (进步扎枪; **Forward-Stepping Stabbing** *Qiang*) / *Jin Bu You Beng Qiang* (进步右崩枪; **Forward-Stepping Right-Smashing** *Qiang*)

1) Do not pause from the preceding movement. The right foot steps forward, passing the inside of the left foot, to form a Zhuang Bu. Simultaneously, while keeping the qiang in contact with the outside of the right leg, both hands pull the qiang to the front of the body; the left hand then slides to the end of the qiang and rotates the wrist inward to drop and press by the yao, while the right hand rotates the wrist counterclockwise so that tip of the qiang draws one vertical circle, thus forming the Zhuang Bu Kou Qiang Stance. Eyes look forward (picture 6.184).

2) Do not pause. The left foot follows immediately with a forward step to form a Smashing Fist Stance. Simultaneously, the body twists to the right as the left hand holds the the qiang and stabs it forward, with force, forming a right Forward-Stepping Stabbing Qiang Stance; the qiang is level at center chest height. Eyes look forward (picture 6.185).

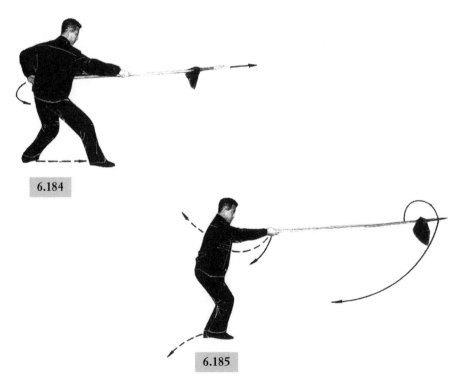

6.184

6.185

PRINCIPLES

  i. In step 1, the body and the qiang must be coordinated, with the qiang and the foot arriving at the same time.

 ii. When stabbing the qiang forward, utilize momentum of the body's turning and the yao-twist; be swift and forceful, with power permeating to the tip of the qiang.

iii. Utilize the curved-stepping momentum to make the movements continuous; do not pause between them.

## 16. *You Che Bu Quan Ti Qiang* (右撤步圈提枪; **Right Retreat-Stepping Circling and Up-Lifting *Qiang***)

The movement description and principles are the same as for movement 13 above, except the left and right are reversed (pictures 6.186 and 6.187).

**6.186**          **6.187**

## 17. *You Hu Xing Bu Dao Ba* (右弧行步倒把; **Right Curved-Stepping Handle-Swap)**

The movement description and principles are the same as for movement 14 above, except the left and right are reversed (pictures 6.188 through 6.192).

6.188          6.189          6.190

6.191                    6.192

## 18. *Jin Bu Zha Qiang* (进步扎枪; **Forward-Stepping Stabbing Qiang**) / *Jin Bu You Beng Qiang* (进步右崩枪; **Forward-Stepping Right-Smashing Qiang**)

The movement description and principles are the same as for movement 15 above, except the left and right are reversed (pictures 6.193 and 6.194).

6.193

6.194

**19.** *Hui Shen Shang Bu Pi Qiang* (回身上步劈枪;
**Turn–Around Advance-Stepping Chopping** *Qiang*)

1) The body turns to the right; the right foot follows immediately with a backward step; the left foot hooks the toes inward as the body turns around, thus forming a Zhuang Bu. Simultaneously, the right hand twists the palm outward to pull the qiang over the right side of the head to above and behind the right shoulder, while the left hand slides along the qiang and drops to behind the left kua, with the palm facing outward. Eyes look to the front of the [right-hand] position (picture 6.195).

2) Do not pause. The body turns to the right; the left foot moves past the inside of the right foot to take one forward step to form a Zhuang Bu. Simultaneously, the right hand grabs the qiang and presses it tightly against the front of the right kua; in conjunction, the left hand flips the qiang past the left side of the head and slides along the qiang to chop it downward; the qiang is at kua level. Eyes look to the front of the qiang (picture 6.196).

PRINCIPLES

    i. In step 1, the body and the qiang must be coordinated; the movement must be natural; gather energy and wait to issue.

   ii. In step 2, the qiang and the foot must arrive at the same time. Borrow the momentum of body's turning, yao-twisting, arm swinging, and sliding down the qiang to chop the qiang forward; furthermore, it's important to tighten the hold when the qiang arrives at the target so as to issue power.

6.195

6.196

## 20. *Jin Bu Beng, Kou, Zha Qiang* (进步崩,扣,扎枪; Forward–Stepping Smashing, Hooking, Stabbing *Qiang*)

The movement description and principles are the same as for movement 3 above, except the direction is reversed.

Up to this point, the first half of Linking Qiang and turn-around is complete. To complete the second half, continue with movement 4, movement 5, and so forth, up to the starting position and turn around, and continue with movement 3, then proceed to the closing movement. For now, practice up to the starting position, turn around, and continue with movement 20 (picture 6.197), then proceed to the transitional movement of the closing movement.

**6.197**

## 21. *Che Bu Hui Shen Wu Hua Jia Qiang* (撤步回身舞花架枪; Retreat-Stepping Turn-Around Spinning Parry *Qiang*)

1) The body turns to the right; the right foot immediately takes one backward step; the left foot hooks the toes inward to form a Zhuang Bu. Simultaneously, the right hand twists the palm outward as it pulls the qiang upward and backward to above the right side of the right shoulder; the left hand slides along the qiang as it drops behind the left kua, with the palm facing outward. Eyes look to the front of the right hand (picture 6.198).

2) Do not pause. The body weight shifts forward to the right foot; continue to turn to the right; the left foot takes one forward Kou Bu past the front of the right foot. Simultaneously, the left hand holds on near the qiang tip and spins it over the head and brings it down on the left side of the body; in conjunction, the right hand slides along the qiang as it sinks downward to rest under the left armpit; thus, the qiang has now passed around once behind the body. Eyes look to the tip of the qiang (picture 6.199).

3) Do not pause. The body continues to turn to the right; the left hand borrows the downward-spin momentum to gua the qiang in front of the body toward the right (picture 6.200).

4) Do not pause. The body continues to turn 180° to the right; the body weight quickly shifts backward to the left foot; the right foot

6.198                                    6.199

immediately retreats in a straight line behind the left foot; the retreating step must be long, by utilizing the left foot's backward deng momentum. As soon as the right foot lands, the left foot also retreats one half-step to form a Zhuang Bu. Borrowing the momentum of the retreat-stepping and turning-around, the right hand slides along the qiang and lun gua the qiang downward, rightward, upward, then backward to the top of the right shoulder. Simultaneously, in conjunction with the right-hand lun gua, the left hand slides along the qiang to point the qiang tip upward, leftward, downward, then rightward so that the tip of the qiang is lifted upward and pushed outward; the qiang is over the head, with the tip lower than the rear. Eyes look forward (picture 6.201).

PRINCIPLES

   i. In this retreat-stepping turn-around spinning qiang, the Kou Bu and Bai Bu must be natural, coordinated, and swift. The body weight must be centered; the hands must be agile. The body and stepping must be coordinated. The spins of the qiang must be verti- cal circles.

  ii. The retreat stepping, the spinning the qiang, the left foot's back- ward deng, the abrupt shifting of the feet, and the solid landing all must be coordinated with the lifting of the qiang to achieve a holistic power.

6.200        6.201

### 22. *Shou Shi* (收势; **Closing Stance**)

1) The left toes hook in by 90°; the body weight shifts to the left leg. Simultaneously, right hand slides along the qiang to push it toward the outside of the left foot before resting just below the left hand; the left hand also drops to the left side of the body. The qiang now stands upright by the outside of the left toes. Eyes look to the qiang (picture 6.202).

2) Do not pause. The right foot moves to be next to the left foot; the body stands up straight. At the same time, the right hand opens to a palm to touch the front of the body, then swings downward, rightward, and then upward to draw half a circle, ending with the palm facing upward at the top the head; then it continues to draw the circle, passing in front of the face to finally rest in front of the left ribs, with the palm facing downward. Eyes follow the hand movement and finally look toward the left (picture 6.203).

3) The right palm drops naturally to press on the right thigh as the head turns to the right to look forward (picture 6.204).

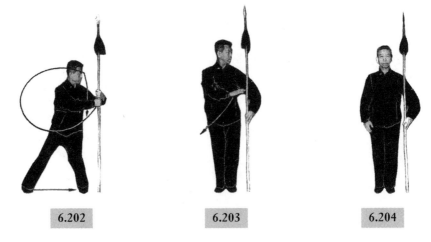

6.202          6.203          6.204

| Pin Yin | Chinese | English Translation/Explanation |
|---------|---------|--------------------------------|
| *Ao Bu* | 拗步 | A stance in which the left hand and right leg are in front while the right hand and left leg are in the back; or vice versa |
| *Bai Bu* | 摆步 | A forward stepping in which the front foot swings outward |
| *Dantian* | 丹田 | Field of elixir: about three inches below the navel |
| *Dao Bei* | 刀背 | Back of a dao, or dull side of a dao |
| *Deng* | 蹬 | Press on the heel of one or both feet to create a springing forward force |
| *Deng Jing* | 蹬劲 | Energy coming from deng |
| *Gai* | 盖 | Swing a palm or a weapon over the head in a curved path to chop downward |
| *Gua* | 挂 | Draw a curve with the tip of the weapon by pointing downward, backward, then upward and forward |
| *Hukou* | 虎口 | Tiger Mouth; the curved area between the thumb and the index finger |
| *Jing* | 劲 | Force |
| *Jian Finger* | 剑指 | With the hand that is not holding the sword, we form a jian finger by pressing the thumb over the ring finge and the pinky; while the middle finger and the index finger are held together. The function of jian finger is to keep balance with the other hand. |

| Pin Yin | Chinese | English Translation/Explanation |
| --- | --- | --- |
| *Kou* | 扣 | Hook; grab with the palm facing downward |
| *Kou Bu* | 扣步 | T-step |
| *Kua* | 胯 | The combination of the groin and the pelvis area |
| *Lao Gong* | 劳宫 | A point in the Pericardian channel that is located at the point, when you make a fist, where the mid-fingertip touches the palm |
| *Lun Gua* | 抡挂 | To draw a vertical circle, in the backward direction, with the tip of the weapon |
| *Lv* | 将 | To brush against the back of the dao |
| *Mai Men* | 脉门 | Gate of pulse: area near the base of the palm where Chinese medical doctors examine the pulse to diagnose the patient condition |
| *Ni Wan* | 泥丸 | An acupuncture point; Mud Pill Palace in Qigong practice, residing in the Great Spiritual Valley of the upper Dantian, which is in the center of the forehead between the eyebrows |
| *Pi* | 劈 | Chop |
| *San Cui* | 三催 | Three pushes: waist pushes the shoulder, shoulder pushes the elbow, elbow pushes the hand |
| *San Guan* | 三关 | Three gates: Jade Pillow Gate, Narrow Vertebrae Gate, Coccyx Gate |
| *San Jian* | 三尖 | Three Alignments: alignment of the nose tip, fist, and toes |

| Pin Yin | Chinese | English Translation/Explanation |
|---------|---------|--------------------------------|
| *San Xing* | 三星 | Three Stars: the dents in the shoulder joint, elbow joint, and the wrist joint, which are formed when holding the fist vertically with the palm facing inside |
| *Shen* | 神 | Spirit; the total manifestation of the internal organ functioning and physical and psychological condition |
| *Shun Bu* | 順步 | A stance in which both the left hand and left leg are in front while the right hand and right leg are in the back; or vice versa |
| *Tang* | 趟 | Move forward with Tang Jing |
| *Tang Jing* | 趟劲 | The energy that comes from the back foot pressing against the ground hard to create a springing forward momentum |
| *Tiao* | 挑 | Lift the tip (of a weapon) upward by pressing on the handle |
| *Yao* | 腰 | Waist region; the midsection of our body between the waist line and the groin |
| *Yao Kua* | 腰胯 | Region between the waist and the groin |
| *Yin Yang* | 阴阳 | A basic theme of Taoist thought used to describe all manner of oppositions and complementarities in the physical and metaphysical worlds |
| *Yong Quan* | 涌泉 | Bubbling well. The starting point of the kidney channel, located in the center of the depression underneath the ball of the foot |
| *Yun* | 云 | Waving the weapon around above the head |
| *Zhuang Bu* | 桩步 | Stance for Post Standing Meditation (70 percent of body weight on back leg) |

# ABOUT THE AUTHORS

LI WEN-BIN was born in 1918. He began his martial arts training at the age of eight, and at thirteen he began to learn Xingyiquan and weapons from Grandmaster Shang Yun-Xiang. In 1996, the Chinese Martial Arts Association named him one of the top ten martial arts masters in the country. Throughout his life, he valued virtues and strived to master the art of Xingyiquan. Through the good example he had set up and his prolific publications, Li Wen-Bin established Shang Pai Xingyiquan as one of the major branches of Xingyiquan. Master Li was also able to apply the concepts and approaches of traditional Chinese martial arts to other fields and was instrumental in helping athletes in fields such as hockey, skating, field and track, basketball and swimming to elevate their skills. Master Li passed away at the age of eighty. His son, Li Hong, carries the lineage of Shang Pai Xingyiquan.

LI HONG has won many Xingyiquan championships. In 1984, he was selected to be an Outstanding Athlete for his performance at the National Martial Arts Exhibition. In 1986, he participated in his father's book project of Shang Pai Xingyiquan Jie, Jue Wei, Volume I. At the same time, he authored Volume II and Volume III for the same book. These three books have been published by People's Physical Education Publishing Company in China. Li Hong is also the founder and president of the International Shang Pai Xing Yi Quan Research Association.

Shang Zhi-Rong is the daughter of Grandmaster Shang Yun-Xiang and one of the demonstrators in the book.

## ABOUT THE TRANSLATOR

Dr. LU MEI-HUI was born into a martial arts family in Taiwan. She began her training at a very young age and is an indoor disciple in the Wudang martial arts system. Besides her outstanding achievements in academia, she has won championships in many national and international internal martial arts competitions for her performance in hand-form, push-hands, and weapons. She is listed in the Encyclopedia of Contemporary Outstanding Chinese Martial Arts Masters. Dr. Lu's publications cover the fields of education, language and culture, Chinese medicine, painting and martial arts, including the translation of The Major Methods of Wudang Sword. She has written the curriculum and textbook for Xingyiquan physical education classes for first- to ninth-grade students in Taigu County in Shanxi Province, China. She teaches at and is the vice president of the International Wudang Internal Martial Arts Academy in Seattle, Washington. For questions about the material presented in this book, please contact her at info@wudangdanpai.com, or visit her school website at www.wudangdanpai.com.